# THE
# FRAMEWORK OF
# WORSHIP

## CLAY HECOCKS

Clay Hecocks is available for consultation and speaking and teaching engagements. He can be reached at checocks@gmail.com.

Copyright © 2014 by Clay Hecocks. All rights reserved.

All Scripture quotations (unless otherwise marked) are from *The Holy Bible, New International Version*, NIV, Copyright © 1973, 1978, 1984, 2011 by Biblica, Inc. Used by permission. All rights reserved worldwide.

Scripture quotations marked NASB are taken from the *New American Standard Bible*, Copyright © 1960, 1962, 1963, 1968, 1971, 1972, 1973, 1975, 1977, 1995 by the Lockman Foundation. Used by permission.

Scripture quotations marked KJV are taken from the *King James Version Bible*, public domain.

Scripture quotations marked NLT are taken from the *Holy Bible, New Living Translation*, Copyright © 1996, 2004, 2007 by Tyndale House Foundation. Used by permission of Tyndale House Publishers, Inc., Carol Stream, Illinois 60188. All rights reserved.

Scripture quotations marked ESV are from *The Holy Bible, English Standard Version*, Copyright © 2001 by Crossway, a publishing ministry of Good News Publishers. Used by permission. All rights reserved.

Scripture quotations marked NKJV are taken from the *New King James Version*, Copyright ©1982 by Thomas Nelson, Inc. All rights reserved. Used by permission.

Scripture quotations marked HCSB are taken from the *Holman Christian Standard Bible*, Copyright © 1999, 2000, 2002, 2003, 2009 by Holman Bible Publishers. Used by permission.

Scripture quotations marked TLB are taken from *The Living Bible*, Copyright © 1971. Used by permission of Tyndale House Publishers, Inc., Carol Stream, Illinois 60188. All rights reserved.

Scripture quotations marked GW are taken from *God's Word*, Copyright © 1995 God's Word to the Nations. Used by permission of Baker Publishing Group.

Scripture quotations marked ISV are taken from *The Holy Bible: International Standard Version*, Release 2.1, Copyright © 1996-2012, The ISV Foundation. All rights reserved internationally.

Scripture quotations marked ABPE are taken from *The Original Aramaic New Testament in Plain English—with Psalms & Proverbs*. Copyright © 2007; 8th edition Copyright © 2013. All rights reserved. Used by permission.

# Table of Contents

# CHAPTER 1

# *Introduction*

## Why another book on worship?

A couple of years ago, a pastor friend of mine encouraged me to write a book, one that would put down on paper my experiences, methods, views, failures and successes, in order to pass them on to others who are involved in worship ministry and leadership. Writing a book was a noble idea, one that I told him I would consider, and then I promptly put it aside.

*Your church, your team, your community demographics and your pastor are unique, and so the solutions to your challenges will likely be unique as well.*

Two years later the idea came back up again. But this time I wasn't able to put it aside. Instead, I felt led to give it some serious thought and prayer. After another conversation with this same pastor friend, and more convincingly, after a sense of prompting by the Spirit that it was time, I began to write in earnest.

Believing that I have some special knowledge, insight or God-given revelation that has never been considered, practiced or even written about would be quite presumptuous. Rather, what I do have is a unique opportunity, a season of time and a sense of responsibility to share my experiences in order to encourage, and maybe even inspire, those who are considering their calling or possibly struggling in their calling. If there is one person who, after reading this book, is encouraged or finds a solution to a challenge, then I'm pleased and fulfilled. That's why I'm writing another book on worship.

In this book, you will find numerous issues I faced over thirty years in worship ministry and leadership. Perhaps more importantly, you will also find the methods and solutions that I used to address and deal with those issues. I share the answers I found most effective, and by effective, I mean the ones that most honored the Lord and produced the most fruit.

Let me clarify one thing from the onset: the solutions offered are not intended to be a "one size fits all," but rather a menu from which you may choose to implement all, some or none of what is shared. My hope is that this book will cause you to pray and consider whether the solutions I presented are right for you and your ministry or whether some kind of hybrid solution would be more likely to produce and sustain fruit. Your church, your team, your community's demographics and your pastor are certainly unique as a whole, and so the solutions to your challenges will likely be unique as well.

*Leadership is all about being okay with failure, but not being okay with giving up.*

As you read this book and consider the ideas contained in it, look for common ground between the issues I faced and the ones you are now facing. In your mind, apply the proposed solutions and envision as best as you can how they will work. Then, if necessary, modify the method a bit and see whether your new, revised solution makes better sense for your circumstances. Cover your whole endeavor with prayer, ask for feedback from trusted friends, and then go for it. It may be exactly what the situation requires. Or it may be a train wreck. In that case, start over, adjust and adapt and try again. And again and again. That's what leadership is all about: being okay with failure but not being okay with giving up.

The fact that you're even reading this book is an honor to me. So from me to you, thank you for the privilege of sharing these thoughts and experiences with you. May you be blessed as you continue on in your calling to ministry. You have an especially high honor and distinct privilege of leading and serving in worship to the Most High.

# CHAPTER 2

# *A Journey*

## Our unique gifting, equipping, calling and life experiences.

My journey began in Michigan when I was seven years old. It started when my dad surprised my mother with an electric organ for her birthday. As part of the deal, the organ came with six "free" beginner lessons. As an accomplished organist, my mom certainly didn't need beginner lessons. My older brother wouldn't have anything to do with the organ or its lessons, and my younger sister was just that, too young. Not knowing any better, I volunteered. After I completed those six lessons, my teacher convinced my parents that I had progressed well enough for them to continue lessons for me (paid, of course).

It was at that point I realized this "thing" was out of my control—I was taking organ lessons whether I liked it or not. My practice sessions were subsequently monitored, enforced and timed, and much to my dismay, strategically scheduled trips to the restroom were deducted from the mandatory half hour. Life as I had known it was forever changed.

Years added up and organ lessons soon transitioned to piano lessons. Half-hour practice sessions became one-hour sessions and this thing was now in full swing.

By the time I reached middle school, I had become infatuated with baseball. Fully convinced that baseball was my new career path, I begged my parents to let me quit piano lessons so I could devote all my time to preparing for the big leagues. Cleverly, my parents convinced me to continue lessons and stick it out just a little longer, at which time I would then be allowed to cease piano lessons.

Predictably, my passion for baseball began to ebb, and I continued piano and theory lessons throughout high school. I went on to college as a piano performance major and finished my four-year degree, and several years later I completed another year and a half of graduate studies in piano performance. (I must say at this point that I owe my parents a great debt of gratitude for their persistence when it came to my lessons and practice. I also owe them for their investment of time and money over all those years of musical training. I'm not sure what I'd be doing if it weren't for them.)

Although my studies were centered around classical music, I developed a fondness for various musical styles including stage band, rock, pop and rhythm and blues. During that time I began to play in various bands, venues and studios, performing and recording as often as I could. To help make ends meet, I also taught piano, theory and improvisation privately.

In the midst of all of the musical training and piano lessons, I was introduced to worship leading quite unexpectedly when, at the age of fourteen, I was approached by a local church to be their accompanist and organist. I was soon playing for every weekend service as well as countless weddings (it was a bicentennial church next to a covered bridge, a perfect photo-op for any bride!), and in short order I was essentially adopted into this church family. I found this extended family to be a wonderful and unexpected addition to my life, and the pay was certainly a welcome bonus. I continued to serve in my capacity as organist and accompanist, and I even became the choir director during my last two years of high school, until it was time to leave for college. I would come back and serve for Christmas, Easter and summers until I left for California following graduation from college.

At this point you may have noticed something missing from this story. "When did you get saved during all of this?" you might ask. I didn't. The people at this little bicentennial church were wonderful and loving; but as I look back, there was a glaring omission: they didn't share the Gospel. They were a works-based church; the Gospel was not at the foundation of their doctrine. A couple years ago I went back with my wife to visit that little church and show her where I started my music ministry journey. It was no longer there—a local government services agency was in its place. So sad . . . but as we will see in chapter three, it was sad but foreseeable.

After graduating from college, I left Michigan and moved to California to "make it big" in the music industry. I had varying degrees of success, but I ended up being asked to lead the music at a small outreach church in Ventura. I needed the work, so I accepted. The summer was just beginning, and the church had also hired a dozen interns from Westmont College to work its summer camp for kids. These college students were amazing—they were filled with joy and they worked hard, loving the kids, loving each other and loving the Lord. They modeled the Lord for me and they shared the Lord with me. That was it! I wanted what they had, and I invited Jesus into my heart and into my life. A couple of years later, one of those student interns, a beautiful young woman named Sheri, would become my wife.

I had been serving and leading worship for eight years. Yet now, for the very first time, I was able to lead worship actually knowing Jesus. What a novel idea! At this time my journey as a worship leader truly began in earnest. This journey would take me to several different ministries and parts of the country, with each step along the way presenting varying challenges that often required unique and creative solutions.

Twenty-three years ago, my journey took me and my family to

a ministry in Fort Lauderdale, Florida. Moving from the cool, breezy coast of Southern California to the hot, humid, tropical-storm- and hurricane-prone east coast of South Florida was a shock to the senses. This shock, along with bugs so big they could qualify as the state bird (in case you didn't know, palmetto bugs, otherwise known as flying cockroaches, can easily reach three inches in length), made for a period of serious adjustment. But adjust we did, and in no time at all we fell in love with the ministry and the people. Our initial commitment of three years was then extended to five years, then to seven years, and then we quit counting.

*Your journey is no less unique than mine.*

When we arrived, we found a church of 500 people who were in love with the Lord. Today, there are ten campuses and over 25,000 people who call this church home. As you can imagine, it's been an amazing journey. Lots of ups, a few downs, of course, and an experience that I could have never, ever imagined, even in my wildest dreams. That's so like the Lord,

> *who is able to do immeasurably more than all we ask or imagine. (Ephesians 3:20)*

Your journey is no less unique than mine. Yet, when it comes to your vision, your hopes, your goals and your challenges  as a worship leader, ministry leader, team member or volunteer, you will undoubtedly find common ground with many, many others, including me.

So let's get started by taking a look at this thing called worship, beginning with the foundation and then moving on to the framework with its overarching concepts as well as the nuts and bolts that hold it all together.

CHAPTER 3

# *Building the Foundation*

## The beginning of the framework.

Before we can begin to contemplate building anything, whether it be a house, a marriage or a ministry, we must first consider the foundation. The beginning of a sturdy framework is in the foundation, and unless the foundation is solid and sure, the framework will, at best, be compromised. Jesus puts it this way:

> *I will show you what he is like who comes to me and hears my words and puts them into practice. He is like a man building a house, who dug down deep and laid the foundation on rock. When a flood came, the torrent struck that house but could not shake it, because it was well built. (Luke 6:47–48)*

Conversely:

> *But the one who hears my words and does not put them into practice is like a man who built a house on the ground without a foundation. The moment*

9

*the torrent struck that house, it collapsed and its destruction was complete. (Luke 6:49)*

*No matter how well the framework is built, it will come to ruin without a firm foundation.*

To have a successful structure, whether it be a physical structure such as a building or an intangible structure such as a marriage or worship ministry, the framework must be built with structural integrity and quality materials. But as the Lord makes clear, no matter how well the framework is built, it will come to ruin without a firm foundation.

*By the grace God has given me, I laid a foundation as an expert builder, and someone else is building on it. But each one should be careful how he builds. For no one can lay any foundation other than the one already laid, which is Jesus Christ. (1 Corinthians 3:10–11)*

Jesus Christ is our foundation, and this foundation is established when we come to Him, hear His words, and then put them into practice:

*But be doers of the word, and not hearers only, deceiving yourselves. (James 1:22 ESV)*

This foundation is all about a genuine and sincere relationship with Christ. Anything short of a sincere relationship is fraud and a deception. Building anything on a Christ-less foundation makes no sense, although many try and fail. For others, it's not a case of a fraudulent relationship but an unseasoned one. Some worship leaders may be incredibly skilled and talented in music but brand new in their faith. However, some in leadership are so desperate for a worship leader that their only spiritual prerequisite is salvation, and, as was the case with me years ago, even that is often negotiable. These new believers are put in harm's way when they are expected to build a framework on top of an incomplete foundation. They need mentoring, they need to grow and they need to mature in their faith, all the while serving and building their own foundation in Christ. Only then can they begin to build a sturdy framework.

*This foundation is all about a genuine and sincere relationship with Christ.*

> *So this is what the Sovereign Lord says: "See, I lay a stone in Zion, a tested stone, a precious cornerstone for a sure foundation; the one who trusts will never be dismayed." (Isaiah 28:16)*

It all comes back to Jesus: read His Word consistently, continue to grow in knowledge and understanding, and put His Word into practice, knowing and trusting that the Author of our faith is the Builder of our sure foundation.

CHAPTER 4

# *Defining Framework*

## How to build on a foundation.

Take a look at the following definitions for *framework*:

- A structure for supporting or enclosing something else, especially a skeletal support used as the basis for something being constructed.[1]

- A supporting structure around which something can be built.[2]

- A structure that supports something built on or around it.[3]

- The initial structure of a building.[4]

- Any underlying structure something is built on.[5]

This aforementioned structure or framework is what holds everything together. Framework gives a building its integrity and keeps it from collapsing; buildings need framework. The same is true for worship: it too requires a framework to support it, to give it integrity and strength and to keep it from imploding when faced with various trials and challenges. Paul gives us some insights on how this framework is to be built on our foundation:

> *If any man builds on this foundation using gold, silver, costly stones, wood, hay or straw, his work will be shown for what it is, because the Day will bring it to light. It will be revealed with fire, and the fire will test the quality of each man's work. If what he has built survives, he will receive his reward. If it is burned up, he will suffer loss; he himself will be saved, but only as one escaping through the flames.*
> *(1 Corinthians 3:12–15)*

If we build our framework with inferior materials and poor workmanship, it won't last long. Oh sure, this framework will last a while, and it will even look fine to most people, but when it is inspected closely, and especially when it is exposed to extreme elements, it will soon become evident to all where the builder cut corners and compromised.

I have been living in South Florida for twenty-three years now. How the framework of a home is constructed here is essential. In other parts of the country you can get away with wood-framed construction but not here. First, wood rots quickly due to the high humidity and tropical climate. Second, wood-framed walls are particularly susceptible to extreme wind. During a period of many years without a direct hit from a hurricane, many homebuilders here became complacent, even lazy. Desiring to maximize profits, they cut corners and began building entire developments using wood framing rather than the standard concrete block. Then Hurricane Andrew came along with 150-plus mph winds. In the aftermath of the destruction, you could drive down a street and on one side observe an older development that was constructed entirely out of cement block. Although there was significant roof damage, all the homes were essentially intact. On the other side of the street was a newer development that had all wood framing.

Nothing was left standing; the entire development was leveled.

The framework of worship is no different: it requires integrity and quality workmanship to stay viable. It requires those leading and serving within this framework to be skilled, uncompromised in their walk and called by the Lord to serve. In addition to these three qualities, this framework requires leaders to build into it a vision and work ethic that equips, trains, evaluates, encourages, directs, redirects, corrects, informs, teaches and mentors those under their care.

*Building a framework sturdy enough to support a culture of relevant, effective and sincere worship takes considerable prayer, hard work, diligence and perseverance.*

I have spent a lifetime learning, understanding and building this framework. I have experienced both successes and failures through the years and been hit by numerous storms along the way. But we must always persevere; we keep building, even rebuilding if necessary, and then one day we look on at the worship experience that this framework is supporting and we are awestruck and humbled to see it bearing fruit. We see people being ministered to and healed, restored and renewed. We see lives being changed and people drawing close to God. We see the Holy Spirit moving in lives and hearts, and the worship, with its framework and foundation, standing firmly against all the forces that conspire to knock it down.

But this doesn't happen by accident; building a framework sturdy enough to support a culture of relevant, effective and sincere worship takes considerable prayer, hard work, diligence and perseverance. But it's undeniably worth it, and the rewards far outweigh any sacrifice.

CHAPTER 5

# *Something*

## Understanding the beauty and simplicity of worship.

Remember that one of the definitions of framework is "a structure that supports *something* built on or around it."[6]

To discuss framework, we must understand what this *something* being built on or around is, and in this case, of course, the something is worship. The subject of worship has been the theme of endless books, conferences and teachings—so much so that one would think that with all the exhaustive resources, there would ultimately be a definitive and conclusive summary that all

> **Worship is faith expressing itself in grateful adoration.**

pastors, worship leaders, and congregations would agree on and embrace.

Nope.

Throughout my years of service in worship ministry, I have grappled with all the various definitions of worship. Some have been pages long, some a paragraph long and some just a simple sentence. Some are understandable, some are inspiring, and some—I don't have the slightest clue what's being communicated. You might ask what's mine. Here's my definition of *worship*:

- Worship is faith expressing itself in grateful adoration.

  Or maybe you'd prefer this version:

- Worship is faith expressing itself personally and corporately in grateful adoration to an immortal, invisible and redeeming God.

  Or better yet:

- Worship is faith expressing itself in a personal and corporate response to God through His Spirit while attaining to a sincere friendship and intimacy with Him, expressing both grateful adoration and reverential submission to an immortal, invisible and redeeming God.

  Or even better:

- Worship is faith and an act of consciousness that expresses itself selflessly and genuinely in and through a personal and corporate response that embodies Spirit and Truth while attaining to a sincere friendship and intimacy with God, fully and wholly acknowledging Christ's redemptive work on the cross while quickening our hearts and affections to express the inexpressible and imagine the unimaginable as we contemplate and embrace an immortal, invisible and redeeming God, thus affirming and capturing the whole reason for our existence.

You can probably see where I'm going with this. They're all accurate, but which one of these four variations is more to your liking? Some will like the simplicity of the first one, although the second one adds some vital qualities of God that bring it home more for others, and yet the third one . . . and so on.

I'm wired a certain way. I prefer the first one; I like simplicity. But that's just me. For curiosity's sake, I Googled "definition of worship" and found what seemed to be an endless variety of definitions. One particular site posted a dozen or more definitions from recognizable leaders of the faith both past and present; some of the definitions were one sentence long, while others were a little longer—some were a paragraph in length, and yet others were even longer than my fourth variation. It's fairly clear that a wide range of personal convictions, preferences, length and detail is needed to adequately convey the various personal definitions of worship.

So what's my point? My point is that there is not a definitive, exhaustive or concise definition of worship but rather personal definitions that are a combination of the Word as it relates to one's personal experience with and unique surrender to the Lord, and one's similarly unique cognitive and emotional response resulting from his or her ongoing and growing relationship with the Lord. Granted, that's a bit of a mouthful, but all that is to say that everyone is unique and each person's definition of worship will be unique to a degree as well. So what's the common thread? God created mankind and gave us life, free will, His Son Jesus for salvation and His Holy Spirit to dwell in us; therefore, God is worthy to be worshipped, and the Bible and all of creation attest to that.

The Old Testament predicted and pointed to Jesus, and the New Testament fulfilled that prediction with the birth, death and resurrection of Jesus, the Lamb that was crucified for the forgiveness of sins.

> *For God so loved the world that he gave his one and only Son, that whoever believes in Him shall not perish but have eternal life. (John 3:16)*

This Good News is beautiful and simple: We are all sinners in need of a Savior. Jesus died on a cross for our sins to bridge the gap between a holy God and sinful man. Whoever accepts God's Son, Jesus, into their hearts and lives are forgiven their sins and promised eternal life in heaven.

It's supposed to be simple; yet we seem to have a knack for complicating things. Always have. Some 2,000 years ago, Paul spent a better part of his ministry coming against and refuting the Judaizers who insisted on adding more and more preconditions to this beautifully simple and uncomplicated Good News. So I suppose it shouldn't come as a surprise, then, that there are those today who similarly insist on adding more and more preconditions to the expression of worship, this simple, sincere and heartfelt response to the Author of this simple, amazing and undeserved Good News.

Thus, once again, we have a knack for complicating things, including worship. We have those, let's call them *worship Judaizers*, who feel the need to dissect and critique every current form of worship expression. They dictate which styles, arrangements, instrumentation, order of service and various other elements are necessary in order to make worship legitimate and authentic, justifying their opinions and preferences with dizzying scriptural precedents and arguments.

Over the years I've read numerous books and articles and listened to just as many sermons and teachings on worship, and it's disappointing how many address what's wrong with worship by confusing personal preference with biblical mandate. Just recently I read a book of well over 300 pages (with small print!) on why essentially every current expression of worship is unbiblical, misguided and completely missing the mark spiritually and musically. Each chapter contains a lengthy, detailed scriptural dissertation that pretends to explain the dismal condition and failure of every present-day worship practice. The overall purpose of the book appears to be to highlight the author's seemingly impressive grasp of biblical doctrine and academic prowess, rather than to provide the reader any practical understanding and application of worship and worship leadership. The author finally concludes with a brief chapter on what a biblically mandated worship service should look like: a completely self-serving, tradition-steeped and liturgically heavy exercise that would be for many the antithesis of a sincere, personal and corporate worship experience.

After reading this book, I found myself incredulous and disappointed. I struggled to see how it (and similar teachings and blogs) could help or encourage. And except for those who are similarly narrow-minded, it doesn't. In fact, it can be horribly discouraging. Consider this scenario: A young man, after having a miraculous encounter with the Lord where he surrenders his life to Him, picks up his guitar and writes and sings a simple song of worship to the Lord. Some of his friends hear him and ask him to sing some worship songs for their small group. He does, and before long, he's leading the group in worship every week. He's loving it and so are his friends. As he grows in the Lord, he wants to become more knowledgeable and have a greater understanding of worship. He goes to the local Christian bookstore to find a book on worship and picks up one of these worship-Judaizer-type books whose back cover claims it will explain the worship leader's biblical role and responsibility. Perfect! He begins to read it and quickly realizes he is confused, inadequate, ill-equipped and unable to be the worship leader that the book, the author and apparently the Bible dictates. He's deflated and discouraged and decides he's not qualified to lead worship any longer. He steps away from his small group and his friends and puts his guitar away.

> *We tend to complicate the Good News, and then we complicate the response in worship.*

Why do we need to complicate things, adding more and more conditions and prerequisites? We tend to complicate the Good News, and then we complicate the response in worship.

Pastor Chuck Smith, founder of the Calvary Chapel movement,

took the Bible and condensed it down to this one simple yet profound sentence: "Love the Lord your God with all your heart, soul, mind and strength, and do whatever you want." Again, I love the simplicity of this statement, but at the same time, this is by no means a call to forgo any in-depth academic study of the Bible by wrongfully suggesting that Bible study is a fruitless, or even counterproductive, effort. Absolutely not! In fact, by loving the Lord with all of our being, we will only desire to understand His Word more fully and do what His will and Word instructs. Again, one of the wonders of the Bible is that, at its core, it points to and presents a very simple offer—the Good News—an offer that all can understand and receive.

*Complexity and simplicity, both at the same time— that's the wonder and mystery of the Living Word.*

But the Bible also offers a wealth of history, prophecy, characters, events, stories, adventures, epic victories and tragic failures, and so much more, that all point to and validate this same Good News. The enormity of this vast treasure, the Bible, can consume one's entire life with academic and scholarly study and still not scratch the surface. Such complexity and such simplicity, both at the same time—that's the wonder and mystery of the Living Word—it has something for everyone from the child to the scholar, while ultimately bringing everyone to the same proposal and offer of Jesus as Savior.

The same is true of worship. At its core is a simple desire to respond with affection and gratitude to our Creator and Savior. That can be done with a simple raised hand or voice, or with a musical expression that is the culmination of a lifetime of study and practice, each response worshipping Jesus with no greater effectiveness or reward but rather with a common faithfulness and devotion.

To avoid any confusion at this time, let me make clear my view of higher education: if you have the desire to pursue a higher level degree in biblical theology, worship arts or anything else, please, go for it! I have completed six years of undergraduate and graduate studies, so clearly I'm not opposed to ongoing study. I'm only opposed to it if it swells your head, puts you in oppressive debt or makes you so heavenly minded you're no earthly good.

So whatever your level of education may be, there's a role for you in ministry. Whether you're a brand new believer or a mature and seasoned believer, there's a place for you in ministry. Whatever your level of musical ability, there's a role for you in worship ministry. And there's a place in worship ministry for any style and expression of music and the arts and for any instrument or voice.

The Good News is not complicated, nor is the response in worship necessarily complicated. Yet the simplicity of both is partnered with a depth that allows us a lifetime of growing and maturing in our understanding without ever abandoning the need for childlike faith in believing and responding.

I hope and pray that I have presented adequately the simplicity and beauty of a heartfelt response in worship to a loving Savior and His simple, yet profound, invitation. Whether the presentation of worship be the young man mentioned earlier singing simple songs with simple chords on a guitar or an accomplished and life-long-trained musician performing with all his might, may their hearts and our hearts be the same: simply offering what we have in worship to God Almighty.

# CHAPTER 6

# *Keepin' It Real*

## Living an authentic life in a world of fakes.

Several years ago when our worship team was touring through New York and New Jersey and we had a day off, we decided to go to New York City and see some of the sights. We went to the top of the Empire State Building, visited Rockefeller Center, ate in Little Italy and saw several other iconic sites. Some of us wanted to get souvenirs and check out the local shopping, and we were told the place to go was Canal Street. So we hopped into a couple of taxis and off we went. We soon realized that we were in the knockoff capital of the world: from Disney prints and Ray Ban sunglasses to Rolex watches and Gucci purses, it was all there for pennies on the dollar. A buddy of mine got an $8,000 Rolex for $45, and I got my wife a nice $800 Coach purse for $30. The similarity to the real thing was stunning! If you were to put those items next to the real thing, a cursory look, or even a closer look, wouldn't reveal the differences. It wasn't until a few weeks later that the inequalities began to appear. I distinctly remember asking my buddy how the "Rolex" was working. He told me, "It's working great, if you don't mind losing twenty minutes every day." The purse? Well, that took a little longer, but the seams began to come apart, the handle came off, the zipper wore out and other telltale signs of substandard quality began to surface everywhere. The purse was soon curbside with the rest of the weekly trash.

Now my wife happens to really like a Coach purse: the look, the functionality and the quality, but she would never consider buying one. She's just way too cost conscious. Then one day I happened to be in a store that carried the Coach line. They were having a significant sale, including the very purse my wife had previously admired from afar. I approached the manager and offered her an even lower price if I paid cash. Much to my surprise, she accepted the offer and I had a Coach purse for a song. My Christmas shopping was done! And my wife still uses that purse. The fake was gone in months, while the authentic one is still going strong years later.

Often, our walk with the Lord can also be a knockoff. Everything looks and sounds great with typical Christianese answers to questions of how's it going: "Oh, I'm blessed brother," or "Just another day of praising the Lord," and so on. Whenever I encounter someone like this, I can't help but wonder if I'm seeing just another knockoff. The overwhelming need for so many in our culture today to present themselves in a perceived acceptable manner, regardless of the truth or the reality, is a sad commentary. But the fact that so many do, and do so in such a convincing way, has made it much more difficult to tell the fakes from the authentic anymore.

I once had a guy call me up and make himself available to serve on the worship team. He had played and sung with the Eagles, the Doobie Brothers and many other big name groups from that era (I know, I'm dating myself). I was excited to say the least. So I asked when a good time would be for us to get together so I could hear him, and his initial response was, "Oh, that won't be necessary. I've played my whole life; I'm a pro." (Dead give-away: if someone has to tell you they're a pro, it means they're not; it just means they got twenty dollars for playing at their nephew's bar mitzvah.) So the audition was scheduled, and he came in with his guitar and proceeded to sing and play a couple of songs for me. It was absolutely awful. There wasn't a thing redeeming about it. At first I was disappointed, then a little angry. I challenged him on his previous statements—he simply wasn't capable of playing for the Eagles, the Doobie Brothers or any other group. Then I confronted him concerning his attempt to deceive me and others. Eventually he came clean and we got to the bottom of it: he had in fact *played* with the groups he had mentioned, actually more like *played along*; he would play and sing with these groups at home while he was playing their records on his stereo.

Another time an "artist" had wanted to join the worship team and his credentials included playing on *The Arsenio Hall Show* (I know, I know). Something in my Spirit, however, told me otherwise. So, much to his dismay, I had one of my staff call CBS to verify his claim. It had never happened. Again, following a confrontation, the truth came out: he had in fact been on *The Arsenio Hall Show* but in the audience, nowhere near the stage.

Fakes look great on display, on paper, at a distance and sometimes in person, and they can even function convincingly for a while. But when scrutinized, or more often, when put to the test or through a trial, fakes don't hold together for very long.

> *Truthful lips endure forever, but a lying tongue is but for a moment. (Proverbs 12:19)*

I think we all can get caught up in this behavior, even if it's for just a moment when your pastor asks: "Were you able to call so-and-so?" You haven't because you put it off, yet you respond, "Yeah, but there was no answer. I'll keep trying and let you know how it goes." Or from a team member: "Did you get that email I sent you?" You did, but if you say yes, you'll be admitting that you haven't bothered to answer your email for two weeks. So instead you answer, "No, when did you send it? Huh, it must not have been delivered; we've been having some problems with our server lately."

If we're comfortable with the little, eventually we can become comfortable with the bigger. I'd be a liar myself if I said I'm not guilty of having gone down this easier route. But I have found that just saying it like it is and apologizing when necessary honors God—and although it's a little more work and possibly a little embarrassing, it's so much easier on the conscience. It also builds trust; you will always be known for being truthful, even in your mistakes. And, believe it or not, you will often be thanked for simply being honest and straightforward.

> *Do not lie to one another, seeing that you have put off the old self with its practices and have put on the new self, (Colossians 3:9–10a ESV)*

"Did you get my email?" "Yes, I did, and I apologize for not getting back to you sooner. I'll make sure to get back to you before the end of the day (or week); thanks for your patience."

"Were you able to call so-and-so?" "No, I didn't. I'm sorry; I really dropped the ball on that one. I'll get right on it and make the call as soon as I get back to my office."

Some would argue that it's not that big a deal—what's the harm in a little white lie that may preserve someone's feelings that the truth would unnecessarily hurt. "Did you like the song I wrote?" "I did, great song!" You know it's a not a great song, not even close, but what's wrong with encouraging this person with a little untruth rather than causing hurt feelings?

The problem is twofold: first, it's misleading. Now this person will spend more time and resources on writing, possibly go into debt to make a CD, only to ultimately find out through various experiences and evaluations that songwriting is not his or her gift or strength. Now this person is not just discouraged but angry, broke and in debt with no way to recoup the cost. Second, you lied. You lied.

I had a staff member who would help me with auditions, and when people played or sang poorly simply because they weren't gifted and skilled, he would invariably tell them, "Nice job, that was really good." I would always tell him afterwards (with a smile), "Stop lying, you're giving them false hope!" The people auditioning would get their hopes up, even share with their friends, "They told me I did a really good job!" But when told that they didn't make the team, and, in fact, they might want to consider serving in another area of ministry, they would leave the church hurt, angry and even bitter for having been lied to.

If these songwriters and auditionees had been told the truth in love, they would likely still be serving, and serving in more suitable areas for their gifts and strengths. No matter how innocent the white lie might seem, it's still a lie and it's misleading, often with heartbreaking results.

When we mislead and misrepresent the truth, no matter how large (I played with the Eagles) or small (great song!), we are presenting something that is not totally authentic but rather a fake.

*So we speak, not to please man, but to please God*
*who tests our hearts. (1 Thessalonians 2:4b ESV)*

We've all had our hearts tested and we've all failed. A lot. Those little white lies? Fail. "Uh, no, I didn't get your email." Fail. "I'm a pro!" Big fail. I'm sure we've all had times in our lives that we can look back on and admit to being a bit of a fake—times when we've presented ourselves in a flattering light, while in our hearts we knew it wasn't quite accurate or maybe not even close. (Can you say *résumé* or *mortgage application*?) Even as musicians, many of us have had to rely on a "fake book," pretending to know and play songs that we've never heard of before. But to be the authentic worship leader God has called us to be requires us to conduct a thorough heart check. Daily.

> *But the things that come out of the mouth come from the heart, and these make a man "unclean." (Matthew 15:18)*

The Pharisees had just confronted Jesus and His disciples, accusing them of eating with unwashed hands and thus becoming "unclean." But Jesus rebuked them and said to the crowd:

> *What goes into a man's mouth does not make him "unclean," but what comes out of his mouth, that is what makes him "unclean." (Matthew 15:11)*

Then Jesus said to the disciples:

> *For out of the heart come evil thoughts, murder, adultery, sexual immorality, theft, false testimony, slander. (Matthew 15:19)*

You may look at the list and feel good about a few of the items; maybe you've had total victory when it comes to murder or theft, and maybe even a couple of the others. But what about evil thoughts (pornography, revenge, hurting someone), or false testimony (lying), or slander (hurtful gossip, character assassination)? Are any of those residing in your heart?

The heart can be an ugly, dirty, unclean place if left unattended. And everything that we say and do is first conceived in the heart, so clearly the condition of our heart is critical and essential to authentic and real worship. If any part of our heart is "unclean," how do we go about changing the condition of our heart, making it "clean" and authentic?

## First, pursue God.

> *You will seek me and find me when you seek me with all your heart. (Jeremiah 29:13)*

30

## Let Him clean house.

*Create in me a clean heart, O God, and renew a right spirit within me. (Psalm 51:10)*

## Trust Him.

*Trust in the Lord with all your heart, and lean not on your own understanding; in all your ways acknowledge him, and he will make your paths straight. (Proverbs 3:5–6)*

## Study His Word.

*I have hidden your word in my heart that I might not sin against you. (Psalm 119:11)*

## Be accountable.

*Search me, O God, and know my heart; test me and know my anxious thoughts. See if there is any offensive way in me, and lead me in the way everlasting. (Psalm 139:23–24)*

## And then protect your heart.

*Above all else, guard your heart, for everything you do flows from it. (Proverbs 4:23)*

If your heart isn't right, then you're just going through the motions. It's an act. It's a fake. And eventually, like a fake watch or purse, it will start to break down, it will come apart at the seams and it will eventually lose all of its value.

Isaiah condemned Israel for this same hypocrisy, and Jesus used Isaiah's words when He confronted the Pharisees' hypocrisy as well:

> *These people honor me with their lips, but their*
> *hearts are far from me. They worship me in vain,*
> *their teachings are but rules taught by men.*
> *(Mark 7:6b–7)*

Their mouths said one thing, but their hearts said quite another. Their worship was fake, fabricated and insulting to the Lord. Their hearts were more concerned about appearance than substance.

> *Therefore once more I will astound these people*
> *with wonder upon wonder; the wisdom of the wise*
> *will perish, the intelligence of the intelligent will*
> *vanish. (Isaiah 29:14)*

This is a scary judgment that God pours out on the people of Israel, not only for their hypocritical behavior but also for their pride in and reliance on their own intelligence and wisdom. The very things they cherish the most and have the most pride in are the very things God takes away from them. This very same people that used to see wonder after wonder as they wholeheartedly followed and worshipped God will now experience a new kind of wonder—an astonishing unfolding of events that will literally cause them to become utter fools as they mock God in their worship.

But wait, there's more . . .

> *The multitude of your sacrifices—*
> *what are they to me?" says the Lord.*
> *I have more than enough of burnt offerings,*
> *of rams and the fat of fattened animals;*
> *I have no pleasure*

*in the blood of bulls and lambs and goats.*
*When you come to appear before me,*
*who has asked this of you,*
*this trampling of my courts?*
*Stop bringing meaningless offerings!*
*Your incense is detestable to me.*
*New Moons, Sabbaths and convocations—*
*I cannot bear your evil assemblies.*
*Your New Moon festivals and your appointed feasts*
*my soul hates.*
*They have become a burden to me;*
*I am weary of bearing them.*
*When you spread out your hands in prayer,*
*I will hide my eyes from you;*
*even if you offer many prayers,*
*I will not listen. (Isaiah 1:11-15)*

The Israelites would give up their livestock for sacrifices, they would give up their incense to be burned, and they would give up their time for "assemblies" (services). They would give up their money and valuables for offerings, but they wouldn't give up their sins. They wouldn't give up their sins. . . .

I have watched in horror, incredulousness, disappointment and even anger as worship leader after worship leader and pastor after pastor have fallen over the years. I have known many of them personally. For many it's been sexual sin. For some, it's been drug or alcohol addiction. Most have shared with me that it all started with a small compromise here, then another one there, then another, then some more, and then it just started to snowball. Some didn't know how to get out of it, others thought they were somehow justified, and still others just liked their sin too much to give it up. What happened? They didn't protect their hearts, they began to spend less and less time in the Word (especially as it began to convict them), they leaned on their own understanding and they began to separate themselves from godly accountability and counsel. And yet they continued leading worship, blinded by their sin—some for months and some for years.

But, as Isaiah makes clear, fake worship won't last forever, and for all of those over the years that I've known who have fallen, it obviously didn't last for them either. Here's what I found to be interesting: all the people I've spoken to who have fallen were grateful and relieved when they were finally caught. I have, on a number of occasions, been the person who initiated the confrontation, and I can still remember the body language, the look in the eyes, the tears and the words that all clearly expressed a huge relief that the masquerade was finally over. As soon as they stopped being fake and became real again, then the process of restoration could begin, and, for the first time in a long time, worship became authentic to them again.

*If the heart's not right, then the worship won't be right. It won't have a spiritual impact. It won't* touch *lives, let alone* change *lives.*

> *For the Lord sees not as man sees: man looks on the outward appearance, but the Lord looks on the heart. (1 Samuel 16:7b ESV)*

Worship may sound great and look great, and the worship leader may have the perfect look and say all the right spiritual things, but the Lord sees the heart. If the heart's not right, then the worship won't be right. It won't have a spiritual impact. It won't *touch* lives, let alone *change* lives. I would much rather have someone say, "Wow, the Spirit was sure moving today during worship; I was really ministered to," than, "Wow, great worship team, cool looking worship leader." My prayer before worship often sounds similar to this: "Lord, may the worship today be spiritual and Spirit led; may our hearts be right before You. Get us out of the way so that You're the One seen and heard."

*Above all else, guard your heart, for everything you
do flows from it. (Proverbs 4:23)*

I know I used this verse earlier, but this issue of the heart is so vital to our worship and its framework (and to our life and ministry) that I felt the need to share it again. Please, guard your heart. If everything you do flows from a real and authentic heart, one that is surrendered to and sincerely honors and worships the Lord, then its impact will reach beyond this life and into eternity, literally!

# CHAPTER 7

# *Must Be Nice*

## Envy: wanting what others have.

When we look at other peoples' cars, homes, jobs, clothes, schedules and maybe even their spouses, and witness their skills, talent, intelligence, knowledge, or even their looks, we can often say, "Must be nice." All this adds up to success in our eyes, and after comparing it to our own lot in life, while shaking our head, we once again conclude: "Must be nice." But clearly the only reason they're more successful than us is because they have a certain advantage. An unfair advantage. An undeserved advantage. It's not fair, and it bugs us.

Once, having been involved in some form of music ministry for thirteen years, I had just gone through a church split and resigned. I chose to take a sabbatical from paid church service and simply serve and volunteer for a season. In the meantime, having a love and knack for woodworking, I opened a little wood shop in the garage of our home and began to pick up some odd jobs here and there to pay the bills. One afternoon, as I was working on an oak fireplace mantle, a friend of a friend stopped by. He came into the garage, we exchanged greetings, and then he just looked at the mantle for a moment. Then he looked around the shop for another moment. Suddenly, out of the blue, he said, "I envy you." Then he left. And I found myself really bothered by his comment.

Here's why I was so bothered: this man had been touring the country with some of the biggest names in Christian music. He was also playing, writing, arranging and producing Christian music and having incredible success. And I wasn't; so to me his comment felt patronizing. But I was terribly wrong.

What I didn't realize, to put it simply, is that his life had become a shambles, and to him my life and circumstances looked pretty darn good. Work had dried up for him—no more touring, writing, arranging or producing—and he sincerely wished he could be a woodworker doing exactly what I was doing.

When I had discovered the reality of his situation, I felt horribly convicted of my own envy. A little later that night the Lord spoke clearly to me and asked, "So do you still want what he's got? The only response I could muster up was a sobering, "I'm so sorry, Lord. . . ." That was the turning point in ministry for me.

I had been preoccupied with what I didn't have rather than taking stock of what I did have and not only being content with it, but grateful as well.

> *Now the works of the flesh are obvious: sexual*
> *immorality, impurity and debauchery; idolatry and*
> *witchcraft; hatred, discord, jealousy, fits of rage,*
> *selfish ambition, dissensions, factions and envy;*
> *drunkenness, orgies, and the like.*
> *(Galatians 5:19–21)*

That's quite an impressive list of bad behavior. I find it interesting to see envy listed in the same category (works of the flesh) as idolatry, witchcraft and orgies. I would imagine most people would rate envy way below the other three in the seriousness of the offense. But Paul makes no differentiation; left unchecked, envy, like any of these works of the flesh, leads to spiritual death.

I would best define envy as follows: awareness and resentment of an advantage enjoyed by another, joined with a desire to possess the same advantage.

Without digging into the topic a little deeper, simply exhorting you to resist being envious and to be content and grateful with what you have would be simplistic. There's the fairness factor to consider. We can easily submit to the need to be content and grateful and still grapple with why someone else has been given an abundance of skills, talents and gifts while we are essentially barren in those same areas. Again, it doesn't seem fair.

> *But who are you, O man, to talk back to God? Shall what is formed say to him who formed it, "Why did you make me like this?" Does not the potter have the right to make out of the same lump of clay some pottery for noble purposes and some for common use? (Romans 9:20–21)*

All this boils down to acknowledging God as sovereign. Sovereignty means that God, as the ruler of the universe, has the right to do whatever He wants. Further, He is in complete control over everything that happens.[7]

> *The Lord does whatever pleases him, in the heavens and on the earth, in the seas and all their depths. (Psalm 135:6)*

Even while acknowledging God's sovereignty, one can still understandably ponder God's seemingly random "favoritism." This can clearly be seen, heard and evidenced with vocalists as an example. I have had many a singer audition, who, in spite of years of voice lessons, thousands of dollars of investment and countless hours of practice and performance, are still unable to sing adequately enough for the team. But how do you explain those few vocalists who walk in having never, ever, had a voice lesson, step up to the mic and blow everybody in the room away? Their voices are clear, pitch perfect, accurate, dynamic and heartfelt. It's an amazing thing to hear and experience, except possibly for those who have made the sacrificial investment with far inferior results.

*Envy continuously desires what it doesn't have, and it can never be satisfied.*

To me, this is a great example of God's sovereignty: He gives whatever He wants to whomever He chooses. He has a reason and we simply aren't privy to it. It's that simple. And although I rejoice for the singer who has amazing God-given natural gifts and talents, my heart does break for those who have worked so hard and invested so much only to come up short of their hopes and expectations. God didn't give them as much. So, what does the Word say about this? How do I explain this?

> *For if the willingness is there, the gift is acceptable according to what one has, not according to what he does not have. (2 Corinthians 8:12)*

The key to finding contentment with God's allotment of gifts to you is to simply use what He has uniquely given you to wholeheartedly serve Him. It's being faithful with what you have rather than envious of what you don't have. If you're willing to generously serve with whatever gift you've been given, the gift and offering is acceptable, and God is honored and pleased. But envy continuously desires what it doesn't have, and it can never be satisfied. Even if by chance envy acquires what it so desperately wants, it is soon unsatisfied once again. Envy is only overcome when we are content and satisfied with what we already possess, serving with the gifts God has chosen in His sovereignty to give us.

In the parable of the talents in Matthew 25, the master has three servants. To one servant he gives five talents; to another, two talents and to yet another, one talent. All three servants are to invest their talents (in this case, a monetary unit) and realize a return while the master is away. When the master returns, he settles up with the servants. The servant who was given five talents used them faithfully, and the master responded:

> *Well done, good and faithful servant! You have been faithful with a few things; I will put you in charge of many things. Come and share your master's happiness! (Matthew 25:21)*

Likewise the servant who had two talents used them faithfully, and the master responded:

> *Well done, good and faithful servant! You have been faithful with a few things; I will put you in charge of many things. Come and share your master's happiness! (Matthew 25:23)*

However, the servant who was given one talent did not use his talent faithfully. In fact, the master considered that servant wicked and lazy for his irresponsibility, and the master had him removed from his presence.

Notice the master's reply to both the first and second servants is exactly the same, word for word. And, given those two servants' experiences, we can assume that had the last servant used and been faithful with his one talent, the master would have responded to him the same way.

Once again, rather than finding ourselves envious of those with more talent, we instead are to take what talents we do have and use them faithfully to serve the Lord and His church. And the Lord's reply—

*Well done, good and faithful servant! You have been faithful with a few things; I will put you in charge of many things. Come and share your master's happiness! (Matthew 25:23)*

I encourage you to hide this truth and reality in your heart and thus be ready to guard against those times when envy can so subtly (and not so subtly) creep in to your life.

Keep this in mind: you may think you see someone with more talent and apparent success than you have, and you may even wish you had what that person has, but the reality of it may be very, very different than what you think it is. I have been the worship leader at Calvary Chapel Fort Lauderdale for over twenty-three years now. It's a huge ministry with abundant resources, incredible musicians, great staff, solid leadership and an amazing congregation. Many have looked on at my circumstances with envy: "If I just had what he has, can you imagine what I could do and accomplish!" But here's the irony: at times at the end of several back to back to back sixty-to-seventy-plus-hour weeks during which hardly any time was devoted to actual worship and music, when everybody expected an amazing spiritual worship experience five times a week, and all the while I was refereeing musicians and staff, coordinating schedules, preparing for and engaging in seemingly endless meetings and responding to letters where one says the music is too loud and another says it's not loud enough, I have envied those who lead at a smaller church. They have only one service, there's much less stress, they're able to invest more into their team and their worship and they can spend more time with their family. Must be nice!

*No matter how many* **talents** *you may have, the opportunity for envy, discontentment and ingratitude will always be present.*

My point is this: no matter how many *talents* you may have, the opportunity for envy, discontentment and ingratitude will always be present. Always. But the greater and wiser opportunity is to be faithful, thankful and content with your talents, neither wanting more nor wanting less. What you have is perfect!

I want to touch on one other area where we're as equally susceptible to having envy take hold: how much we're paid. Or not paid. Especially compared to someone else. Very few things validate our worth as much as our pay (besides a solo, of course). The subject of pay is also one of the most challenging and delicate areas of my job. As of this writing, I oversee around thirty full time and fifty part-time employees, and I alone am responsible for determining their pay rates, their increases (or, in some cases, decreases), and even their bonuses, if warranted. Pay increases can be directly attributed to increased job responsibility, improved job performance and, in some cases, a growing family. In each situation, I need to determine the rate and then justify that rate to my pastor, the board, and ultimately the employee. I never publicize who makes what, but invariably some employees become privy to what others are making, and, on rare occasions, they have been surprised and disappointed with what they discover, desiring a greater understanding of why they only make what they do and someone else makes more. I will always be open and honest in discussing people's value and contribution to the ministry and the team, how their particular set of skills, talents and work ethic play a part in their pay determination as well as what areas they can concentrate on and grow in that would increase their "value" and warrant a pay increase or bonus in the near future.

When confronted with team or staff members who are struggling with envy as it relates to issues of compensation, I'm quick to take them to the book of Matthew, specifically the parable of the vineyard workers:

> *For the kingdom of heaven is like a landowner who went out early in the morning to hire men to work in his vineyard. He agreed to pay them a denarius for the day and sent them into his vineyard.*

*About the third hour he went out and saw others standing in the marketplace doing nothing. He told them, "You also go and work in my vineyard, and I will pay you whatever is right." So they went.*

*He went out again about the sixth hour and the ninth hour and did the same thing. About the eleventh hour he went out and found still others standing around. He asked them, "Why have you been standing here all day long doing nothing?"*

*"Because no one has hired us," they answered.*

*He said to them, "You also go and work in my vineyard."*

*When evening came, the owner of the vineyard said to his foremen, "Call the workers and pay them their wages, beginning with the last ones hired and going on to the first."*

*The workers who were hired about the eleventh hour came and each received a denarius. So when those came who were hired first, they expected to receive more. But each one of them also received a denarius. When they received it, they began to grumble against the landowner. "These men who were hired last worked only an hour," they said, "and you have made them equal to us who have borne the burden of the work and the heat of the day."*

*But he answered one of them, "Friend, I am not being unfair to you. Didn't you agree to work for a denarius? Take your pay and go. I want to give the man who was hired last the same as I gave you. Don't I have the right to do what I want with my own money? Or are you envious because I am generous?"*

*So the last will be first, and the first will be last.* (Matthew 20:1–16)

Like the servant with two talents who received the same reward as the servant with five talents, the vineyard workers who worked an hour received the same pay as those who worked the whole day. In both cases, the five-talent servant and the first-hired workers weren't treated unfairly or cheated, but rather the two-talent servant and the one-hour workers were generously blessed. Can we accept someone being blessed and treated generously? Even if it appears they're blessed more than us?

Numerous times I've stepped in to help an employee through an unforeseen difficult time. It might be a sudden health and medical issue, a blown engine on the family's only car or some other emergency, and I'll surprise and bless that person with a bonus or a raise to help through the tough times. Is that okay? Or is that not fair? Should I give a matching bonus or raise to every staff member?

Matthew 20:1–16 makes it quite clear that each circumstance is unique, God chooses to bless as He desires—His reasons are His, we are to be content with what we've agreed to and not be envious of the Lord's generosity. Nor your boss's, since someday you just might be the recipient of that very same generosity.

Recently, a well-known professional athlete signed a long-term contract averaging over twenty million dollars a year. It was a signed contract, he agreed to it and it made him the highest paid athlete in that particular position. Then, during free agency the following year, another athlete in the same position signed a contract that paid him slightly more per year than the other athlete. The other athlete decided to not report to training camp but instead to hold out, demanding a new contract that would pay him

*Let the Lord have the opportunity to be generous with you, but first be content with what you have.*

more and once again make him the highest paid athlete in his position. How embarrassing. That's the world, not us. If you agreed to your pay rate, be sure to honor it, work hard for it and be content with it. Then watch God give you a raise when you least expect it, or maybe even a job opportunity you never saw coming with a commensurate pay raise to go along with your increased responsibilities. Let the Lord have the opportunity to be generous with you, but first be content with what you have.

Guarding against envy is crucial to effective and sincere worship. Look for the warning signs and be proactive, never allowing envy to distract you from your calling or keep you from putting your talents to work. Be content and faithful with what you've been given, serving and worshipping the Lord with a thankful and satisfied heart.

Paul sums it up best:

> *I have learned the secret of being content in any and every situation, whether well fed or hungry, whether living in plenty or in want. I can do everything through him who gives me strength. (Philippians 4:12a–13)*

Amen!

# CHAPTER 8

# *You Can't Have It; It's Mine*

## The unattractive quality of jealousy.

In the previous chapter, *Must Be Nice*, we looked at envy and its impact on effective worship. Along with envy in the works of the flesh (Galatians 5:19–21) is another not-so-attractive quality: jealousy. At first glance the two can seem somewhat similar, but a closer look reveals that they're quite different.

To understand the difference, I'll present a simple contrast: Envy is *wanting* what someone else has. Jealousy is being fearful of *losing* what one already has.

> *Envy is* wanting *what someone else has; jealousy is being fearful of* losing *what one already has.*

While envy employs a sense of resentment, jealousy is more fear based. And that fear comes from a selfishness and self-centeredness. But there's also a righteous jealousy, also defined as zealousness: a strong passion for and desire to protect something that's close to our hearts.

*You shall not make for yourself an idol in the form of anything in heaven above or on the earth beneath or the waters below. You shall not bow down to*

> *them or worship them; for I, the Lord your God, am*
> *a jealous God. (Exodus 20:4–5a)*

God is jealous, but in this use of the word, zealous. He is zealous for Israel, and He has set apart Israel for Himself. He asks for complete devotion, as a wife for a husband, but soon Israel disregards God's commands and leaves the protection and affection of her God for others, for idols.

> *For they provoked him to anger with their high*
> *places; they moved him to jealousy with their idols.*
> *(Psalm 78:58 ESV)*

So God left the people of Israel to their own desires, and they became a defeated people, a despised nation. Yet even in the most hopeless and dire situations, God can still redeem and restore:

> *"To me this is like the days of Noah,*
> *when I swore that the waters of Noah would never*
> *again cover the earth.*
> *So now I have sworn not to be angry with you,*
> *never to rebuke you again.*
> *Though the mountains be shaken*
> *and the hills be removed,*
> *yet my unfailing love for you will not be shaken*
> *nor my covenant of peace be removed,"*
> *says the Lord, who has compassion on you.*
> *(Isaiah 54:9–10)*

Let me illustrate a similar righteous jealousy that I personally encountered: I had a certain band member who over time began to greatly overvalue his worth and importance to the team, to me and to the ministry. He ultimately demanded a level of pay that I was unwilling to comply with, and, not surprisingly, he left the team shortly thereafter. Even more disappointing than his diva-like behavior were his efforts to communicate to the entire team his complaints and his case, and his attempts to rally the team to his "side" and create division. These efforts were further carried out by invitations to private gatherings in his home.

The work this man went through to divide the team was unprecedented in my experience. I immediately found myself absolutely and completely jealous for my team, the kind of jealousy that wanted to protect them, to warn them and to keep them from harm. I even surprised myself. So after speaking to my pastor and getting his okay, I confronted this man and we had a lively chat. I clarified my position with him: "If I find out you have one more meeting with anyone on my team, say or communicate one more thing to any of them or do anything more to cause division and confusion on my team, I will do everything in my power to expose you for who you are, to make sure you never set foot in this ministry again and to come against you with all of my strength and every resource available to me." That's how jealous I was and am for my team. That's also the same approach I take if a "wolf" approaches any of my female team members or if someone confronts one of my team members with a complaint that should be addressed to me. I'm jealous for my team and my staff. Even Paul says to the Corinthians:

> *I am jealous for you with a godly jealousy.*
> *(2 Corinthians 11:2a)*

That's a *good* jealous. What about a *bad* jealous?

> *"This Jesus I am proclaiming to you is the Christ,"*
> *he said. Some of the Jews were persuaded and*
> *joined Paul and Silas, as did a large number of*
> *God-fearing Greeks and not a few prominent*
> *women.*

> *But the Jews were jealous; so they rounded up*
> *some bad characters from the marketplace, formed*
> *a mob and started a riot in the city.*
> *(Acts 17:3b–5a)*

Paul and Silas and their message were beginning to get a lot of attention and response. The Jewish leaders, though they had so much to gain from Paul and Silas' message, were only concerned over the potential loss of their position, power and wealth. The message for many was great gain, but for the Jewish leaders, it was nothing but loss of what they had selfishly enjoyed for so long. This realization caused them to behave completely irrationally, losing their minds in a fit of jealousy as they attempted to silence Paul and Silas.

Likewise, in Genesis 37, Joseph's brothers were so jealous of their father Jacob's love and affection (and especially that really nice coat) being poured out on their little brother that they initially planned to kill Joseph. Not wanting their brother's blood on their hands, they instead sold Joseph into slavery, likely assuming he wouldn't survive for long. And you thought your family was dysfunctional!

And yes, irrational responses to jealousy can and do happen on our teams. New musicians join the team, and some of them are good. Really good. Some of those that currently hold similar positions on the team now feel threatened. They become jealous of their position and begin to do irrational things, not wanting to lose their position. They may not kill the new members physically (thankfully), but they can assassinate their character; and though they can't send them off into slavery, they often treat them as lepers.

Paul, seeing similar irrational behavior, presents his concern to the Corinthians:

> *You are still worldly. For since there is jealousy and quarreling among you, are you not worldly? (1 Corinthians 3:3)*

Paul is essentially telling the Corinthians to stop dwelling on and being controlled by their own selfish desires and fears. Our teams and our leaders need to let go of and not be jealous of their positions, their performance and even their popularity. It's all gonna change some day. It's not a matter of *if* but *when*. So rather than worrying and being jealous of earthly positions and possessions, we're to focus our efforts and concerns on the things of God:

*Be jealous of nothing; be filled with the peace of God and have a light grip on everything.*

> *If then you have been raised with Christ, seek the things that are above, where Christ is, seated at the right hand of God. (Colossians 3:1 ESV)*

And as we seek and dwell on the things of God, consider what God replaces jealousy with:

> *Do not be anxious about anything, but in everything by prayer and supplication with thanksgiving let your requests be made known to God. And the peace of God, which surpasses all understanding, will guard your hearts and your minds in Christ Jesus. (Philippians 4:6–7 ESV)*

Be jealous of nothing; be filled with the peace of God and have a light grip on everything.

# CHAPTER 9

# *Looking Out for Number One*

## Recognizing and overcoming selfish ambition.

Selfish ambition. It's right up there with envy and jealousy in the works of the flesh. This behavior is only concerned with one's own interests, not the interests of others. It serves and glorifies one's self over others, even over God. Selfish ambition trumps God's will, refuses to listen to His calling and ignores His Word. It has no desire to serve but rather to be served.

Ambition in and of itself isn't the problem:

- *Ambition*: an earnest desire for some type of achievement or distinction.[8]

Even Paul has ambition:

> *It has always been my ambition to preach the gospel where Christ was not known, so that I would not be building on someone else's foundation. (Romans 15:20)*

It's when our ambition becomes self-serving rather than God-serving that conflicts begin.

There are many instances of selfish ambition in the Bible, with just as many tragic endings. One example that stands out is the story of King David's son Absalom. Absalom's overriding ambition was to be the king of Israel, even though he knew that God had ordained Solomon, another of David's sons, to be Israel's next king. Absalom's ambition was so selfish and so self-consuming that he deceived, lied and even made plans to attack and destroy his father, his family and all who were with them. He was so consumed with being king that nothing was going to stop him. Ironically, one of the objects of his pride, his hair, would be his final undoing. In his attempt to flee the battle he himself had initiated against King David, Absalom got caught by his hair in a low-hanging branch and was subsequently killed by King David's men. His selfish ambition had finally caught up to him—he knew God's plan and will for his life, but he was completely consumed by his own selfish ambition, and in his own blindness he lost everything, including his life.

*It's when our ambition becomes self-serving rather than God-serving that conflicts begin.*

> *Do nothing out of selfish ambition or vain conceit, but in humility consider others better than yourselves. Each of you should look not only to your own interests, but also to the interests of others. (Philippians 2:3–4)*

Selfish ambition exalts us above others and looks only to our own interests. It calls on us to exalt ourselves, to promote ourselves and to lift ourselves up. However, the Word of God clearly contradicts that attitude:

*Humble yourselves, therefore, under God's mighty hand, that he may lift you up in due time.*
*(1 Peter 5:6)*

We read in Matthew:

*Then Jesus said to the disciples, "If any of you wants to be my follower, you must turn from your selfish ways, take up your cross and follow me."(Matthew 16:24 NLT)*

We're clearly left with two choices: forsake our selfish ambitions and follow Christ, who gives life, or embrace and pursue our selfish ambitions, and, like Absalom, disregard God's Word and will, which leads to certain death, both spiritually and literally.

*Your attitude should be the same as that of Christ Jesus:*
*Who, being in very nature God,*
*did not consider equality with God something to be grasped,*
*but made himself nothing,*
*taking the very nature of a servant,*
*being made in human likeness.*
*And being found in appearance as a man,*
*he humbled himself*
*and became obedient to death—*
*even death on a cross!*
*Therefore God exalted him to the highest place*
*and gave him the name that is above every name,*
*that at the name of Jesus every knee should bow,*
*in heaven and on earth and under the earth,*
*and every tongue confess that Jesus Christ is Lord,*
*to the glory of God the Father. (Philippians 2:6–11)*

What an incredible picture and example: Jesus humbled Himself, having left heaven to come to earth as a man and to give His life for us and denying Himself to serve His Father and fulfill His Father's will. And God exalted Him to the highest place. Now God asks us to humble ourselves and serve Him so we, too, can be exalted:

> *Whoever exalts himself will be humbled, and whoever humbles himself will be exalted.*
> *(Matthew 23:12 ESV)*

How does selfish ambition manifest itself on our worship teams? It's when we begin to consider how our efforts on stage might benefit or serve us. It's when we no longer desire to write and record a CD to edify the body but rather to make a name for ourselves, to promote ourselves and to find commercial and financial success. It's when we no longer want to sing a solo to honor the Lord and bless the church body but rather as an opportunity to be "discovered." For some, rather than humbly serving the Lord with their gifts and talents, their efforts become an opportunity to be paid, to attract a mate, to have some sort of prestige, and more. It all comes back to these two questions: who is it for and whom is it serving?

*If you pursue your ambitions by seeking and serving the Lord rather than yourself first, you'll almost certainly avoid the temptation of serving yourself over God.*

Again, there is nothing wrong with ambition. In fact, ambition can be healthy and can drive us to pursue greater excellence in order to serve the Lord more fully. There's also nothing wrong with finding commercial and financial success, being "discovered," being paid or finding a mate. *But*, let that be the blessing rather than the motive.

To safeguard our hearts and expose our motives, we must always precede ambition with this initiative:

*Seek first his kingdom and his righteousness, and all these things will be given to you as well. (Matthew 6:33)*

If you pursue your ambitions in that order, seeking and serving the Lord rather than yourself first, you'll almost certainly avoid the emptiness, futility and temptation of serving yourself over God.

\* \* \* \* \* \* \* \*

I hope you never grow tired or give up serving the Lord. The world will tell you that you have to look out for number one, yourself, to get what you want. But the Lord admonishes us instead to look to Him in all our ways and to serve Him only, not ourselves. When we do so, He'll watch out for us, lift us up and give us the desires of our heart.

# CHAPTER 10

# *Can't We All Get Along?*

## Dealing with team dynamics.

I would say without a doubt that the biggest and most challenging part of my job is juggling all the egos and personalities on my team in order to get them all to play nicely together. I have often jokingly referred to my job title as "playground monitor." This is by no means a slight to my team. They're the first to recognize and admit the obvious challenges. Rather, it's a reality that any leader of any group faces. We're all covered in flesh, so naturally there will be envy, jealousy, gossip, dissention and even rebellion, and the bigger the team, the more challenges. This is not a fatalistic view of a worship team or any other ministry team but rather a sober reality. The apostle James said it best:

> *Consider it pure joy, my brothers and sisters, whenever you face trials of many kinds. (James 1:2)*

It's not a matter of *if* you'll face any challenges and trials but *when*. However, these issues can certainly be mitigated and managed. These trials should never compromise, divide or destroy a team but quite the opposite: in God's economy, trials can actually grow and mature a team, depending on how they're handled.

> *The testing of your faith develops perseverance.*
> *Perseverance must finish its work so that you may*
> *be mature and complete, not lacking anything.*
> *(James 1:3b–4)*

So the team leader's job is a matter of developing a culture that understands the reality of trials and challenges and seeks to minimize any detrimental impact on the team while simultaneously allowing the team to grow from its trials. This takes cultivation (preparation), correction (boldness) and care (unconditional love).

## Cultivation

Cultivating your culture is preparing your team and the ministry to receive scriptural expectations and mandates, and translating those to specific guidelines for your team, or any team, for that matter. It's defining and ingraining these standards into the culture of your team and ministry. Without them, there's nothing to direct or correct since there's nothing to define what's right or wrong, acceptable or unacceptable.

> *What shall we say, then? Is the law sinful?*
> *Certainly not! Nevertheless, I would not have*
> *known what sin was had it not been for the law. For*
> *I would not have known what coveting really was if*
> *the law had not said, "You shall not covet."*
> *(Romans 7:7)*

So again, there have to be standards that determine what behavior is acceptable and what is unacceptable, and the standards that I employ use scriptural precedent, cultural relevance and personal preference to define them.

***Scriptural Precedent*** doesn't need much explanation. The Bible makes it clear what disqualifies someone from ministry. Whether it's sexual immorality, unrepentant sin or false doctrine, the Bible sets a standard that transcends time and culture.

***Cultural Relevance*** requires us to carefully consider codes of conduct as they relate specifically to our culture and time. The Bible deals with many cultural issues, and although the specific biblical remedy doesn't necessarily apply to our current culture, the bigger-picture issue is still prevalent today. For example, in 1 Corinthians 11, we read that women are to wear head coverings. So then, are we to wear head coverings today? No, we're not. There's a much bigger picture being presented here: two cultures were colliding in the church, Jewish and Greek. Jewish women wore head coverings; Greek women did not. The big-picture issue wasn't head coverings; it was overcoming division and creating unity in the church. Although head coverings were the solution for that time and in that culture, those particular cultural conditions are no longer present in our church today. But the need for unity in the church is still relevant today (and always will be), so the need for solutions continues, and the most effective solutions will be ones that are relevant to today's time and culture.

Here in South Florida, we also have a divergence of two cultures: the young, casual group and the more seasoned, traditional group. For us, our "head covering" issue became the issue of attire. On one extreme were sandals, shorts, t-shirts and baseball caps, and on the other extreme were suits and ties and dresses. To create unity, I had to find a reasonable balance. For starters, now I don't allow sandals to be worn on stage. They're sort of the poster child for a relaxed, carefree kind of living (not to mention that the exposed foot is not always an attractive feature), and I felt we needed to kick it up a notch. Also gone are t-shirts with messages or advertisements, shorts and, for the men, hats. Instead, on weekends, nice jeans or dress pants, button-up shirts, appropriate length dresses and no tennis shoes. Midweek services are more casual; nice t-shirts and tennis shoes are okay. Again, we found a respectable balance that took into account both sides of the issue and brought peace and unity to the church.

Another example of conflict in our church has been over body piercings and tattoos. I don't have an issue with either (although it creeps me out to think of what some of those tattoos are going to look like when the wearers are in their sixties, seventies or eighties), but for many, body markings and piercings have derogative associations. So in order to promote unity, before being on stage, I have my team members remove any visible piercings (other than earrings) and wear clothing that can reasonably cover any visible tattoos, such as long-sleeved shirts to cover arm tattoos. Again, this isn't an indictment on tattoos or body piercings but rather a promotion of peace and unity in the body of Christ. We're finding a reasonable balance while keeping our eyes and hearts focused on Jesus.

*Worship is bringing attention to Jesus, so we should always use great care, consideration, discretion and balance in taking steps to reduce distractions.*

Paul dealt with this balancing act as well and came to this conclusion:

> *"Everything is permissible"—but not everything is beneficial. "Everything is permissible"—but not everything is constructive. Nobody should seek his own good, but the good of others.*
> *(1 Corinthians 10:23–24)*

That's the point of cultural relevance, not insisting on one's own rights but rather on the well-being of others. That's why they wore head coverings in the early church, and that's why I don't allow sloppy clothing, body piercings, visible tattoos (if possible) or other distractions on stage. Not because it's not permissible but because it's not beneficial. Worship is all about bringing attention to Jesus, and to that end there should always be great care, consideration, discretion and balance used in taking steps to reduce any unnecessary distractions.

These are decisions all leaders have to make for their teams and ministries; what is permissible and what is beneficial. Lots of factors go into determining cultural relevance, so be sure to pray for wisdom, know your pastor's heart and look at the big picture.

***Personal Preference*** is also fairly self-explanatory. These are standards that are not scriptural directives but nonetheless have roots in the Word—and they aren't necessarily culturally relevant either, although the prevailing culture may push back against them to some degree. These are standards that I personally insist on, whereas another leader may not have the same inclination to pursue them with the same persistence I do. Although I do feel they contribute to order and excellence on the team in a significant way, again, they're my personal preferences, and you'll have your own preferences as well.

My personal preferences could generally be summed up with the following standards: punctuality, preparation and performance.

**Punctuality.** I expect my team members to be on time, whether to a rehearsal, a sound check or a special event. I don't expect them to just be present on time; I expect them to be set up, tuned up, warmed up and ready to go on time. No excuses (except for legitimate emergencies or death!). And then I do my part. Rehearsals, for example, are only an hour. We start on time and we end on time. After rehearsal is when team members may socialize, not during rehearsal time.

Quite honestly, people from all over the country consistently share with me that their worship team rehearsals usually start at least an hour or two late, and, once started, they continue for another two, three or even four hours! I'm stunned. Is there no concern for the family? Is there no respect for people's time and busy schedules?

> *Simply let your "Yes" be "Yes," and your "No,"*
> *"No." (Matthew 5:37)*

If rehearsal starts at six o'clock, it's six o'clock. Not six fifteen, not six thirty, not seven o'clock, and not eight o'clock, for crying out loud. When somebody joins the team, I ask "Can you make rehearsals at six o'clock and service sound checks on time?" They always say "yes," so I expect their "yes" to be "yes," not an hour or more late. That, to me, is unacceptable.

**Preparation.** I have a saying I often share with the team concerning rehearsals: "We're here to polish the apple, not plant the tree." I expect everyone to come prepared, ready to play and sing. I give them all the tools they need a month at a time: MP3s, charts, Planning Center access, and schedules and song lists. They should be prepared and ready to go. Now, rather than spend time on basics, we can proceed to working on blend, feel, transitions, dynamics and so many other facets that, once again, "polish" our presentation.

> *Do your planning and prepare your fields before*
> *building your house. (Proverbs 24:27 NLT)*

Team members are to get their individual work done ahead of time and practice on their own, and then when we all get together as a team, we can "build our house" together during rehearsal.

**Performance.** We've all had people freeze up in auditions only to hear them say, "I just sang it great at home and in the car on the way here. I really do know the song; I'm just nervous." But once in a while someone will keep his or her nerves in check through auditions, and even on rare occasion through rehearsal and sound check, only to freeze up and choke during the actual service. The standard I have for performance can only be tested and met on the stage during live worship, and, unfortunately, that performance usurps all other performances that may have taken place during auditions, rehearsals, at home or in the car.

The fear and anxiety that some team members encounter during those clutch moments are debilitating and defeating. Some overcome it in time; for others it only gets worse. Now, some people will launch into the message that fear is of the devil and share Scriptures such as:

> *For God has not given us a spirit of fear.*
> *(2 Timothy 1:7a ABPE)*

or

> *There is no fear in love, but perfect love casts out*
> *fear. (1 John 4:18a ESV)*

But I challenge that thinking.

The *fear* that these Scriptures mention is a cowardly fear that causes one to "be deterred from the work of the Lord, the preaching of the Gospel, opposing the errors of false teachers, and reproving men for their sins."[9] This fear should not be confused with a type of performance anxiety that is more of a gift deficiency than a prevalence of fear. Leaders have to be very careful and discerning. All that some team members will hear is that their anxiety is now their sin, and their inability to overcome this sin will likely push them over the edge and discourage them from serving in any ministry ever again. I prefer this approach:

> *Anxiety weighs down the heart, but a kind word*
> *cheers it up. (Proverbs 12:25)*

A kind word tells them, "It's okay. This doesn't define who you are, and if this only causes you stress and anxiety, then let's take a break and pray about how we can best use your gift in a way that will bring you peace rather than terror." I say this with a reassuring smile, making sure they know that I'm not disappointed in the least. And I leave the door open for them to try again in the future if they want to (but it's up to them), with my full and complete support.

There's also the possibility of something in between: a few years ago, there was a girl on the worship team who sang with the vocal team but hadn't sung any solos. I decided to give her an opportunity at a solo, and, after the final weekend service, she pulled me aside in the back hallway and said in a panicked voice, "Don't *ever* do that to me again. Some of the others may want solos, but I don't. It's way too much pressure and stress, and my family can't wait for this weekend to be over so they can have me back. Just let me sing with the group and no more solos." I laughed and never gave her another solo, and she couldn't have been happier!

So to recap: we've looked at cultivating the culture in order to prepare our team members for standards based on scriptural precedent, cultural relevance and personal preference. What follows, then, is the need to enforce those standards in order to maintain order, direction and vision.

## Correction

Maintaining order once standards have been integrated into the culture requires correction and confrontation. By definition, *correction* is

- "to make right, to conform to an established standard,"[10]

and *confrontation* is

- "to face boldly, to bring face to face."[11]

When my kids were little and one of them began to cross the street without looking, I would stop him and gently explain the need to look both ways for his own protection. I would correct him. If the next day he tried to cross the street once again without looking, I would stop him, confront him and sternly tell him (in an age-appropriate way) that his behavior was unacceptable; it was going to get him hurt. A consequence was now in order, a time out. I would confront (rebuke) him and subsequently discipline him with a consequence.

I use a very similar process with the team. If someone is late, a friendly correction is in order: after the fact, one on one, not in public. If late again, then a face-to-face confrontation takes place privately that now has me questioning this person's commitment to the team. I have this team member take a break from the team for a week or more (depending on the circumstances and attitude) to pray about his or her future involvement. The response is almost always, "But I know God's called me to be on the team," to which I respond with, "But your actions and behavior have betrayed your calling. Take a couple of weeks and pray about it, and at that time if you still feel God's calling you to be a part of the team, then jump back in. Then the challenges you've been having with punctuality (or being unprepared, having a lousy attitude or whatever it happens to be) shouldn't be an issue moving forward."

Start with correction:

> *Listen to advice and accept correction, and in the end you will be wise. (Proverbs 19:20)*

Follow up with confrontation, rebuke or discipline, if necessary:

> *For the moment all discipline seems painful rather than pleasant, but later it yields the peaceful fruit of righteousness to those who have been trained by it. (Hebrews 12:11 ESV)*

And finally, if a team member simply isn't responding but is purposefully being disrespectful, divisive and self-serving, then it's time to remove him or her from the team:

> *As for a person who stirs up division, after warning*
> *him once and then twice, have nothing more to do*
> *with him. (Titus 3:10 ESV)*

I haven't encountered this scenario often but certainly a few times over the years. Each time it's disappointing and heartbreaking. At this point, make sure you've already shared your concerns and experiences with your pastor and that you have your pastor's support and blessing for this person's removal from the team. You'll always want to have a unified front when dealing with this level of discipline.

Each one of these three levels of enforcement requires boldness. This is not something you can shy away from, naïvely hoping it will go away or solve itself. In fact, quite the opposite will happen. The problem will only grow and fester, and the person creating the division will feel more emboldened when confrontation is avoided. As a result, morale on the team will suffer, especially when confrontation is avoided due to exceptional skills, irreplaceable position or privileged position due to a favored relationship. Don't allow this to happen; instead, confront the situation immediately:

> *Be strong and courageous. Do not fear or be in*
> *dread of them, for it is the Lord your God who goes*
> *with you. He will not leave you or forsake you.*
> *(Deuteronomy 31:6 ESV)*

I had an electric guitarist on my team who was an amazing and truly gifted musician and player. But he showed up when he felt like it and made it quite clear that punctuality was not an option. The whole team was watching to see what I was going to do.

Would I make an exception because of this man's incredible gift, or would I follow through on my standards? I did correct and confront but to no avail. So, I removed him from the team. That doesn't mean I wasn't sad to see him go, but yes, it was imperative that I follow through on my standards and enforcement, and I did just that. The end result: a team that was pleasantly surprised, that felt their diligence and effort was honored and that now has a greater level of respect for my integrity and commitment to team unity.

*A team that's unified is one whose members understand their roles and expectations, honor and respect each other and care for and support each other even in times of correction and discipline.*

Let me finish this section with a scenario that I have been asked about at literally every single conference I've taught at, bar none: "What do I do if a team member is never on time and never prepared, but I can't remove her because she's the pastor's wife?" It's actually quite simple: you follow the same standards you hold the rest of the team to. If her behavior warrants correction, confrontation and subsequent dismissal, then proceed with exactly that. If dismissal is ultimately warranted but you're not allowed to follow through due to her relationship to the pastor, then it's time to dismiss yourself and find another ministry and pastor to serve under. If compromise is happening there, it's happening elsewhere, so get out now before things get worse. Trust me, things will get worse.

> *Preach the Word; be prepared in season and out of season; correct, rebuke and encourage—with great patience and careful instruction. (2 Timothy 4:2)*

In all instances of correction, confrontation and discipline, employ the Word at all times, doing so patiently so as not to make any rushed or rash decisions. In every instance, be sure to provide counsel that is thoughtful rather than impulsive and reactive, allowing the greatest opportunity for repentance and restoration to take place in hearts and lives.

## Care

As much as correction, confrontation and discipline are necessary and biblical, it's just as important to restore those who have been through a season of discipline. We want to neither "shoot our wounded" nor neglect them but rather to walk alongside them, caring for them and welcoming them back with open arms and open, forgiving hearts.

> *Therefore, as God's chosen people, holy and dearly loved, clothe yourselves with compassion, kindness, humility, gentleness and patience. Bear with each other and forgive whatever grievances you may have against one another. Forgive as the Lord forgave you. And over all these virtues put on love, which binds them all together in perfect unity.*
> *(Colossians 3:12–14)*

For those who have been corrected, disciplined or even removed for a season, reengaging can be awkward—but it doesn't need to be. Part of the restoration process is training your team members: training them to forgive as they've been forgiven, to pray for their teammates and to restore them even in their own hearts. When that happens, those rejoining the team feel welcomed, they're truly restored and there's unity on the team.

A team that's unified is one whose members understand their roles and expectations, honor and respect each other and each person's uniqueness, and care for and support each other even in times of correction and discipline. The Lord loves us and forgives us in spite of ourselves. When we do the same for each other, we have a team that gets along. That's not only a key aspect of the framework of worship, but it's a whole lot of fun.

> *Above all, love each other deeply, because love covers over a multitude of sins. (1 Peter 4:8)*

Amen!

# CHAPTER 11

# *I Don't Feel Like It*

## The discipline of worship.

At Calvary Chapel Fort Lauderdale, we have one Wednesday evening and four weekend services. This happens every week of every month of every year, and has been for the last couple of decades. I'm the worship leader and I love my job. I really, really do. But every once in a while, I just don't feel like leading worship. Would it surprise you to learn that when the alarm goes off at six fifteen every Sunday morning, I don't always bounce out of bed overflowing with utter excitement and anticipation for what awaits me, the team and the church in our times of worship? I do look forward to worship, just not all the time, not every week.

Sometimes it's the song list: it just happens to be a collection of songs that aren't my favorites. Other times it's that some key people are missing due to sickness, vacation or something else. Sometimes I'm just plain tired: it was a long week of meetings, planning, meetings, counseling, meetings, practices and some more meetings. Other times I'm worn out spiritually from some particularly tough confrontations, stupid behavior on the team or by staff (yes, my stupid behavior, too) or conflicts at the leadership level or at home. Maybe it's a rehearsal that's not planned out or a song list with no songs. Or it could be that my daily devotion has become weekly—or even monthly. You get the point. Whatever the reason, sometimes I just don't feel like leading worship.

Let me illustrate it this way: I enjoy working out, often going to the gym three to four times a week. Most of the time I look forward to going, sometimes I can take it or leave it, but other times, I just don't want to go work out. At those times when I'm just not into it, I employ a little self-discipline. I look at myself in the mirror from the neck down (to remind myself of why I need to go), and then I'm off to the gym. Once I'm there and get started, I'm into it. Ironically, those workouts are often the best. By the end I'm energized, feeling good about myself and my health, and pleased with the results that the self-discipline accomplished.

> *But I discipline my body and keep it under control, lest after preaching to others I myself should be disqualified. (1 Corinthians 9:27 ESV)*

I particularly like this Scripture. While using the illustration of an athlete in training, it simultaneously links the flesh (body) to the Holy Spirit. When I don't feel like leading worship, I need to discipline my body, my lazy and selfish body. And if I don't control my body, the obvious result is that my body will control me. The apostle Paul spells it out very clearly:

> *For those who live according to the flesh set their minds on the things of the flesh, but those who live according to the Spirit set their minds on the things of the Spirit. (Romans 8:5 ESV)*

And the repercussions are:

> *For to set the mind on the flesh is death, but to set the mind on the Spirit is life and peace.*
> *(Romans 8:6 ESV)*

When "I don't feel like it," the reality is that my flesh is struggling against the Spirit. A few times when I *really* didn't feel like leading worship, I wanted to call in "sick." It crossed my mind. But when I took my mind off the body and set it on the Spirit, I pushed on, much like the runner who is at a similar crossroads, "Should I quit or keep going?" and upon continuing he gets a second wind. I have gotten countless second winds in the Spirit, that extra perseverance that carries us through. And not just carries us through but takes us to a place of such victory that there's an overwhelming awareness of having just narrowly escaped missing an amazing blessing and experience because the flesh almost won out over the Spirit.

But there has also been at least one time in the past when I did give in. I didn't feel like leading worship, so I called my assistant and asked him to take the service for me. He did— and everything went great. But like Romans 8:6 says, *"to set the mind on the Spirit is life and peace"* (ESV). I can distinctly remember feeling unsettled over my decision and reason for taking the time off. There was no peace that day.

> *Worship requires a sacrifice. It requires us to give up something, and that something is our flesh.*

Now, I know there are extenuating circumstances that require all of us from time to time to miss a service on short notice. But again, just check your motive and what your mind is set on. Are you being flexible and available to respond to another need or ministry opportunity that God has presented to you or are you simply being a bit lazy? Or maybe, just maybe, you're being just a little irresponsible because of an athletic event, concert or Star Trek movie release that's conflicting with service time. Just asking. . . .

Of course, we all have the need, and even the responsibility, to take time off to recharge and to be refreshed—this is addressed in the upcoming chapter *Road Trip*. Taking days off or taking a vacation is a very different animal than waking up in the morning, not feeling like leading worship (or whatever your responsibility may be) and acting upon your feelings. Having days where you don't feel like leading worship is understandable, but giving in to that mindset one too many times will eventually lead you down a path of ineffectiveness and apathy, at which time you might want to consider another calling or career.

Which brings me to my final point: in addition to discipline, there's also an element of sacrifice involved in worship. While discipline is a form of training that corrects and molds behavior, sacrifice is a surrender and an offering that costs something.

> *Through him then let us continually offer up a sacrifice of praise to God, that is, the fruit of lips that acknowledge his name. (Hebrews 13:15 ESV)*

- *Continually:* At all times and through all circumstances.

- *Sacrifice of praise to God:* Giving up our selfish wants and desires in order to praise God.

Worship requires a sacrifice. It requires us to give up something, and that something is our flesh. That means when we don't *feel* like it, we sacrifice our *feelings*. If there are other things that we would rather do than lead worship, we sacrifice them as well. It's not about us; it's about Jesus, who willingly gave His life on a cross for our freedom. But just like we have a choice when we don't feel like it, Jesus had a similar choice when He didn't feel like it:

> *Going a little farther, he fell with his face to the ground and prayed, "My Father, if it is possible, may this cup be taken from me. Yet not as I will, but as you will." (Matthew 26:39)*

Jesus had an agonizing choice to make, one that I can't even begin to fathom. He chose the cross because of us. With that as a backdrop, I don't think it's asking too much to choose to set our minds on the things of the Spirit. Especially on the days we don't feel like it.

# CHAPTER 12

# *That's How We've Always Done It*

## Understanding and navigating the influence of tradition.

*Tradition*:

- an inherited, established or customary pattern of thought, action or behavior.[12]

It's Christmas morning, and this morning, like so many Christmas mornings before it, Sheri and I get up, turn on the Christmas tree lights, get everything situated and then tell the kids they can come out of their rooms—a huge relief for them since they've been awake since four a.m. We sit around the tree and the kids marvel at the gifts awaiting them. We read the Christmas story from the Bible, and I pray, thanking God for His Son whose birthday we celebrate. Then I thank Him for all of His goodness and good gifts to us as we prepare to open our gifts from one to another. "Amen!" That being the signal, the kids all rush to the gifts. Those will always be amazing memories for me, our own little tradition every Christmas morning.

Well, my oldest boy is now married with two little ones, so they won't be coming on Christmas morning anymore; they're starting their own family traditions for Christmas. They'll come over later, splitting their time between the in-laws and us. My middle child just got married, so she won't be coming on Christmas morning either; she and her husband will be alternating Christmases with us and his family in Ohio. And my youngest, although he's still single at twenty, doesn't consider a six a.m. gift call a tradition worth maintaining anymore.

So the tradition that had been an integral part of our Christmas for years is no longer celebrated or honored. Well then, it's sad but true: Christmas no longer holds any value or purpose. It's dead, void of any real meaning. Christmas is worthless now, wrecked by a bunch of self-serving and insensitive kids who have ingloriously traded our rich heritage for their own empty and meaningless routines, effectively snubbing their noses at the very fiber and substance of a previously holy and blessed Christmas experience, which has now been relegated to a mere memory and footnote. Thanks, kids.

Sound familiar?

Tradition is a powerful thing. Whether right or wrong, it evokes strong emotion and loyalty. Although I made up the last paragraph of my Christmas story as it pertains to my family, the content is a collection of quotes from hundreds of letters and emails I've received over the years. And right about now one might expect me to launch into a bit of a righteous tirade directed at the denominational church structures and their hierarchy, along with the older, purse-string holders that are responsible for holding back many an attempt to contemporize and personalize the worship experience. But I won't. Not exclusively anyway.

The push back against the denominational church and its older members is based on the *inherited* element of tradition. These people have done church a certain way for most of their lives, and they hope to pass their traditions on to the next generation. The problem is that the next generation isn't all that excited about its inheritance. So are we to assume then that contemporary, nondenominational churches don't have tradition issues? Reading all of the books and articles on tradition, one could come to that conclusion. And from an *inherited* element of the tradition definition, I would obviously have to agree. But from an *established* element of tradition, I would have to say that the contemporary church most certainly does have tradition issues.

Let me attempt to clarify this distinction between *inherited* tradition and *established* tradition by giving an illustration of the two:

Back in the '80s I was brought on as the minister of music (the precursor to the worship leader) of a Baptist church in Southern California. It had approximately 2,500 members (which means about 800 attended church) and had been in existence for well over a hundred years. The worship consisted of hymns only, accompanied by an electronic pipe organ (played by a particularly mean old lady) and a piano, with choir songs and occasional "special music" rounding out the worship experience. The newly installed pastor had a great vision for moving the church forward, and the worship was a major component of that vision. The pastor tasked me with the following: transition from traditional worship to a predominantly contemporary worship format; develop a praise band consisting of drums, keyboards and acoustic, electric and bass guitars; bring in praise songs (or choruses as they were known then) and accomplish this in a two-year time frame.

That seemed like a long time, but I ended up needing every minute of those two years. I immediately knew I was in for a long rough road ahead when one of the very first changes I made was to sing a praise chorus, "In Moments like These" instead of the Doxology at the close of the offering. We lost four families due to that one change alone. (It's the truth; I couldn't make this stuff up.) But with the full support of the pastor and board, I continued to move forward. I reshuffled staff, brought in one praise band instrument at a time (hoping to keep the shock to a minimum) and began to incorporate more and more praise choruses.

Slowly the balance from hymns to praise songs began to shift, and I used every ounce of charm I possessed to try to win over those who had fought me every step of the way. At the end of the two years, we had a great thing going; the church was growing and the congregation was becoming a wonderful mix of young and old. All was good!

Then the pastor resigned and the old guard came back to life. Then I resigned. And now the old guard was back in business, and in short order they got back everything they had lost, including the hymns, the organ, the choir and even the mean old organ lady.

Within a few years attendance plummeted, giving sank, and, after some 125 years in existence, the church was forced to liquidate and sell its property. There weren't enough people left to even relocate. Gone. The old guard was so determined to have their way and maintain their traditions that they would sacrifice anything in order to achieve that. And they did. They sacrificed everything. Today the church building is a pet food warehouse. So sad.

A few years later I went to Calvary Chapel Fort Lauderdale, at that time a small but growing group, to join around five hundred believers as their worship leader. The worship consisted of worship and praise songs only (no hymns), led by an acoustic guitar, accompanied by more acoustic guitars and the usual praise band instrumentation. I was tasked with expanding the breadth of the worship experience, raising the skill level and investing in the team musically and spiritually. I immediately, but not purposefully, introduced a slightly new and different sound than what they were used to simply because I led from the keyboard rather than the acoustic guitar. In addition, I decided to change things up a little by introducing a hymn into each of the worship sets over the first two weekends: current arrangements of "Nothin' but the Blood" the first weekend and "How Great Thou Art" the following weekend. It seemed like a nice touch and a healthy mix. Seemed. The vast majority enjoyed those two hymns. However, some did not, particularly the writers of the two letters I received. One said, "We don't sing hymns here; only dead churches sing hymns," while the other was a little less subtle, "Go back to where you came from!" Great start. These people's tradition wasn't inherited—the church was too young—but their tradition was established. They had determined what their worship would look like and sound like and what style of songs would define them. This group at Calvary Chapel was just as protective of their tradition as those at the Baptist church were. Over time and with scriptural exhortation, the Calvary group came to fully understand that hymns don't make a church dead, people do. And this church has gone on to become one of the largest churches in the country.

"But doesn't your earlier example of the Baptist church going back to hymns prove that hymns do in fact make for a dead church?" No, it doesn't. It was the insistence on maintaining tradition that killed the church. Hymns were simply one of the objects of their tradition.

"But wait; you say it was tradition that killed the church. But Paul says that traditions are good, that we should hold to them and maintain them."

> *So then, brothers, stand firm and hold to the traditions that you were taught by us, either by our spoken word or by our letter.*
> *(2 Thessalonians 2:15)*

> *Now I commend you because you remember me in everything and maintain the traditions even as I delivered them to you. (1 Corinthians 11:2 ESV)*

These traditions Paul refers to are the Word of God passed down from generation to generation before there was a Bible. In this usage, tradition is defined as "the handing down of information, beliefs and customs by word of mouth or by example from one generation to another without written instruction."[13]

*The overriding obstacle of tradition is the worship of tradition itself.*

There weren't any Bibles or written form of the Scriptures for the masses, just the traditions passed on by oral communication and the content of that communication lived out by example. These are God's traditions (truth passed on) unlike man's traditions (preferences passed on).

Jesus confronted man's traditions in a strongly worded rebuke directed at the Pharisees; but beware, lest any of His words should ring true for us:

> *Then some Pharisees and teachers of the law came to Jesus from Jerusalem and asked, "Why do your disciples break the tradition of the elders? They don't wash their hands before they eat!"*
>
> *Jesus replied, "And why do you break the command of God for the sake of your tradition? For God said, 'Honor your father and mother' and 'Anyone who curses his father or mother must be put to death.' But you say that if a man says to his father or mother, 'Whatever help you might otherwise have received from me is a gift devoted to God,' he is not to 'honor his father' with it. Thus you nullify the word of God for the sake of your tradition. You hypocrites!" (Matthew 15:1–7)*

Or, as Mark quoted Jesus:

> *You have a fine way of setting aside the commands of God in order to observe your own traditions! (Mark 7:9)*

The overriding obstacle of tradition is the worship of tradition itself. Tradition often sets itself up as the preeminent element of a ministry, its liturgy and its worship, necessitating a greater adherence to its form and substance than to the Word of God itself. Strictly aligned to preference and familiarity, tradition dictates what songs can and cannot be sung and how they are to be performed. Determining that there are *no* new songs that have any value worthy to be implemented into this tradition-based worship is absolutely ludicrous, shortsighted and unbelievably self-serving. I'm not a fan of doing away with anything and everything associated with tradition, but rather I am a huge fan of doing away with the culture that blindly and selfishly advocates the selection, style and format of songs while indiscriminately disparaging and condemning everything else. It's maddening, and it's turning church after church into private country clubs.

> *Psalm 33:3 says to sing a new song, but it doesn't say to sing **only** new songs.*

So how do we transcend this culture? How do we overcome tradition in worship? At the risk of sounding simplistic:

*Sing to him a new song. (Psalm 33:3a)*

Yes, sing a new song. We're told to. Not asked, told. And it makes perfect sense: if we keep singing new songs, the old ones don't get a chance to become tradition. And if the church already has its own traditional songs, then we can slowly and gradually wean them off their tradition. Wherever you go, wherever you lead, be prepared for push back. Not everyone will like your new song, but you still have to sing it.

Psalm 33:3 says to sing a new song, but it doesn't say to sing *only* new songs. Wherever you serve as a worship leader, you don't have to love their songs (or even like them), but you do need to show respect. And if you do that, if you show sincere respect and appreciation for their songs and play them on occasion, the people will be more inclined to respect and appreciate your songs. And who knows—as their worship experience deepens and broadens, they might actually like your new songs! I have seen this done, and I have done this myself. Though it does take time, it does bear fruit.

But, whatever you do, don't go into any place with an approach and attitude that proclaims, "I'm the new sheriff in town," and proceed to throw out everything they know and love. They will run you and your new song out of town. Then you'll be mad at the church and blame it for your failure, when, in reality, you blew it. You didn't love on the people, nor did you respect them or their songs. But if instead you love on people, learn their culture, respect their songs and are consistent and persistent in committing everything to prayer, you will win them over and endear them to you and your songs. Share your passion for Christ and for worship with them the entire time, and they will eventually love you and your songs. They just need time.

*The church will always need a new song; otherwise it will stagnate and become irrelevant.*

A few years ago my team and I were asked to lead worship for services at a church in Southern California. As we were warming up and running through one of our newer, upbeat arrangements, a very old, frail woman slowly shuffled down the aisle toward us. When she finally made it all the way to the front, she stopped, looked right at us and yelled, "This kind of music belongs in a club, not a church!" She immediately turned and began to shuffle back up the aisle. It was so surreal. We all stopped playing and singing, and just stared at the woman as she slowly faded out of sight. After a moment, we all kind of shook it off and chuckled a little, then continued with our sound check. Not too long after that encounter the service began, and as we led the church in worship we all had an amazing time in the Spirit. And the song that "didn't belong in church"? It was the highlight of our worship experience. It *did* belong in church. And that little old lady? My heart broke for her. We all got together and prayed for her, that her heart would be softened and not so consumed and blinded by tradition and preference.

The church will always need a new song; otherwise it will stagnate and become irrelevant. Soon tradition will be worshipped while worship itself is marginalized, even frowned upon.

No, it should never be that way—don't let it be that way.

> *Because of the Lord's faithful love we do not perish, for His mercies never end. They are new every morning; great is your faithfulness.*
> *(Lamentations 3:22–23 HSCB)*

He's given us new life, new hope and a new heart, and He gives us new mercies every day. Why wouldn't we worship Him with a new song?

# CHAPTER 13

# *Seasons*

## Adapting to changing times.

*There is a time for everything, and a season for
every activity under heaven:*

*a time to be born and a time to die,*
*a time to plant and a time to uproot,*
*a time to kill and a time to heal,*
*a time to tear down and a time to build,*
*a time to weep and a time to laugh,*
*a time to mourn and a time to dance,*
*a time to scatter stones and a time to gather them,*
*a time to embrace and a time to refrain,*
*a time to search and a time to give up,*
*a time to keep and a time to throw away,*
*a time to tear and a time to mend,*
*a time to be silent and a time to speak,*
*a time to love and a time to hate,*
*a time for war and time for peace.*
*(Ecclesiastes 3:1–8)*

I have been involved in leading worship in some capacity for well over thirty years, and in that time I've seen countless programs, ministries, songs, styles and even artists and teachers come and go. At one time they all were embraced, admired and raised up as examples. Now they're mostly forgotten, maybe fondly remembered but no longer valued by most. They've been replaced, as they themselves replaced others who preceded them, who replaced others before them. . . . The very nature of *seasons* points out this reality: things change and they're supposed to. Besides false doctrine, one of the biggest impediments to successful and fruitful ministry is our innate resistance to change. Especially when it comes to worship. But is it always the church that resists change, or could it also be us, the worship leaders?

> **Besides false doctrine, one of the biggest impediments to successful and fruitful ministry is our innate resistance to change.**

Having looked at tradition in the previous chapter, we initially can easily see a great similarity between it and the subject of seasons, especially as these subjects relate to the tension and necessity of change. They're both founded on a sense of preference, but those very preferences are, in fact, what make tradition and seasons very different and unique, especially in their formation and establishment.

Tradition is based on a set of preferences that are corporately established and generationally honored, gaining almost sacred status (and, in some cases, equal or even higher status than biblically mandated practices) and that are often labeled as a church's (or institution's) heritage.

Seasons, however, are more a set of personal preferences resulting from environmental influences; these preferences can significantly shape and define a person's identity and personality. Seasons can often become known as "the glory days" or "the good ol' days," and are typically generational (fifteen to twenty-five years); whereas traditions can last for centuries. An example of tradition could be the weekly playing of the Doxology after the offering or the closing of the service with the reading of a benediction. A perfect example of a season could be acoustic-guitar-led '70's praise songs. The list goes on and on.

I recently read a blog where the writer was lamenting how worship had "lost its way" after the '70s. I then read the multitude of comments from people who chimed in with their own similar grievances. And, once again, another faction is born that concludes that all other manifestations of worship, including style, production and instrumentation, that don't line up with their own preferences and experiences are misguided and inauthentic.

This is unfortunate. Are there examples of misguided and inauthentic worship happening today? Of course. How about during the '70s? Absolutely. If you want to find a gripe about any and every season, you won't have to look hard. The dispute arises when people look at the problems of every other season but their own, thus concluding that theirs was the apex of the authentic worship experience. And, unfortunately, it happens more than we'd like to admit.

Things change, seasons change, and we either adapt or we don't. If we choose not to adapt, then we tend to surround ourselves with others who choose not to adapt for similar reasons, often initiating (whether consciously or unconsciously) some form of division. It's like wearing a t-shirt and shorts in the summer but refusing to wear warmer clothes when fall comes. A little odd, but whatever. But when winter comes and there's snow on the ground and we're still wearing a t-shirt and shorts, now it's getting weirder, and we become further isolated and our circle of influence is diminished. If people don't want to adapt or change, if they want to stay in their shorts, in their glory days, even though it's snowing outside, that's completely up to them. But to now impose their glory days on everyone else, to belittle everything that's not in line with and similar to what they're doing and what they've always done, is counterproductive, divisive and a bit embarrassing.

Rising above the traditions and personal preferences of any particular church body is challenging enough. But to be additionally burdened by other leaders (some of recognized status) who continue to live out their glory years as if theirs is the only valid representation of authentic worship creates unnecessary tension in the worship community. I want to make something as clear as I can right now: I don't have any issues whatsoever with any style, arrangement, instrumentation or anything else that somebody may want to lead worship with. Enjoy it, as will others, and honor God with it. Just don't impose it on everyone else or marginalize what someone else is doing. But I will ask: why don't you just try another season? "Because this is what I do; it's who I am." I disagree. That's all you've chosen to do, and it certainly shouldn't define you. Why not venture out and try a new style, a new arrangement? I'm not asking you to eliminate your style; simply add another one to your repertoire.

*A static, unchallenged mind settles for status quo, but a renewed mind and new attitude embraces a new season and new challenges.*

I began piano lessons at an early age. Before long I was playing simple classical music, and over time I began to perform some of the most challenging pieces written by Rachmaninoff, Chopin, Beethoven and others. I became known for my classical piano chops. I could have easily stayed in that world, poo-pooing all the contemporary music of that time as trite and worthless (as most of my peers did), never changing and never experiencing another season. But after playing in various rock bands, dance bands, jazz bands and even some country bands, I began to have an understanding, and even appreciation, for these different genres.

Following my salvation experience, I began to explore and embrace season after season of worship music, purposing to never settle on any one style or genre but to rather continue to grow my repertoire. I don't want to be defined by a specific style or genre, nor do I ever want my evolving musical tastes and preferences to atrophy. I'm committed to changing seasons. It's challenging—yet it's fun—and it results in greater relevance and influence far beyond just one season. This is the point I hope to get across more than any other: the goal is to influence others for Christ, and allowing seasons into your life and ministry will help accomplish that goal so much more effectively and for so much longer.

So how do you go about accepting, and even embracing, these seasons?

• **For starters, understand that even our lives have their seasons: the old, and yes, the new:**

> *Therefore if anyone is in Christ, he is a new creation. The old has passed away; behold, the new has come. (2 Corinthians 5:17 ESV)*

In this case, holding on to the good ol' days is a really, really bad idea.

• **Understand that everything we do, our call to ministry and all we do to support and accomplish that ministry, including our songs, arrangements and styles, has a time limit:**

> *There is a time for everything, and a season for every activity under heaven. (Ecclesiastes 3:1)*

When it's time for a particular season to change, we have the choice of accepting that change, maybe even instigating it, or resisting it. Resisting, and even resenting, these new seasons is the very reason for much of the division in the body today. People may find themselves holding onto the past and the good ol' days too tightly, only to have a new season imposed upon them (often by a pastor or the leadership) against their will. Instead, willingly and gladly accept these new seasons; it's much more enjoyable and profitable for everyone involved.

- **Don't completely throw out the old.** Changing seasons doesn't require us to eliminate altogether or no longer incorporate any of what we've used in a previous season. Those things just no longer define who we are. We start a new season with new challenges, new unknowns and new risk. Whether you decide to change your worship style, songs, arrangements, look or whatever, don't throw out the baby with the bathwater, but instead let your previous season take more and more of a back seat as you slowly and purposefully progress into the new season.

- **Renew your mind.** A new season requires a new mind or mindset:

> *Do not be conformed to this world, but be*
> *transformed by the renewal of your mind.*
> *(Romans 12:2a ESV)*

> *Be made new in the attitude of your minds.*
> *(Ephesians 4:23)*

*Though your seasons change, His promises and His faithfulness remain unchangeable.*

A static, unchallenged mind settles for status quo, but a renewed mind and new attitude embraces a new season and new challenges and gives new opportunities for God to manifest Himself. Now there's neither a sense of nor need for self-preservation but rather a renewed sense of adventure and walking out one's faith. Don't pine for the good ol' days, but rather look forward to a new season with a new attitude.

* * * * * * * *

Be encouraged knowing that in the midst of change and a new season, there is One who will never change:

*Jesus Christ is the same yesterday, today, and
forever. (Hebrews 13:8)*

Though your seasons change, His promises and His faithfulness remain unchangeable.

Amen!

# CHAPTER 14

# *They Love Me; They Love Me Not*

## Are we pleasing man or pleasing God?

*In Lystra there sat a man crippled in his feet, who was lame from birth and had never walked. He listened to Paul as he was speaking. Paul looked directly at him, saw that he had faith to be healed and called out, "Stand up on your feet!" At that, the man jumped up and began to walk.*

*When the crowd saw what Paul had done, they shouted in the Lycaonian language, "The gods have come down to us in human form!" Barnabas they called Zeus, and Paul they called Hermes because he was the chief speaker. The priest of Zeus, whose temple was just outside the city, brought bulls and wreaths to the city gates because he and the crowd wanted to offer sacrifices to them. (Acts 14:8–13)*

The people of Lystra thought Paul and Barnabas were gods—they could do no wrong. Then in just a few days' time:

> *Then some Jews came from Antioch and Iconium and won the crowd over. They stoned Paul and dragged him outside the city, thinking he was dead. (Acts 14:19)*

The people in church and on the worship team can be the same way, figuratively speaking. You're the new worship leader; you arrive in town to great fanfare. You can do nothing wrong, everybody wants to know you, they all want to have you over for dinner, they tell you how you're an answer to prayer and, like the Lycaonians, they even bring you sacrifices (cookies, brownies, maybe even a pie). Then it happens. In just a short time they're now ready to stone you and throw you out of town. What happened?

When I arrived in Fort Lauderdale many years ago, I arrived to great expectations. I, too, was told I was an answer to many prayers. And immediately the lobbying began. Some sincerely welcomed me and my family, truly concerned for us and our well-being during this time of transition—and I'll always be grateful to them for their kindness and caring hearts. Others, however, welcomed me out of concern for their own well-being, to gain greater position and favor and to advance their personal agendas and preferences. "We're so glad you're here!

*Instead of trying to win man's approval, seek only to please God, and as a result, you'll find you have man's approval after all.*

We've been praying for someone to liven things up around here because the worship is so boring." Or, "We're hoping you can make the worship more holy and reverent and not so loud all the time." And, "We're hoping you'll bring in some new singers instead of using the same ones all the time." On and on it went. And my favorite came from one of the team members: "I'm gonna be your right-hand man!" How nice, I didn't even have to ask.

There's a natural inclination to want to please man and win his approval, but that can become akin to a hamster on a wheel where you just keep trying and trying and trying to please everybody's wants and preferences. Pretty soon you're exhausted and defeated. And, worst of all, you quickly realize that all your efforts to please everybody backfired, and now you're getting run out of town because you apparently couldn't please anybody after all.

There's nothing wrong with trying to please people. A courteous servant's heart sincerely desires to please people and be kind to them. That's good. But pleasing that seeks approval and favor for one's own benefit is not good and creates conflict:

> *For am I now seeking the approval of man, or of God? Or am I trying to please man? If I were still trying to please man, I would not be a servant of Christ. (Galatians 1:10 ESV)*

If I'm honest with myself, sometimes I tried to please man in order to gain his approval but more often, his favor. This approval and favor profits me and has me in mind rather than the other person.

> *Just as I also please all men in all things, not seeking my own profit but the profit of the many, so that they may be saved.*
> *(1 Corinthians 10:33 NASB)*

So my goal then is to please men for *their* profit and *their* edification, not mine.

For example, as our Latin community here in South Florida grew, so did the Latin population in our church. I began to introduce some Latin-style worship and an occasional chorus in Spanish. I sincerely wanted to please the people for their profit and edification so that the Latin community could worship in a culturally relevant way and have their hearts truly touched. And I wanted the rest of the body to broaden its experience and be blessed by seeing others being blessed as well. However, if I had done this only to increase the sales of Spanish worship CDs, I'm back to profiting myself and promoting my agenda. It can be a tricky road to navigate and one that requires constant examination before the Lord.

If I spend my time and effort trying to please man for my own profit and to win his approval and favor for my gain, I am no longer in the Spirit; now I'm in the flesh:

> *And those who are in the flesh cannot please God.*
> *(Romans 8:8 ABPE)*

So how do we please God?

> *And we pray this in order that you may live a life worthy of the Lord and may **please him in every way**: bearing fruit in every good work, growing in the knowledge of God, being strengthened with all power according to his glorious might so that you may have great endurance and patience, and joyfully giving thanks to the Father, who has qualified you to share in the inheritance of the saints in the kingdom of light.*
> *(Colossians 1:10–12, emphasis mine)*

Bear fruit, grow in the knowledge of God, be strong in the Lord, have endurance and patience and give thanks with great joy to the Father. It's all right there. Surprisingly, instead of trying to win man's approval, seek only to please God, and as a result, you'll find you have man's approval after all:

> *For the kingdom of God is not a matter of eating and drinking, but of righteousness, peace and joy in*

*the Holy Spirit, because anyone who serves Christ in this way is pleasing to God and approved by men. (Romans 14:17–18)*

Though you may attain man's approval by meeting his selfish wants and preferences, you'll find his approval fleeting, and maintaining it will require more and more attention and ongoing servicing. Eventually you'll come up short, and that's when you'll begin to get chased out of town. But by pleasing God and not man, we are often required to reject man's needs and wants rather than meet them, all for his own benefit (whether he realizes it or not). Ironically, it's then that we gain man's respect and approval. That's the amazing economy of God!

But wait; there's more:

*When a man's ways please the Lord, he makes even his enemies to be at peace with him.*
*(Proverbs 16:7 ESV)*

Here's the picture I see Scripture paint and one that I aspire to every day: to so rightly represent the Lord and please Him in all my ways that the congregation, my team, the leadership and my pastor find approval with me—and my "enemies" (those that would attempt to divide and slander), having found no charges to bring against me that bear witness, are at peace with me as well.

The person mentioned earlier who proclaimed he was going to be my right-hand man actually caused more turmoil and division than any worship team member I have worked with since. Had I sought to please the Lord rather than to please and pacify this person, I would have made

> *Pleasing man will always be at best a short-term solution that will ultimately fail, while pleasing God will always, always prevail.*

different decisions at that time. Those decisions would have benefitted him in the long run and saved the team and me a lot of unnecessary headaches and heartaches along the way. Pleasing man will always be at best a short-term solution that will ultimately fail, while pleasing God will always, always prevail.

So what happened to Paul after he was dragged outside the city and left for dead?

> *But after the disciples had gathered around him, he*
> *got up and went back into the city. (Acts 14:20)*

You might get beat up in the process, but keep seeking to please God. Get up, dust yourself off and go back in!

CHAPTER 15

# *Who's in Charge?*

## The many roles and challenges of worship leadership.

"Who runs your worship ministry?" If I were to ask several attendees at a worship conference that question, I'd probably get the following answers:

- the soundman,
- one of the sopranos,
- this week?
- the pastor,
- the pastor's wife,
- nobody,
- I don't know, or
- the worship leader, of course.

In fact, these are actual answers I've received. Of course, many of the answers were intended to be humorous, yet a lot can be gleaned from someone's humor.

It's no surprise the worship leader's position is often fraught with dysfunction and instability, though not always at the fault of the acting worship leader. Sometimes the position of worship leader is simply filled by the wrong person. Other times there's dysfunctional leadership overseeing the worship leader. More often than not, there's simply an incomplete understanding of the necessary roles of the worship leader according to Scripture. What are the scriptural mandates? What are the specific ministry needs? And what does it take to lead this uniquely created and gifted worship community?

The necessary qualities of a worship leader are not unlike those of other leadership roles within a ministry, whereas the challenges presented by the worship community and the church body's expectations and the roles required to meet those challenges are significantly unique. On one occasion I went to my pastor to get his thoughts on how to best handle a particularly bizarre situation. Upon hearing the scenario, he stopped what he was doing, looked at me and said in utter amazement, "Only in the music ministry!" Another time a pastor with several degrees in ministry and counseling remarked concerning my role of overseeing the worship ministry, "How do you do it? Those people scare me!"

Without a doubt, there's a disconnect between left brainers and right brainers, making the role of the worship leader that much more critical. If done well, worship leadership is a bridge between the two worlds. If done poorly, it simply becomes another confirmation of unflattering stereotypes.

I have on my bookcase upward of two dozen books on leadership alone, and they barely scratch the surface of the plethora of resources available on the subject. While this is not an attempt to rewrite the book on leadership, it is, however, an opportunity for me to highlight some attributes I feel are vital to effective leadership and worship leadership—attributes that have served me well throughout the years.

## Qualities of a Leader

*Integrity.* Soundness, honesty, sincerity, unimpaired conditions and completeness are some terms that define integrity. But the one word that really spells it out for me is undivided. The root of the word integrity is integer, which is a whole number, one that cannot be divided, and likewise a leader with integrity cannot follow two separate paths—one that satisfies the flesh and another that honors God. Most of us have heard and subscribe to the expressions "walk the talk" and "practice what you preach" because we abhor the boss,

> *Integrity doesn't work with one foot in the world and the other in the Kingdom of God.*

the leader, the politician and the pastor who say one thing, yet do the exact opposite. That's why hypocrisy is the antithesis of integrity. Jesus pointed out this same practice of hypocrisy concerning the Pharisees:

> *But do not do what they do, for they do not practice what they preach. (Matthew 23:3b)*

And Jesus' indictment:

> *Woe to you, teachers of the law and Pharisees, you hypocrites! (Matthew 23:13a)*

Integrity doesn't work with one foot in the world and the other in the Kingdom of God. You cannot be divided or your leadership will ultimately fail, and you don't have to look very hard or very far to see example after example of leaders who have proven this reality.

> *Whoever walks in integrity will be delivered, but he who is crooked in his ways will suddenly fall. (Proverbs 28:18 ESV)*

**Humility.** The quality or state of not thinking you are better than other people.[14] That's the definition for humility. Now look at how the Bible describes a life of humility:

> *Your attitude should be the same as that of Christ Jesus: Who, being in very nature God, did not consider equality with God something to be grasped, but made himself nothing, taking the very nature of a servant, being made in human likeness. And being found in appearance as a man, he humbled himself and became obedient to death— even death on a cross! (Philippians 2:5–8)*

Those who consider themselves of no greater value than others are able to learn and glean from a multitude, increase in wisdom and grow in their ability to lead. Those who think themselves higher than others will value no one's input or wisdom but their own. They're a *know-it-all* who will in no time even begin to craft God's Word into their own thinking and likeness, unknowingly digging their own hole.

> *Whoever exalts himself will be humbled, and whoever humbles himself will be exalted.*
> *(Matthew 23:12 ESV)*

To humble yourself is to become teachable and to be led and taught in the ways of the Lord:

> *He leads the humble in what is right, and teaches the humble his way. (Psalms 25:9 ESV)*

**Generosity.** Generosity is a willingness to give of one's assets, time and talents to others in need without expecting anything in return. It's having a heart to help others, to come alongside them giving freely and selflessly to comfort them, to be Christlike:

> *"For I was hungry and you gave me something to eat, I was thirsty and you gave me something to drink, I was a stranger and you invited me in. I*

*needed clothes and you clothed me, I was sick and you looked after me, I was in prison and you came to visit me." (Matthew 25:35–36)*

Jesus goes on to give even greater meaning to His words:

*"I tell you the truth, whatever you did for one of the least of these brothers of mine, you did for me." (Matthew 25:40)*

We're to meet the needs of the hungry, the thirsty and the lonely, to be a covering for those who have none, to care for the sick and to encourage the oppressed. And we're to do so generously and unto the Lord.

If we're not giving generously, we're keeping selfishly and blending in with a society that cares for its own needs and wants while neglecting and ignoring the needs of others. God's economy contradicts that of the world:

*One gives freely, yet grows all the richer; another withholds what he should give, and only suffers want. (Proverbs 11:24 ESV)*

Be generous with all things, to all people, at all times and likewise lead generously, giving yourself fully to those God has entrusted to you.

*A generous man will prosper; he who refreshes others will himself be refreshed. (Proverbs 11:25)*

## Lead by Example

*Remember those who led you, who spoke the word of God to you; and considering the result of their conduct, imitate their faith. (Hebrews 13:7 NASB)*

We're to remember those leaders in our life who did it right and finished well. Then we're to imitate them so that one day others whom we have led will honor our leadership and conduct and in turn purpose to imitate us. This is so important. We're teaching believers and leaders by our example, and without a right example, our words condemn us:

*We set the example for others by doing what we say and saying the truth according to God's Word.*

> *Dear children, let us not love with words or tongue but with actions and in truth. (1 John 3:18)*

We set the example for others by doing what we say and saying the truth according to God's Word. Paul, in one of his letters to Timothy, expounds on this action-in-truth admonition and gives us some relevant and practical ways to lead and live as an effective example for others:

> *Be an example to all believers in what you say, in the way you live, in your love, your faith, and your purity. (1Timothy 4:12b NLT)*

### What You Say—Your Words

> *Do not let any unwholesome talk come out of your mouths, but only what is helpful for building others up according to their needs, that it may benefit those who listen. (Ephesians 4:29)*

Say nothing that is rude, racist, sexually suggestive or condescending, but instead use words that encourage rather than discourage, correct in love rather than in anger and build up rather than tear down.

## *The Way You Live—Your Life*

> *Watch your life and doctrine closely. Persevere in them, because if you do, you will save both yourself and your hearers. (1Timothy 4:16)*

Your life will reflect what you believe. Know and study God's Word, hide it in your heart and live accordingly with steadfastness so you will see the Lord face to face at the end of this life. Then those that follow and imitate your example in life will also see the Lord face to face because of you. It's a heavy responsibility. Make sure you undertake it in His strength and not your own.

## *Your Love*

> *Love is patient, love is kind. It does not envy, it does not boast, it is not proud. It is not rude, it is not self-seeking, it is not easily angered, it keeps no record of wrongs. Love does not delight in evil but rejoices with the truth. It always protects, always trusts, always hopes, always perseveres. Love never fails. (1 Corinthians 13:4–8a)*

This area of Scripture is often associated with a wedding ceremony, but, in fact, it's how we are to live and how we are to lead. Love is the opposite of lust. Lust takes; love gives. Lust is consumed with meeting our own needs and wants, but love cares deeply, even sacrificially, for others.

*Lust is consumed with meeting our own needs and wants, but love cares deeply, even sacrificially, for others.*

*We love because He first loved us. (1 John 4:19)*

Jesus went to a cross because of love; will we give our lives for others as well?

## *Your Faith*

*Now faith is being sure of what we hope for and certain of what we do not see. (Hebrews 11:1)*

*If you're not living by faith in God, you're living by faith in something else.*

When we face trials, when challenges come, when opposition rises against us, do others see us trusting God and relying on His Word and His promises? Or do they see us filled with anxiety, doubt and fear? If others see our confident and sure faith in the midst of uncertainty, their faith is strengthened and they are encouraged.

*And without faith it is impossible to please God, because anyone who comes to him must believe that he exists and that he rewards those who earnestly seek him. (Hebrews 11:6)*

If you're not living by faith in God, you're living by faith in something else—yourself, man's wisdom, the government or some other idol or false god. You cannot approach faith in God like some kind of test drive or trial run. It's all or nothing, hot or cold. Let your faith be sold out for God, overcoming every trial that comes your way, not in your strength but in God's power for all to see!

*That your faith might not rest in the wisdom of men but in the power of God. (1 Corinthians 2:5 ESV)*

## *Your Purity*

*Religion that God our Father accepts as pure and faultless is this: to look after orphans and widows in*

*their distress and to keep oneself from being
polluted by the world. (James 1:27)*

Purity is sincerity and genuineness in faith. It is responsibility in action, and it is morality, unaffected and unstained by the world and its pleasures, temptations and distractions. Imagine buying a beautiful ring after being told that it was made of pure gold. But after time and some wear and tear, you notice the top layer of gold starting to wear off, and you realize you were duped. The ring is not pure gold; it's gold plated. Now as the elements attack the inferior materials underneath, the ring begins to dull and tarnish, rendering it useless and worthless. We find ourselves in disbelief when we encounter a believer who mirrors this gold-plated ring, but imagine the horror when we realize we're the ones who have become this picture. How do we keep ourselves pure and uncorrupted, and if we have become tarnished, how do we make ourselves pure again?

*Finally, brothers, whatever is true, whatever is
noble, whatever is right, whatever is pure, whatever
is lovely, whatever is admirable—if anything is
excellent or praiseworthy—think about such things.
Whatever you have learned or received or heard
from me, or seen in me—put it into practice. And
the God of peace will be with you.
(Philippians 4:8–9)*

We make the very nature of God and all that He has for us our focus and our priority. It's a choice and a discipline, but it's also our hope. That's what keeps our hearts after the Lord, and for those who have lost their way, it's what brings them back to Him. It's hope that gives us a future; it's hope that purifies:

*And everyone who has this hope in Him purifies
himself, just as He is pure. (1 John 3:3 HCSB)*

111

Hold onto this hope and all of the promises that His Word gives us. Have nothing to do with the world and its tarnished pleasures, but honor God with all your heart and in all your actions, and, as Paul admonished the Philippians, "put it into practice" (Philippians 4:9).

> *Therefore, since we have these promises, dear friends, let us purify ourselves from everything that contaminates body and spirit, perfecting holiness out of reverence for God. (2 Corinthians 7:1)*

## Lead with Authority, Not by Position

> *Some Jews who went around driving out evil spirits tried to invoke the name of the Lord Jesus over those who were demon-possessed. They would say, "In the name of Jesus, whom Paul preaches, I command you to come out." Seven sons of Sceva, a Jewish chief priest, were doing this. One day, the evil spirit answered them, "Jesus I know, and I know about Paul, but who are you?" Then the man who had the evil spirit jumped on them and overpowered them all. He gave them such a beating that they ran out of the house naked and bleeding. (Acts 19:13–16)*

These men were calling on the name of Jesus to establish their authority over demons while having no relationship whatsoever with Jesus—a classic case of "name dropping." And all they got in return for their circus act was a good beating, right before they ran away in their birthday suits!

And so it is in the church. There are some leadership who call on the name of the Lord in all their authority for all to see, all the while living a life of hypocrisy that renders their authority impotent, forcing them to instead rely solely on their position. In most cases, those who lead from position alone will eventually be exposed.

Once I witnessed a pastor who was appropriately challenged by a subordinate for his compromised behavior. His response: "How dare you talk to me like that? I'm a pastor!" This leader's life no longer reflected a right relationship with Christ, and it had become obvious to those around him that his position was all that he had left to lead from.

*True authority comes from a right relationship with Christ, and when we lead as Christ leads, authority begins to look completely different from that which the world espouses.*

True authority comes from a right relationship with Christ, and when we lead as Christ leads, authority begins to look completely different from that which the world espouses:

> But Jesus called the disciples and said, "You know that the rulers of the unbelievers lord it over them and their superiors act like tyrants over them. That's not the way it should be among you. Instead, whoever wants to be great among you must be your servant, and whoever wants to be first among you must be your slave. That's the way it is with the Son of Man. He did not come to be served, but to serve and to give his life as a ransom for many people." (Matthew 20:25–28 ISV)

A servant's heart affirms true authority. A servant's heart provides leadership that others will readily follow. The position of authority is certainly to be honored and respected, but we can't necessarily assume the person filling that position will be similarly honored and respected. You have to know Jesus to have authority, not just know *of* Him, and to know Jesus is to serve others just as He came to serve.

> *Be shepherds of God's flock that is under your care, serving a overseers—not because you must, but because you are willing, as God wants you to be; not greedy for money, but eager to serve; not lording it over those entrusted to you, but being examples to the flock. (1 Peter 5:2–3)*

## Roles of a Worship Leader

Up to this point, we've looked at various elements of leadership that apply to ministry in general. But as we look at the specific roles of a worship leader, I want to explore the various responsibilities that are, for the most part, unique to this area of ministry and consider ways to effectively manage these roles and lead the people they affect. As you read and reflect on the following roles, see which ones, if not all, are currently on your plate:

***Pastor.*** In this role, you help reconcile the lives of those in your circle of influence to the Word of God. This includes helping broken and hurting lives that are affected by fallout from broken relationships, lost jobs, illness, family struggles, finances or the death of a family member, a friend or even a pet.

***Manager.*** The manager coordinates various day-to-day administrative duties, such as worship team schedules, song lists, purchase orders, check requests, rides for musicians whose cars are in the shop (or who don't have one), equipment purchases and inventory control, toner and paper for the printer—and the list goes on and on and on. . . .

***Music Director.*** This role is pretty much what it sounds like: the music director coordinates and directs all aspects of live music, including rehearsals, services, concerts, Easter and Christmas celebrations and various other special events. This role determines the desired song list, arrangements and sound and goes about achieving it.

***Service Programming Director.*** Another directing role, but in this one you coordinate all of the elements of a service into a seamless flow and presentation, including teaching, worship, video, media, fine arts (drama, dance, music), audio, lighting, and environmental projection.

***Artist.*** "One who is skilled in any of the fine arts."[15] This role requires significant knowledge and skill, which are achieved and maintained through consistent study and practice. It's often necessary to learn other instruments and various styles of music in order to be relevant and relatable.

***Performer.*** One who carries out, executes, renders music as by playing or singing.[16] This role, unlike that of the artist (private development) is the public expression of the culmination of study and practice. This role can be rewarding, though surprisingly challenging. To be successful, the performer must overcome nerves, noises, people, reactions, varying sound mixes, atmospheric conditions (too hot or cold) and subsequent reviews, critiques, observations, opinions and comparisons. Performing can be nerve wracking and exhausting. After a weekend of services, I'm beat and I feel like I've just worked two 16-hour days.

***Motivator.*** The motivator helps others overcome discouragement and fear, challenges them to a greater level skillfully and spiritually and inspires them to keep going even when they feel like quitting. It's about encouraging a team member who's totally blown a solo, played the intro in the wrong key or started to sing a second chorus when everyone else had ended after the first.

***Technical Director.*** Often referred to as the "soundman," the technical director makes sure all of the technical aspects of the service are in order and working, helping to provide a flawless worship experience void of any inappropriate levels and mixes and, of course, feedback.

Many worship leaders who had no idea all those roles even existed find themselves fulfilling most, if not all, of them. We might assume that this multi-role necessity would be relegated to smaller ministries where the budget is likewise smaller and staffing is limited, and that the larger the ministry, the more these roles could be delegated to assisting staff. I submit that no matter the size of your ministry, you will still function in and be responsible for all of these roles to some degree.

I have been blessed with a large and competent staff to help handle many of these roles for me. However, although I may not function in all these roles directly with the worship team, I now fully function in every one of these roles with my staff. The bottom line is this; you need to be prepared and equipped to function and lead effectively in all these roles whether you are full time, part time or a volunteer. Your unique skills and giftings will determine what percentage each of these roles take out of your available time, but be assured that an awareness of and ability to function in these various roles when necessary and called upon is essential.

*We can be extremely busy at our jobs but not performing any of our job responsibilities and calling.*

Now, it's one thing to be prepared and capable to function in these roles, but it's quite another to manage them all while attempting to fulfill your calling and responsibility, (i.e., your job).

But wait—there's more! Just for fun, add to all of that a spouse, some kids, a house and a pet or two.

My calling and responsibility (my job description) is to manage and lead worship, to be creative in the dispensation of that responsibility, to lead, train and build up the worship team, to write new songs and to record and produce worship CDs and live DVDs. But if I don't manage the multitude of roles that come along with this broad responsibility and expectation, I will end up working sixty to seventy hours a week while not being creative, writing any new songs or producing any new projects. In other words, I can be extremely busy at my job but not performing any of my job responsibilities and calling. Sound familiar?

Managing and balancing all these roles is challenging, yet necessary. You might be able to do them all yourself for a little while but not for long. If you're unable to get a handle on these responsibilities and roles and everyone's expectations, you'll eventually burn out and leave the ministry. Or you'll be let go. And divorced.

## Practical Applications for Maintaining Balance

Over the years I have grappled with these same roles, responsibilities and expectations and the pull they exert on my calling and time. To help in this balancing act, I've filtered all the efforts and ideas used in attempting to manage this incessant pull—the successes, the dismal failures and everything in between—down to a list of nine practical applications that have proven the most effective for me in finding and keeping a balance between public ministry, personal ministry and family.

***Prepare for distractions.*** They're gonna happen. So get used to it and allow room for them. To help with distractions, adjust your expectations and your schedule. If you've scheduled every waking moment of your day to accomplish the goals you've set for yourself, then you've set yourself up for guaranteed frustration.

When you're frustrated, the temptation to respond in the flesh (anger, selfishness) increases; whereas if you're prepared for distractions, there's a greater chance you'll respond to them in the Spirit (love, joy, peace . . .). Again, allow some breathing room in your schedule for distractions. Don't let them bother you; realize that sometimes a distraction can be a blessing.

***Delegate.*** Get help! I turn to others to help me in two ways—advice and action. For advice, I'll run ideas, plans, problems and potential solutions by those I trust: other worship leaders, close friends, often my staff and, at times, the worship team. They all can give me ideas I hadn't considered and show me potential problems and hazards I hadn't thought of. This advice has saved me a lot of wasted work and unnecessary headaches over the years.

Recruit staff, volunteers or both, depending on the expertise needed and the budget available. Put the word out for volunteers via your church bulletin, program and website, social networks, announcements and the worship community. You'll be surprised by the number of people who would love to help if they only knew there was a need. Then assess your volunteers' abilities, strengths and weaknesses, keeping in mind that they don't necessarily need to have a background in music. Can they return phone calls, host fellowships, coordinate food for events, make copies, help with auditions, coordinate Planning Center, assist with budgets and purchase orders or perform computer tasks? Volunteers with a music background may be able to run rehearsals or sectionals (vocal, band or individual instruments), score charts, program loops, run sound or lights, help set up for rehearsals and services or pick up gear and music supplies from the local music store. The list is endless, but you do need a list. And help your volunteers succeed and feel valued. Give them specific

*You'll be surprised by the number of people who would love to help if they only knew there was a need.*

tasks, clear directions, a picture of what the end result should achieve or look like, and dates and times that they are needed. Then be ready for them when they arrive. Don't micromanage and don't be afraid to let them fail. Understand that not everything will be done as well as you might expect or do yourself, so get over it.

***Train.*** You may have a volunteer who is available to help but doesn't know how to do all of the things you need help with . . . yet. Training people how and in what manner to do basic tasks is a simple matter that you should be able to accomplish yourself. Once the people you've trained become adept at particular tasks, they can then train others to either assist or take over; this frees them up to tackle other needs.

If a task requires greater expertise or a specialized skill set that you don't possess, you'll need to enlist someone with the ability to train your volunteers and staff. If, for example, your volunteers need more training in order to effectively help with sound and audio needs, consider contacting a local sound company, church or studio that has a reputable sound engineer to see if you can hire someone to run a workshop for some of your volunteers. Consider taking a similar course of action with volunteers and staff who would benefit from further training in various musical or computer skills, counseling, video production or other areas. Pursue potential trainers from local universities, churches, trade schools and private teaching studios to assist in training.

There's an invaluable pool of talent all around you. Some people are ready to go and others are "diamonds in the rough." Either way, get them trained up to help you with many, if not all, of your roles.

***Manage.*** As noted in the first point, we need to prepare for distractions. But that doesn't mean we can't organize our time and schedules to avoid unnecessary distractions and interruptions as much as possible. For example, I used to have an open-door policy.

That was my noble way of staying connected and in touch with my staff and team. It was a noble failure. First of all, the open-door policy became an invitation to socialize and "shoot the breeze." Second, it was a diversion for anyone who was bored or needed a break. Third, it became an invitation for opinions and song suggestions that I hadn't asked for. It clearly wasn't working, but I didn't want to permanently close my door and become antisocial either. So I admonished my staff that there would be no more 24/7 open-door policy for any of us. Rather, I advised us all to set aside a specific time (like Fridays from two to four, for example) for open-door access and communicate the time with the team and fellow staff members. After this change was adopted, several staff members relayed to me how their productivity had dramatically increased as a result.

Let me also encourage you to do away with your open-door policy when it comes to phone calls, emails and texts (unless they're from your spouse or pastor . . .). I've been in countless meetings and conversations when the person I was with was suddenly interrupted by a phone call, email, text or some other digital notification that immediately became more important than the conversation we were having. Not only is this a distraction and time waster, but, quite frankly, it's rude. Control and manage these devices before they begin to control you.

With those examples in mind, consider all of the time wasters in your day and schedule. Your goal is to find more time to accomplish work and ministry while minimizing time spent on unproductive activities.

***Say no.*** This has saved me more time and unnecessary stress than any other application, and it's the most simply instituted of all. But I didn't say it was easy. It can be difficult to tell someone or some ministry no when there appears to be a genuine need. But you'll begin to realize that the people and ministries you politely turned down somehow manage, miraculously, so it seems, to meet their needs without you. You then discover one of two things about yourself: (1) you're pleased that there are others who can handle your role quite competently, thus freeing you up, or (2) you're bothered that there are others who can handle your role quite competently, thus forcing you to realize that you're not, in fact, as indispensable as you were led to believe when you were being asked.

If your response was number one, good for you. If it was number two, time for a heart check. See, we can often have this inaccurate and inflated sense of self-valuation that if we say *no*, we assume there's no one else who can take our place or take our place as competently. All the while, we've completely missed the possibility that our *no* is someone else's *yes*, someone whom God has chosen to bless and to be a blessing— except our pride gets in the way. Never say *yes* out of pride, and never say *no* out of laziness, but prayerfully consider the bigger picture and all that you have on your plate. Then make a wise decision that your schedule reasonably allows for and that your spirit agrees with.

***Prioritize.*** Determine what must be done now (creating a song list), what needs to be done soon (charting new songs), what can be done later (planning a worship fellowship) and what can be done any time (playing Words with Friends).

Prioritizing our tasks runs counterintuitively to one of the right brainer's greatest tendencies (mine included): tunnel vision. I describe tunnel vision as an obsession with completing a current project or task before considering or moving on to another task, regardless of the new task's urgency or importance. But I've discovered something about tunnel vision. If I can somehow walk away or disengage from what I'm doing, even momentarily, it's as if the spell is somehow broken and I can then move on to something else and come back to finish the prior task at another time. That's what prioritization does.

Prioritization forces us to determine the importance of all the various tasks, the order in which they should be addressed and how much time should be spent on each task before moving on to the next. Thus, it's the infant stages of multitasking! One final thought: leaving a task before tunnel vision takes over (to return to it at a later time) allows for a more creative and fresh approach that otherwise would have been lost. I cannot tell you how many times I've worked on a song or task only to hit a roadblock, looking for a solution for hours with no success. Yet if I walk away to work on something else, then return to the song or task later on or the next day, I always, always find the fix in a matter of minutes. It never fails. Prioritization works. It keeps us from getting stuck on one thing and promotes a productive and creative workflow.

*Always be open to a different outcome than you expected.*

**Stay in touch.** Call, text, email, visit or have a meal with members of your team. This shows you care, encourages your team and often allows you to deal with personal sin issues before they become a public crisis, and it's the balance to the technological tools at our disposal. Staying in touch keeps it personal; and when it's personal, it's family.

**Stay flexible.** Always be open to a different outcome than you expected:

> *In his heart a man plans his course, but the Lord determines his steps. (Proverbs 16:9)*

We make plans, and we're supposed to. But sometimes the Lord, although pleased with our heart and effort, changes those plans. Sometimes He chooses to bless us beyond our expectations; other times He changes our plans to protect us. Either way, if the Lord's in it, don't resist and don't be frustrated, but rather enjoy the ride, knowing that the outcome will be much better than your original plans.

### *Stay focused on Christ.*

> *As Jesus and his disciples were on their way, he came to a village where a woman named Martha opened her home to him. She had a sister called Mary, who sat at the Lord's feet listening to what he said. But Martha was distracted by all the preparations that had to be made. She came to Him and asked, "Lord, don't you care that my sister has left me to do the work by myself? Tell her to help me!"*
>
> *"Martha, Martha," the Lord answered, "you are worried and upset about many things, but only one thing is needed. Mary has chosen what is better, and it will not be taken away from her." (Luke 10:38–42)*

Mary, unlike Martha, chose to focus on Christ, rather than all of the preparations. May we be ever so careful not to be like Martha, as well intended as she was, and get so caught up in all of our roles and expectations that we lose sight of Christ, our eternal hope whom we're called to serve. When we keep our eyes on Jesus and sit at His feet, everything else will have its proper place and perspective, perfectly aligned to His will and His Word. It's a great place to be!

## Your Turn

It's fairly obvious that ministry leadership is not about having power and position but rather about being a servant. And worship leadership has the added benefit of leading the body of believers in worship: unholy people communing with a holy God because of

His Son, Jesus, who came to serve and give His life as a ransom for us. What an amazing privilege and responsibility it is to be a worship leader!

There's no doubt that we need more honorable leaders to set the example and for others to follow. Do all you can to be one of them, following the examples of great leaders before you, and above all, following the example of Jesus Christ.

# CHAPTER 16

# *I Need Glasses*

## Having a vision for the future.

Actually, I do need glasses. A recent eye examination simply confirmed what I already knew: I can see just fine close up, but seeing objects in the distance is a challenge. I'm nearsighted.

Sometimes our vision for the ministry and in our leadership can be nearsighted as well. Now, before anyone jumps to an inaccurate conclusion, let me explain and clarify. V*ision*, as I see it (no pun intended), is not trying to foresee or predict the future, nor is it what some church leaders do as in "vision casting," which is more often an effort to increase church attendance, build more impressive buildings and accomplish personal agendas. No, I see *vision* as an imaginable and long-term solution to a current or impending problem.

> *Sometimes our vision for the ministry and in our leadership can be nearsighted.*

Consider this definition of *vision*:

- "Something that you imagine, a picture that you see in your mind."[17]

Our house once had a blank sixteen-foot wall. My wife suggested I build a custom entertainment center for that space and, having had several years' experience as a cabinetmaker, I readily accepted the task. (It meant getting more tools. Who can turn that down!) The reason for building an entertainment center was to solve several problems: We had a shortage of storage, so it would have lots of drawers and doors. We also needed a place for the TV, computer and printer, a built-in desk to sit at and work, plus several shelves and lighting for displaying *stuff.* So I stood in front of that wall and stared at it and began to imagine and picture in my mind what it might look like—and soon I had a vision that would solve all of those problems long term. (A short-term solution would have been to raise the bed, creating more storage space underneath.) Yes, I had a vision. I shared my vision with my wife and she was on board (with a few minor adjustments, of course). I drew up plans, came up with a materials list and calculated costs, labor time and a projected completion date. My wife approved the final plans; we determined we could afford it; I had the time and the completion date was sufficient to solve the problem in a timely manner. That's vision!

Can you see why vision is so important? Imagine the alternative: my wife suggests an entertainment center that I agree to build. But rather than come up with a vision, I instead show up with a bunch of lumber and just start cutting. I'm going to waste a lot of material; the project will take a lot longer and cost a lot more and I'll probably end up with all shelving and little or no storage. The problems aren't solved, and, in fact, more problems have been created for a lack of vision. Not a good solution.

Vision is vital. And for those who might still have some reservations about it, I submit you have your definitions crossed.

About ten years ago our church leadership decided to develop satellite churches. This was their vision to overcome the problem of overcrowding and avoid the burdensome cost and incurred debt of building a larger facility. Every satellite campus would have the senior pastor displayed on a large screen via fiber optics, but the worship would be live. This meant we'd need multiple worship teams and worship leaders simultaneously. I was already short staffed, so I needed to come up with a solution to this upcoming dilemma. My first priority was to pray about it and to search the Scriptures. And one day I can honestly say the Lord gave me a vision. It was clearly implanted in my mind and heart that I was to start a worship school to train up worship leaders, artists and team members to carry on the work of the worship ministry. It made perfect sense. It was not unlike the scriptural mandate to go and make disciples; this school would be doing just that. I couldn't have been more excited about and confident of this vision from the Lord.

Now, was this vision a future prediction or was this a vision of the solution to a coming problem? Without a doubt, it was a vision of the solution. I began to put a plan together, seek counsel, develop a budget, create a time frame, determine curriculum, equipment and staffing needs and put in place manageable benchmarks. I presented the vision to the leadership, received their blessing and funding, and as I write this ten years later, we've just started our eighth year of Ocean's Edge School of Worship. The results so far have blown away our highest expectations.

*The number one vision, the solution to all of our problems, is Christ Jesus.*

Without vision, there are no long-term solutions but rather a series of urgent decisions to meet urgent problems with expensive short-term solutions—a perfect formula for frustration, burnout and failure.

Once you have a vision, it will take faith and involve some risk to carry it out. Faith to do things you've never done before and risk of failure and of being embarrassed by those who will doubt, question and even oppose your vision.

The Bible gives us a perfect picture of this vision, along with the typical hesitations and the godly assurances. In the third and fourth chapters of Exodus, we see a fascinating conversation between Moses and the Lord. The Lord has heard the plight of the

Israelites and has a solution to their problem, and He has called on Moses to implement His vision of the solution. The Lord says to Moses:

> *"So now, go. I am sending you to Pharaoh to bring*
> *my people the Israelites out of Egypt."*
> *(Exodus 3:10)*

At this point Moses begins to share five instances of resistance and hesitation: (1) *"Who am I, that I should go to Pharaoh and bring the Israelites out of Egypt?"* (2) *"What should I say to them?"* (3) *"What if they won't believe me or listen to me?"* (4) *"O Lord, I have never been eloquent, neither in past nor since You have spoken to Your servant. I am slow of speech and tongue,"* and (5) *"O Lord, please send someone else to do it." (Exodus 3:11, 3:13 NASB; 4:1 NLT, 4:10, 4:13)*

God's response? If you'll allow me to paraphrase: (1) Don't worry, I'll be with you. (2) Tell them I sent you. (3) Relax, I'll give you plenty of miraculous signs. (4) Don't panic, I'll give you the words to say. And (5), your brother can help you.

This is perfect! When we have a vision similar to Moses', we're bound to have the same doubts and hesitation. Why me? What do I say? They won't listen to me. I'm no good at this. And, I can't do this by myself. Sound familiar? But the Lord's answers to Moses ring true still to this day as He gives us the same assurances and comfort He gave Moses: "Don't worry, I'm with you. I called you; expect a miracle. I'll guide you and I'll bring you help."

All the elements needed to carry out your vision are right there. And as the Lord calmly and reassuringly addressed every one of Moses' reservations rather than blasting him for his lack of faith, it's nice to know that in the same way God will walk alongside us through all of our hesitations and concerns. Remain confident in this.

*But one thing I do: Forgetting what is behind and straining toward what is ahead. I press on toward the goal to win the prize for which God has called me heavenward in Christ Jesus.*
*(Philippians 3:13–14)*

The number one vision, the solution to *all* of our problems, is Christ Jesus—to know Him more fully and to serve Him more faithfully. Don't let past failures and shortcomings determine your future, but instead continue to look ahead with vision for your ministry, your faith and your future.

# CHAPTER 17

# *Investment Strategy*

## Putting our gifts to work for the Kingdom.

It's a simple concept: take an asset, invest it and, over time, it will produce earnings. The original asset becomes more valuable. It's smart, it's wise, and it's biblical. Whether it's the story of Joseph saving up in the abundant years to prepare for the lean years (Genesis 41), the example of the industrious ant in Proverbs 6 or the parable of the talents in Matthew 25, we see a responsibility to invest our money, to prepare for the future and, in addition to that, to have an inheritance to give to our "children's children" (Proverbs 13:22).

*Investing our money prepares us for our future here on earth (temporal), investing our gifts prepares us for beyond and into the Kingdom (eternal).*

Apart from the sluggard and fool that Proverbs describes, we all have assets available to invest. It may not seem like it, but we do. And the amount of assets available to invest is directly related to our level of income and, of course, our level of consumption.

In addition to monetary assets, we all have gifts from the Lord:

*Each of you should use whatever gift you have received to serve others, as faithful stewards of God's grace in its various forms. (1 Peter 4:10)*

And they're not all the same:

*We have different gifts, according the grace given us. If a man's gift is prophesying, let him use it in proportion to his faith. If it is serving, let him serve; if it is teaching, let him teach, if it is encouraging, let him encourage; if it is contributing to the needs of others, let him give generously; if it is leadership, let him govern diligently; if it is showing mercy, let him do it cheerfully. (Romans 12:6–8)*

Whatever our gifts are and whatever the proportion of those gifts, we are called to be faithful with them—to invest them. And to invest them into others. Whereas investing our money prepares us for our future here on earth (temporal), investing our gifts prepares us for beyond and into the Kingdom (eternal).

*Again, it will be like a man going on a journey, who called his servants and entrusted his property to them. To one he gave five talents of money, to another two talents, and to another one talent, each according to his ability. Then he went on his journey. The man who had received the five talents went at once and put his money to work and gained five more. So also, the one with the two talents gained two more. But the man who had received the one talent went off, dug a hole in the ground and hid his master's money. (Matthew 25:14–18)*

The talent was the largest unit of weight mentioned in the Bible, a monetary instrument (I suppose you could say it was the largest denomination). But in this passage, *talent* also refers to the various gifts and skills that God gives us or, closer to home, the gifts and skills used in worship. So what does it mean, then, to those of us in worship to take our talents and "put them to work"?

Well, again, consider the concept of investing: you invest in something in order for it to become more valuable over time. It's no different with our talents. We invest in our gifts and skills, and over time they also become more valuable and have greater worth. And with greater skills come greater opportunities and responsibilities:

> *Kenaniah the head Levite was in charge of the singing; that was his responsibility because he was skillful at it. (1 Chronicles 15:22)*

Get better. Become skillful.

A gift is something that's been received, but a skill is a gift that's been invested and developed. You're not given a skill but rather a gift. And whether you have a five-talent, a two-talent or a one-talent gift, when you invest it you make it more valuable as you become more skillful.

On Sundays I would rotate teams for each of the services. Same songs, different teams. On this particular weekend, one song was exceptionally challenging, especially for bass players. My first-service bass player was at a three-talent level, whereas my second-service bass player was clearly at a five-talent level.

*A gift is something that's been received, but a skill is a gift that's been invested and developed.*

At the first service, the three-talent bass player outdid himself. He played exceedingly well, much better than I could've asked for. Afterward I pulled him aside and gushed on him. I told him how proud I was of his hard work and diligence, and that it certainly had paid off. I was blessed, the team was blessed, and subsequently, he was blessed.

At the second service, my five-talent guy bombed. Obviously unprepared, he hadn't practiced, and he essentially phoned it in. Afterward I pulled him aside and confronted him for his lack of effort and his irresponsibility. I was really disappointed in him and so was the team. But here's the irony: during the services, my five-talent guy actually played better than the tree-talent guy. So then, why did I chew him out?

> *From everyone who has been given much, much will be demanded; and from the one who has been entrusted with much, much more will be asked. (Luke 12:48b)*

I expected a whole lot more from my five-talent guy simply because he had a whole lot more to start with. I gushed on the three-talent guy because he worked hard, whereas I rebuked the five-talent because he was lazy, regardless of the comparative results.

When someone on my team makes an obvious mistake, I consider one of two causes; it's either a result of being unprepared or it's simply an *oops*. I've certainly had my share of oops, when I've played something a hundred times and for some unknown reason my fingers hit a note other than the one intended. Oops. There are times after a service when one of the team members is distraught over a wrong note. He or she attempts to apologize to me, but I dismiss it simply stating, "It was an *oops;* don't worry about it." There's rarely a service where a mistake happens due to laziness; that's usually weeded out at the rehearsal. But even if the oops are just that, and not laziness, there still has to be a level of skill that keeps the oops to a minimum. Too many oops and people get distracted.

I have visited many churches over the years, and some of their worship has been incredible, taking me right to the throne room. Other times, it's been not so good. On a few occasions, the worship was so poorly executed—out of tune with wrong notes, wrong chords and a bad mix—that I couldn't even begin to worship. I was too distracted. Some might respond and say, "All that matters is the condition of their hearts in worship, not their performance." In private worship, I would agree. In public worship, I disagree:

> *Even in the case of lifeless things that make sounds, such as the flute or harp, how will anyone know what tune is being played unless there is a distinction in the notes? Again, if the trumpet does not sound a clear call, who will get ready for battle? (1 Corinthians 14:7–8)*

There simply must be a level of competency to lead and participate in public worship. There just has to be. That's why we see the various levels of talents listed in Matthew 25, and those various levels have various roles in worship. If you're a one-talent person, then sing in the church, in your home Bible study or even in the shower, but sing as a personal expression. And there's nothing wrong with that. If you're investing your one-talent gift like that, God will give you a return on your investment, and it will be special and precious to you because it's between you and God. If, however, you're a five-talent person, then get out of the shower (get dressed) and get to the stage! You should be in public ministry: leading others, singing solos, participating on challenging worship teams, writing worship songs, maybe even touring or recording. Who knows? But if you're investing your five talents, the return on that investment will be amazing.

*There simply must be a level of competency to lead and participate in public worship. There just has to be.*

How do you increase the value of your investment? Through training and experience.

Training can involve lessons, conferences, workshops, seminars, classes and school, to name a few. Training develops the technical aspect of the gift, and I can't say enough about this subject, especially about lessons. I have encouraged countless musicians to get lessons, whether for ongoing development or simply as a refresher. The rewards are unlike any other type of training. But lessons themselves won't accomplish much unless there's practice to apply and hone the instruction. Lots of practice. Consistent practice. This is where the investment really pays off. Again: lots of practice, lots of return.

A few years ago, when I felt it was time to start playing some Latin worship music due to the growing Latin community in our church, I first needed to learn how to play it. So I found a local guy that had killer Latin chops and took some lessons from him. I practiced, a lot, and pretty soon my Latin chops became fairly competent. But eventually the time comes when we take all the instruction and all the practice and put it to the test—and thus we gain experience. Soon I put a Latin worship song on the list for the weekend services.

The first service came and I was feeling some nerves for sure. But things went okay. We were all a little uptight, but still, it went well. Second service ... okay, that felt better. Next service ... now we're feelin' it. Fourth service felt great. I could have practiced that song for months and as a group we could have practiced for even longer, but as soon as we hit the stage it's like we forget how the song even goes. Now when we play the same song, we don't even think twice about it. The training and practice to play it is there, and now the experience is there to worship from the heart with it. In a musician's vernacular, "It's one thing to play it, but it's another thing to own it." And the more you grow through training, the greater the opportunities for experience. They both go hand in hand.

But the reverse is quite true as well. If you have money and assets and choose not to invest them but instead stuff them between your mattresses or put them in a can in your closet somewhere, then when the future comes, not only will you have no return, you'll have actually lost money due to inflation. The same goes for your talents. If you choose not to practice, not to invest in your talents, you won't be able to keep up with "inflation." Your skills will begin to atrophy, and the very things you were able to do with ease will soon become difficult at best. Subsequently, your opportunities for experience will dry up as well, and when the future comes, you'll be kicking yourself as the reality of all you've missed out on hits you.

*Our talents have been* **entrusted** *to us.*

How does that happen? What keeps people from investing their gifts? In the case of the one-talent servant in Matthew 25, it's laziness and contempt for his master.

> *Then the man who had received the one talent came. "Master," he said, "I knew that you are a hard man, harvesting where you have not sown and gathering where you have not scattered seed. So I was afraid and went out and hid your talent in the ground. See, here is what belongs to you."*
>
> *His master replied, "You wicked, lazy servant!" (Matthew 25:24–26a)*

Laziness and contempt for our Master is also what keeps us from investing our gifts:

• *Lazy*: Choosing not to practice or be prepared, showing no faithfulness with your God-given gifts.

• *Wicked*: Showing contempt and apathy for the Lord by ignoring or refusing His call on your life.

Our talents have been *entrusted* to us. They are not ours to be lazy or apathetic with, but they are gifts from the Lord to be greatly valued and diligently invested. The framework of worship won't be built with your talents residing in a hole, so "go out at once," start investing and enjoy the return on your hard work!

# CHAPTER 18

# *What's the Plan?*

## Getting the worship team organized.

Musicians (i.e., right brainers, creative types, artists) are easily, and often rightfully so, stereotyped and lumped into the nebulous category of being inherently unorganized and undisciplined. They have a reputation for being scattered rather than organized, "winging it" instead of being prepared, and procrastinating rather than planning. I get it. I used to fit that category. Used to.

Notice the past tense, "used to." It's past because I don't fit into that category anymore. I was trained out of it. And if I can be trained out of it, so can my team. And that's exactly what has happened: I've challenged and trained my team to be on time, to be prepared, to have consistent devotionals and to love, respect and serve each other. The Bible states,

> *Train a child in the way he should go, and when he is old he will not turn from it. (Proverbs 22:6)*

I'm not at all insinuating that I treat and respond to my team as children (although there are times . . .) but rather that the concept and application is no different for my team, my staff or me than it is for my children. If we're trained in the way we should behave, work and serve, no matter our age, then we will be less likely to fall back into our old bad habits. Conversely, a team that is untrained, undisciplined and self-serving will continue on in its bad habits, maintaining a constant state of chaos and confusion until it eventually implodes. It's not a matter of *if* the team will implode but rather *when*.

Overcoming chaos requires organization, and organization demands a plan:

> *Good planning and hard work lead to prosperity,*
> *but hasty shortcuts lead to poverty.*
> *(Proverbs 21:5 NLT)*

• *Good planning*: A purposeful set of actions put into place to serve the whole after much counsel, consideration and prayer.

• *Hard work*: Diligent, faithful effort that perseveres against opposition.

• *Prosperity*: Gain, success, fruitfulness, peace.

• *Hasty shortcuts*: Impulsive, thoughtless and selfish decisions made without any counsel, consideration or prayer.

• *Poverty*: Loss, failure, heartache, anxiety.

Planning is hard work. It takes effort, requires goals, looks ahead, identifies problems and creates solutions.

**Effort.** Yes, you have to work at it; it just doesn't happen. You have to be purposeful and dedicate time to accomplish the task at hand.

**Goals.** What is it you're trying to accomplish? Is it putting together the song list and schedule in August for Christmas? Is it a handbook that will clearly explain the new worship team requirements and expectations? Or is it determining a more effective system to better communicate with the team? Make a list of things you'd like to change for the better and accomplish as a team, then develop a plan and a timeline to achieve those goals.

**Look ahead.** Literally sit down with a calendar and look ahead a month, three months, six months, a year (and, in some cases, even more) and determine which events need your attention and when to schedule potential events, including ministry-related, personal and family events. (Take it from me; avoid scheduling a leadership retreat during a family vacation!)

**Identify problems.** Discover where there are conflicts in a schedule, in a team, in systems or in relationships. Schedules can have events that overlap or are too close together—straining support staff and resources—and some of those events may not fully reflect your vision or the vision of the ministry. A team can often struggle with inconsistent availability and effort from various members, personality conflicts, communication breakdowns, equipment issues or any number of other conflicts. System conflicts are various processes that can include auditions, scheduling, team correction or rehearsals that are functioning ineffectively. And relational conflicts are breakdowns in the ability of various team and staff members to serve together with a like-minded purpose, as well as breakdowns in relationships between some team members and their spouses. Look thoroughly at all of these areas and monitor them continuously so you can be aware of and deal with problems and conflicts before they spiral out of control.

**Create solutions.** Come up with a plan to fix and resolve the problem or conflict.

As you plan, Scripture provides the following instructions:

• Commit your plans to the Lord.

> *Commit to the Lord whatever you do, and your plans will succeed. (Proverbs 16:3)*

This is kind of a no-brainer, and yet we're all guilty of occasionally jumping headfirst into a project only to realize we've pursued our plans without first committing them to the Lord in prayer. It takes discipline to always, always start any plan and project with prayer.

• Get advice.

> *Plans fail for lack of counsel, but with many advisers they succeed. (Proverbs 15:22)*

Thinking we have all the answers can border on arrogance. I always strive to get input from trusted friends and colleagues, and that diversity of gifts, wisdom and insight will invariably help me recognize a few deficiencies and blind spots in my plans. I want nothing more than for my plans to succeed and be fruitful. To neglect others' input and insight is foolish.

• Be okay with a change of plans.

> *In his heart a man plans his course, but the Lord determines his steps. (Proverbs 16:9)*

Several years ago I had planned a Night of Worship for New Year's Eve a couple of months ahead of time. (A Night of Worship is an evening where we worship for one-and-a-half to two hours. I share briefly from the Word between groupings of songs to bring greater understanding and clarity to the purpose of worship in our lives and to the particular theme for that evening.) I had the team, the theme, the songs and the arrangements all planned, distributed and ready to go. A couple of days before the event, I heard/sensed the Lord say, "I want you to give an invitation," to which I reminded the Lord that it was New Year's Eve and there's no way anybody who's not saved would be coming to church on that night. No way. We went back and forth a few times, and then I came to my senses. The reality was that I was more concerned about potentially making a fool of myself by giving an invitation on New Year's Eve than stepping out in faith and letting the Lord lead. "What if nobody comes forward?"

*Always plan, but always let the Lord redirect your steps and adjust your plans.*

I changed the plans on New Year's Eve day and gave an invitation that night. To my shock and amazement, over 200 people came forward to surrender their lives to Jesus that night! It was one of the greatest highlights of my entire life. What an incredible blessing I and many others would have missed out on if I had stuck to my plans and ignored the Spirit's prompting to redirect my steps.

Always plan, but always let the Lord redirect your steps and adjust your plans since His plans are always infinitely better than yours. Always!

As you can tell, I'm a fan and advocate of planning. I believe Scripture is clear-cut in its call to plan, to be organized and to be flexible all at the same time. There's an old saying, "If you fail to plan, you plan to fail." It's absolutely true. But be alert and careful not to be swayed by those who attempt to spiritually justify laziness. They claim that planning quenches the Spirit, preferring their worship, therefore, to be Spirit led. The assumption is that worship will either be planned, thus a work of the flesh, or it will be spontaneous, thus Spirit led. The assumption is flawed and inappropriately polarizing. I believe with all of my heart than you can not only plan but that you can also plan for spontaneity. I always tell my team to keep an eye on me on a particular song and to be ready in case I repeat a chorus or have the church sing it a cappella or make some other detour. I also have the flexibility of sharing between songs if I feel led to or of even adding a familiar chorus if appropriate and everyone on stage is familiar with it. But to show up on a Sunday morning with no plan and to just start singing songs without any particular arrangement or order is not only just plain lazy, it's contrary to Scripture:

> *May he give you the desire of your heart and make*
> *all your plans succeed. (Psalm 20:4)*

What plans? How can He make our plans succeed if we don't have any?

A team that is never fully prepared, never at its best and whose best option is the hope of survival rather than the joy of success will be continually frustrated and discouraged. Over time, as I stated before, this constant state of confusion, uncertainty and chaos is misguided and unsustainable. Consider this: if the Spirit can give the plans for the temple to David two decades ahead of time for David's son Solomon to build (1 Chronicles 28), then it's certainly not a stretch for the Spirit to give us appropriate and inspired song lists a week, a month or even more ahead of time. Now that's Spirit-led worship!

And finally, as worship leaders or any kind of leaders, we need to set the example if we expect anyone to follow us. Be trained, organized and disciplined with a plan, and then teach your team to be trained, organized and disciplined, following your lead.

Paul, writing to the Corinthian church concerning confusion in their worship, sums it up this way:

> *For God is not a God of disorder but of peace.*
> *(1 Corinthians 14:33a)*

*But all things must be done properly and in an orderly manner. (1 Corinthians 14:40 NASB)*

Have a plan, get your team organized and then focus on worshipping in Spirit and in truth instead of in confusion and chaos!

# CHAPTER 19

# *It Goes like This . . .*

## Getting the most out of rehearsals.

I purposed to present this chapter on rehearsals right after the chapter on planning since any rehearsal is going to need a game plan to be productive and effective. What are we going to rehearse? What are we rehearsing for? What results are we hoping for? And the defining question: how do we go about achieving those results?

Let's start from the premise of rehearsing for weekend services:

What are we going to rehearse? We'll rehearse the song list for this upcoming weekend's worship service.

*The overriding purpose of a rehearsal is to get better.*

What results are we hoping for? We're hoping to improve the execution of the songs, arrangements and transitions so as to honor the Lord with our gifts, talents and efforts, to facilitate a holy worship experience and to eliminate as many unnecessary musical distractions as possible. Really, the overriding purpose of a rehearsal is to get better.

How do we go about achieving those results? This is where the game plan comes into place.

Before a rehearsal starts, the following elements should be addressed and planned: the people, the songs, the arrangements, the expectations, the tools and finally, the surrender.

## The People

You might be surprised to know that my first step in preparing for a rehearsal is to determine the team personnel for the weekend. For me, the group of musicians that are available and subsequently scheduled can have a significant impact on the songs I choose. For example, if I have an accomplished and seasoned drummer available, I might be inclined to pull out one of our challenging Latin- or gospel-style songs; whereas if I'm plugging in a drummer who's new to the team and not as experienced, I would probably hold off on the more challenging songs that weekend. The same approach applies to my vocalists. Whether their voices are stronger and more cutting or softer and more blending directly affects the style and arrangement of songs I choose, as does the availability of particularly gifted vocal soloists. I will scrutinize all the musicians available for any given weekend, while also attempting to balance everyone's involvement so as not to burn out one person while neglecting another.

I would also point out that I schedule the teams and the songs a month at a time. This is accomplished by requesting everyone's availability for the following month, and with that master list in hand, I then begin to plan the entire month all at once. This accomplishes several things: (1) It's simply easier and more efficient for everyone involved to schedule once a month rather than every week. (2) The team members love it since they can plan their families' weekend activities around the worship schedule. (3) I'm able to schedule new worship team members near the end of the month to give them the most time to be as prepared as possible.

Now that the team is in place and scheduled, I can move on to the song selection.

## The Songs

I have a master list of songs that I continually rotate, retiring songs over time as well as introducing new ones. I usually don't introduce more than two new songs a month; otherwise the congregation might get a little frustrated. I purpose to incorporate songs into each set list that present a reasonable mix of celebratory and intimate worship, varying genres, and traditional hymns (often with contemporary treatments) and current and popular worship songs. I'll also present these songs with various vocal arrangements, alternating between vocal solos, duets, small group vocals and occasionally a large gospel choir. I plan ahead to use a reasonable combination of songs, striving to meet the cultural mix unique to South Florida and the multi-generational makeup of our church body. Your situation will likely be different, so plan your songs accordingly; meet the needs of your church members and they will be blessed.

Another element of planning song lists is picking songs that work together well:

• Choose songs that have a common thread or theme, if so desired, especially if you're coordinating with your pastor's teaching.

• Make sure there's a reasonable flow between songs in relationship to tempo. Going from an upbeat song to a slow song then back to an upbeat song can be a little unsettling to the church body.

• Have a consistency between songs that sing *of* Jesus and *to* Jesus. It can get a little awkward when opening with a song that proclaims "God is great," followed by a song where we intimately sing, "God, You are so faithful," and then back to singing about God again—back and forth between *of* and *to*. This isn't a hard and fast rule, but when done to excess, this back and forth can create an unsettled worship experience that can easily be avoided by planning accordingly.

- Choose songs that transition easily by key. This is nowhere near being any kind of a rule either, but it's really dynamic to seamlessly go right into the next song in the same key. Also, transitioning to a song using a relative key modulation (C major to A minor), a parallel key modulation (C major to C minor) or a common chord modulation (C major to F major or G major, the IV and V of the key of C) can really make for a smooth and effective transition as well.

Now that you've chosen the songs, it's time to plan out their arrangements.

## The Arrangements

This is the opportunity to transform a song into a slightly, entirely, or everything-in-between different-sounding experience. The arrangement can refresh an older song, improve a new song and, with a little imagination, allow a song to fit into almost any genre. This is where a song list can come alive, and where a song can be transformed to fit the skill level of your team, the preferences of your church body and even your pastor's vision for worship—all at the same time. There are countless ways to arrange a song, so I'll only mention a handful that I think will have the most effect, not in any particular order:

- **Key.** Transpose a particular song to a key that allows a male to lead a song that's normally led by a female, or vice versa.

- **Instrumentation.** Arrange for varying groups of instruments. "Unplug," for example, so that a box drum or djembe is providing the rhythm rather than a drum set, or use two acoustic guitars minus an electric guitar, and so on.

- **Vocals.** Try different vocal arrangements: use a prime unison where both the female and male singers sing the very same notes, or a simple two part (but not rigidly parallel, making sure it aligns reasonably with the chordal structure), or closed three part (where there's no other possible harmony parts between the existing three notes of the chord, and all three notes are aligned with the chordal structure). There are certainly other bigger combinations, but these are some potent combinations that work very well, especially when rotated between choruses or other parts of a song.

- **Style.** Take a hymn and add a rhythmic feel to it, or take a slow song and give it a reggae feel (if you feel brave), or any other style change you can think of. There's no need to change the melody; the song's still singable but just with a new paint job.

- **Tempo.** Slow it down and add more movement beneath the melody, then bring it back to tempo the second time around. Or speed it up a bit to add a little spice to it.

- **Texture.** Change up the *thickness,* for example. Change a chorus to a prime unison vocal only with only acoustic guitar or simple keyboard, then go back to the fuller sound for the repeat chorus (big sound vs. intimate sound).

- **Key Change.** Nothing says *goose bumps* like a key change on the last chorus. But try going down a key for the verse, then back up for the chorus, or experiment with other creative key changes.

- **A Cappella.** Drop all of the instruments out on a verse, chorus or both, or drop everybody out and have the church sing a chorus all by themselves. That's a great sound!

- **Layer.** Fatten the sound with pads via keyboards, loops or, if you have them, live strings, or any combination of those. Pads work well since the notes are sustained, vs. rhythmic instruments such as acoustic guitar or piano that can muddy the mix if overused. Adding layers can also create a wonderful contrast, especially following a simple, bare-bones instrumental accompaniment such as a solo acoustic guitar.

- **Chords.** Change them up. Switch them around. Take one chorus and totally change the chord progression while keeping the melody intact for a very cool effect.

- **Ending.** Finish the song differently. End on something other than the I chord, maybe a IV, or make the root the major third of a flat VI, or any other creative idea you might have. Also try ending a song abruptly, in an unpredictable way; on beat 4 of a 4/4 time signature, for example.

- **What's that?** Add unusual instruments. Try adding a banjo, chimes, glockenspiel, harmonica, orchestral bass drum or accordion (or whatever other instruments you may have access to). But not all at once. . . .

- **Length.** Make a song shorter, or maybe longer. Many current worship songs are being recorded well beyond five minutes in length, but you don't have to play them that way. You can cut out some of the redundancy, or even cut out a really boring bridge, to make the song your preferred length. Maybe the song is only three minutes long and you'd like it to be longer: double a chorus or another part using one of the aforementioned treatments.

- **Create.** Write your own bridge or intro or close. A new intro or close could especially help in transitioning to or from another song.

- **Graft.** Take a familiar chorus from one song and graft it into an existing song (purposing to match keys or effectively changing the key). This can be especially effective at the end of a song, or even more dramatically, closing the time of worship.

Like I mentioned earlier, these are just a few options for creatively transforming a song. I'm sure you'll have many more ideas of your own, so go for it!

## The Expectations

This is pretty straightforward. I expect the team members to be on time for rehearsal, to be prepared for rehearsal and to exhibit the fruit of the Spirit during rehearsal. And they rightly expect the same from me. They expect me to be prepared and organized ahead of time in order to have a plan for them to access so they can be prepared, and thus:

## The Tools

These are such things as

*A Schedule.* As I mentioned earlier, a timely list of services and who is scheduled to serve at each service.

*A Song List.* This speaks for itself.

*Charts.* These are valuable tools for many to learn from. They should contain the melody, the lyrics, the chords and the road map. They should not be a typed-out paragraph with handwritten chords all over it. If you don't know how to chart, then find someone who does; or, better yet, learn how to chart yourself. The "paragraph" charts are useless (except possibly for recalling lyrics); there's no indication of rhythm, melody, timing of chord changes, the road map (a scribbled out "repeat here" doesn't count) or any other useful information. Please provide viable charts for your team members. In doing so, you'll gain their favor and respect. If you provide a more traditional worship experience and have the privilege of incorporating an orchestra or similar ensemble, then be sure to have all of the individual parts charted out, coordinated and available well ahead of time.

***MP3s:*** These listenable representations of the songs are especially useful in conveying the feel of a song and the arrangement. They are essential for those rare musicians who only play by ear. I do not require the worship team members to read music; if they can be prepared by studious listening to the MP3s and they have a unique gift of being able to make and remember arrangement adjustments and employ their own understandable set of written notes or instructions, then why not use them? If there's a plan in place ahead of time, this is very doable. I do, however, encourage any and all musicians to learn a basic understanding of reading music. At the very least, have them learn topography, that is, reading music by following the ups and downs and the corresponding intervals. I have had many talented and gifted "play-by-ear" musicians join the team, only to see them, with some effort and training, become competent readers in a matter of months.

Once all these tools are planned and prepared, it's time to gather them together and organize them at into one centralized, accessible place:

***Planning Center.*** I'm not endorsing Planning Center, nor do I derive any benefits whatsoever from this company—but if you don't use this tool already, start. It puts the schedules, song lists, charts, MP3s and pertinent comments in one place accessible by any computer, laptop, electronic tablet or phone. Planning Center is easy to use, it will organize all of the tools into one location, it's accessible from any Internet connection or Wi-Fi (so you can learn songs at Starbucks) and it's a huge time saver. Great tool!

## The Surrender

Quite the opposite of "I give up" (which is where many could end up after a rough rehearsal), this surrender is when we close the rehearsal in prayer as we all agree to surrender the team, the songs and the worship service to the Lord. We did our part. We practiced diligently and prepared faithfully, and now it's in the Lord's hands to use the worship for His glory according to His plan.

## What Rehearsal Is

Let's take a step back and see how the individual elements previously addressed can work together, determining what the goal of rehearsal is and how that goal can be accomplished.

As mentioned in a previous chapter, I see the purpose of a rehearsal as a time to "polish the apple," not as a time to plant the tree. The reason I expect the team to be prepared when coming to rehearsal is so we can fine-tune various elements of the songs, work on unifying the approach or the *feel* of a song, drill and tweak vocal harmonies, work on vocal blend and tone, incorporate musical dynamics and work on stage presence.

My role, in addition to planning and preparing for the rehearsal ahead of time, is to manage and direct the actual rehearsal. I know in advance what we need to focus on and work on. I'll call out a song and then give instructions. It might be, "Let's run this one and see what we've got," or "Let's go to measure so-and-so and let me hear the vocals," or "Let's work on the intro," or countless other options. We'll rehearse those specific areas until I feel we're ready to move on to the next one, while also allowing for flexibility to work on unforeseen problems as they arise.

I also manage the interactions on stage. I don't allow opinions or input from the team during rehearsal. I've always told the team members that it's not a democracy; I'm in charge, not them. That's just a reality. No matter how you try to dress it up, no matter the extent of collaboration and input, someone still has to be accountable and responsible—and if I'm the worship leader, that someone is me. I've learned that by soliciting and accepting opinions on stage, I set myself up for a no-win scenario: when there are more than one opinion, only one has a chance of prevailing. This means one or more opinions will be publically rejected, thus hurting feelings and causing those who offered the free "rejected" advice to feel marginalized. The solution: no unsolicited opinions, input or suggestions from the team on stage. Team members can talk to me off stage before or after rehearsal all they want and I'll listen to and consider their opinions and suggestions but not on stage during rehearsal. I already have a plan.

Another role is setting the mood. I try to keep rehearsals fun, interjecting humor here and there in order to keep our time together interesting, even unpredictable. Sometimes rehearsals can get a little intense, even counterproductive, and when that happens it's time to lighten it up, push less and switch songs. Alternately, rehearsals can sometimes get a little loose and lose focus. Personally, I know of no other setting where multiple conversations can simultaneously and spontaneously break out within a matter of seconds of downtime, with all participants suddenly oblivious to their surroundings. It's truly astounding! And it's not just the vocalists; sometimes the band can give the singers a run for their money when it comes to chattiness. When that happens, don't even try to stop it—you could get hurt. Instead, just jump right back into a song and they'll all snap right out of it and join the rehearsal once again. And then avoid any further downtime, if at all possible. (Honestly though, to me a chatty team is a healthy team. And although it takes a little more effort to manage and keep them focused, it's well worth it!) Keeping everyone on track, focused and productive while maintaining a pleasant and enjoyable atmosphere is definitely a challenging role but also a vital one and a fun one that goes a long way toward building morale and preparing the team for the weekend ahead.

## What Rehearsal Is Not

Rehearsal is *not* the time to "plant the tree," that is, to introduce the song list to the team for the very first time. Yet so many times I've seen or heard of a worship leader who pulls his (insert "her" along the way, if appropriate) team together for a rehearsal with zero preparation and planning, starts late, announces to the group the songs he's "thinking" of doing, and then drops the following dreaded phrase: "It goes like this." He then plays the song poorly on the guitar, offers some half-hearted vocal rendition, uses strange vocal inflections to attempt to emulate how the drum part goes, uses foreign adjectives to describe the sound the rest of the band and vocals should aspire to, and then says "Let's give it a try." There's no excuse for that; there just isn't. It's an incredible waste of everyone's time, and the end result is at best marginal—only to be forgotten by Sunday since there are no tools to allow for personal practice. So another rehearsal is required two hours or more before Sunday service, wasting even more time. If I've just described you, don't be angry with me, but instead be challenged—challenged to take your worship leading to the next level, to utilize the tools I've described, and to honor not only your team's time but your own as well. Start with prayer, follow it up with action, and then watch God honor your effort and diligence. You'll be blessed, as will those whom you lead.

Having a plan and being prepared allows the rehearsal to be equitable. Here's what I mean: if I present the songs at the time of rehearsal, the veterans already know the songs and are bored to tears while the rookies want and need more time to learn them since they've never heard those songs before. The rehearsal ends with no one happy. With all of the tools available, the veterans can now be prepared with less than an hour of work, and the rookies can practice hours upon hours if they so desire, bringing both groups to rehearsal on level ground musically.

Rehearsal is also *not* a Bible study. I'm sure this will surprise and maybe even offend some people, but I've witnessed some

157

rehearsals that I honestly wondered if they were, in fact, a rehearsal or a church service. I will often share a one- to three-minute devotion, a Scripture I'd read earlier in the day or week or some other relevant gem from the Word but thirty to forty minutes of preaching? Seriously, if you have the need and call to preach, then start a new church plant, but let a rehearsal be a rehearsal and let church be church. I'm a fan of exhorting and helping the team to understand the message of the various songs, to apply them and to respond to them appropriately but not of usurping the role of the pastor and preaching to the team while the intent and goal of the rehearsal is compromised or disregarded altogether.

Rehearsal is also *not* a time of fellowship. Fellowship is welcome before rehearsal, and it is certainly welcome and even encouraged after rehearsal but absolutely not *during* rehearsal. Fellowship time is for fellowshipping, and rehearsal time is for rehearsing.

And rehearsal is *not* endless. When I hear time after time about rehearsals that go three to four hours or more, I'm just amazed. That's not a rehearsal, that's a sleepover. The common theme goes like this: team members slowly meander in, there's some fellowship time mostly because there's no urgency for anyone to be on time, and then about forty-five minutes after the scheduled start time there's a thirty- to forty-minute "devotion" and prayer time. Then there's set up, and by the time the actual rehearsal starts, it's around two hours past the start time. Now the rehearsal drags on. The leader and team are both unprepared (by no fault of the team), and at about three and a half to four hours past the start time, there's a prayer time again to close the rehearsal, followed by a conversation about when to rehearse again because they didn't get through all of the songs.

My regular rehearsals are one hour long, 6:00 to 7:00 p.m. They start late enough in the day for members to come from work and end early enough to accommodate parents who need and want to get home to dinner and family. (For a Night of Worship, rehearsal is an hour and a half, and for a major Christmas or Easter production, rehearsal is two hours.) Then, after rehearsal, there's time for fellowship, which can often go on for hours; yet those who need to go, can go. I plan and prepare ahead of time and so does my team, making one hour for rehearsal plenty of time. And with similar planning and preparation, I guarantee a one-hour rehearsal would be sufficient for any team. If you prefer, after rehearsal you can work with any team members who need or would like some extra rehearsal time, which still allows those who have families, homework or other pressing responsibilities to leave at a reasonable time. This shorter rehearsal time frame is also conducive to allowing more new members to participate who otherwise wouldn't be able to give up an entire evening.

* * * * * * * *

All of these tools and methods make for an enjoyable and productive rehearsal. And when rehearsals go well, we're able to look forward to services with anticipation and excitement rather than with anxiety; we're no longer filled with uncertainty over the next note, chord or lyric, but instead we're focused on the bigger picture: leading God's people in worship.

# CHAPTER 20

# *Am I Good Enough?*

## Accessing gifts and skills for effective service.

People regularly approach me and comment, "I'd like to be on your worship team, but I don't know if I'm good enough." Some will ask, "What do I need to do to be on the worship team?"

At our church, to be a part of the worship team or worship choir requires an audition. I'm a huge fan of auditions. I advocate for auditions wherever I teach, wherever I lead, wherever I go. Not just because it's a personal preference but because it's a biblical mandate as well.

I recently read a blog where the writer boldly proclaimed, "If your church has auditions for the worship team, then you should leave." He went on to rant about the evils of auditions and how they crush and destroy people and blah, blah, blah. Truly one of the more ignorant writings I've ever had the privilege to read! The problem is that ignorant writings like this find a receptive audience in those who have been on the receiving end of a perceived "rejection." They, in turn, choose to join with others who have been similarly wounded to attack churches and worship ministries for their supposed immoral behavior, rather than addressing the real issue: their wounded pride.

If you want to see similar behavior in the world, just watch the first couple weeks of any American Idol season. Watch how contestants who can't find a note or a rhythm, let alone any kind of recognizable melody, respond with bleeped out words and blurred out middle fingers when they are rejected.

*We're trying to determine gifts and skills and what role best suits those very gifts and skills.*

First of all, what is it that we're trying to accomplish with auditions? For starters, we're trying to determine gifts and skills and what role best suits those very gifts and skills.

In Matthew 25:14–30, we see that there are different levels of *talent* (gifts and skills). In 1 Corinthians 12:26, we see that there is one body but different parts. Regardless of how many talents you possess, the reward for diligence with those talents is the same. And regardless of what part of the body you are, the concern for each part is equal. So although God loves us all the same, He has nonetheless given us different roles within the body of Christ and different levels of talents to carry out those roles.

How do we determine what our roles are? Can we simply declare what we want to do, or is there a need or even a responsibility to assess our gifts and discern our roles? The Bible is full of instruction in this area:

> *They must first be tested; and then if there is nothing against them, let them serve as deacons.*
> *(1 Timothy 3:10)*

> *Do not be conformed to this world, but be transformed by the renewal of your mind, that by testing you may discern what is the will of God, what is good and acceptable and perfect.*
> *(Romans 12:2 ESV)*

*Dear friends, do not believe every spirit, but test the spirits to see whether they are from God, because many false prophets have gone out into the world. (1 John 4:1)*

*A man ought to examine himself before he eats of the bread and drinks of the cup. (1 Corinthians 11:28)*

*Test everything. Hold on to the good. (1 Thessalonians 5:21)*

So I'm to test and examine to see if someone should be a leader, what the will of God is, if the spirits are from God, and if I'm prepared to take Communion in a worthy manner. In fact, I'm to "test everything," but heaven forbid that I or anyone else should test and examine to see if someone is called, equipped and capable of serving in worship!

*"But you're judging!"*

Of course I'm judging. There, I said it.

"Aren't you aware of what Scripture says about judging?"

*"Do not judge, or you too will be judged. For in the same way you judge others, you will be judged, and with the measure you use, it will measured to you." (Matthew 7:1–2)*

Of course I'm aware of it. I have to defend against this baseless and tired argument all the time. Ironically, if you continue to read this area of Scripture, you'll find that Jesus teaches that we are, in fact, to judge but rightly and justly and without hypocrisy:

*"Why do you look at the speck of sawdust in your brother's eye and pay no attention to the plank in your own eye? How can you say to your brother,*

*'Let me take the speck out of your eye,' when all the time there is a plank in your own eye? You hypocrite, first take the plank out of your own eye, and then you will see clearly to remove the speck from your brother's eye." (Matthew 7:3–5)*

As I disciple and mentor my staff and team, it is my responsibility to bring to their attention various shortcomings (i.e., specks) that they may not see and to address them. But shame on me if, in the meantime, I'm covering up my own sins (i.e., planks) that would likely mean my dismissal if they were exposed.

In *Gill's Exposition of the Entire Bible*, this use of "judge" in Matthew 7:1 is described as being "of rash judgment, interpreting men's words and deeds to the worst sense, and censuring them in a very severe manner; even passing sentence on them with respect to their eternal state and condition."[18]

We are not to judge harshly or hypocritically, nor are we to judge as to condemn. But we are to judge in a way that discerns, corrects, commends and recommends. Jesus exhorts us to judge but with honesty and integrity:

*"Stop judging by mere appearances, but instead judge correctly." (John 7:24)*

Paul tells us to judge those in the church and to have nothing to do with anyone who embraces sin:

*But now I am writing you that you must not associate with anyone who calls himself a brother but is sexually immoral or greedy, an idolater or a slanderer, and drunkard or a swindler. With such a man do not even eat. (1 Corinthians 5:11)*

Paul even rebukes the Corinthian church for not judging:

> *I say this to shame you. Is it possible that there is nobody among you wise enough to judge a dispute between believers? (1 Corinthians 6:5)*

So I think we can move on now to the process of auditions. We've established that the Word confirms that we are called to rightly and fairly judge, discern, evaluate, test and examine, and that the Matthew 7:1–2 argument is not even remotely applicable in this context. Right? Not quite yet.

## "Anyone should be able to be a part of the worship team if his or her heart is right."

Just rereading that comment makes me cringe. The problem is that you can't put a microphone on a heart, only on instruments and voices.

Some time ago I knew a pastor who invited anyone in the church who wanted to be on the worship team to come out for rehearsal. I happened to witness that rehearsal in person. It was an utter disaster. So was the weekend.

Likewise, a long time ago I decided to start a worship choir to join the worship team on occasion during services. I put out the word for interested singers to come out and join the choir without auditioning. Just show up and sing. I really should have known better. Although the strong singers outnumbered the weaker singers, I discovered an interesting phenomenon: the singers' abilities were directly related to their volume. The worse they sang, the louder they sang—which threw off those who were, in fact, capable of finding their notes and pitches, and created unpredictable harmonies. The result was a choir where the majority was annoyed with and frustrated by the louder minority. I quickly disbanded the choir, only to restart it a few months later with auditions.

Believing that anyone should be able to be on a worship team simply because his or her heart is right is not only misguided, it's just not accurate. It can even be dangerous.

The two personal examples I just gave are described perfectly in Scripture:

> *Even in the case of lifeless things that make sounds, such as the flute or harp, how will anyone know what tune is being played unless there is a distinction in the notes? Again, if the trumpet does not sound a clear call, who will get ready for battle? (1 Corinthians 14:7–8)*

In Old Testament times, trumpets directed battles. There was no other form of communication. There were no radios, field telephones or intercom systems, just trumpets. The combination of notes and rhythms the trumpeters played would signal the armies to charge, retreat, flank or perform any number of other critical tactical maneuvers. Imagine now if some guy shows up to battle with a trumpet and says, "I want to play for your army." "Do you have any experience; have you played before?" "Well, yes, a little. But more importantly, I love the Lord with all my heart, and it's my desire above all else to serve the Lord with my trumpet. With God all things are possible, and He told me I was supposed to play trumpet in your army!" "Well, okay. Why don't you grab your horn and join us on the battlefield. Now, to start with, go ahead and play the part that calls us to go to battle." And as the tune is played so poorly that it's unrecognizable, the armies aren't able to discern whether they're hearing a call to charge or a call to retreat. The armies are now in confusion and chaos and they're subsequently attacked by the enemy and defeated with great loss of life.

*To play skillfully is not an option or a suggestion; it is an expectation and an exhortation not to be taken lightly.*

That's an extreme and absurd illustration, yet that's exactly what some propose I do with my worship team as it gets ready to do battle. A worship team that plays so poorly that the songs and lyrics are unrecognizable causes distraction and confusion. Rather than having an encounter with the Lord that fills us with joy and strengthens us for whatever lies ahead, we miss the cue to worship, and the door is opened for the enemy to attack and defeat us.

If a good heart were all that it took to be effective in worship, then I would expect that to be affirmed and corroborated in the Word. We see quite the contrary, however:

> *Sing to Him a new song; play skillfully and shout for joy. (Psalm 33:3)*

To play skillfully is not an option or a suggestion; it is an expectation and an exhortation not to be taken lightly. Look at what happened during the dedication of the temple and consider if this could have happened without skillful participation:

> *All the Levites who were musicians—Asaph, Heman, Jeduthun and their sons and relatives— stood on the east side of the altar, dressed in fine linen and playing cymbals, harps and lyres. They were accompanied by 120 priests sounding trumpets. The trumpeters and singers joined in unison, as with one voice, to give praise and thanks to the Lord. Accompanied by trumpets, cymbals and other instruments, they raised their voices in praise to the Lord and sang:*
> *"He is good;*
> *his love endures forever."*
> *Then the temple of the Lord was filled with a cloud, and the priests could not perform their service because of the cloud, for the glory of the Lord filled the temple of God. (2 Chronicles 5:12–14)*

Can anyone, even the guy who wrote the blog that started this chapter, read this, absorb all that has happened and, having considered the sheer number of musicians involved, honestly think that this was accomplished by a bunch of folks with only a "good heart"? You simply can't have that many instrumentalists and singers all joined together "as with one voice" without some serious training and skill.

The Levites, one of twelve tribes of Israel, were set apart for service to God, and they were assigned to various duties, including worship, for the temple. First Chronicles 25 describes those who were in charge of the worship we just read about:

> *All these men were under the supervision of their fathers for the music of the temple of the Lord, with cymbals, lyres and harps, for the ministry at the house of God. Asaph, Jeduthun and Heman were under the supervision of the king. Along with their relatives—all of them trained and skilled in music for the Lord—they numbered 288.*
> *(1 Chronicles 25:6–7)*

These guys were trained, skilled and set apart. You never saw a guy from the tribe of Benjamin stop by the temple and ask to join the worship team just because he was into it. In the same way, why would I be expected to bring people onto my worship team who aren't trained, skilled and set apart (called)—regardless of their hearts? It's foolish, it's unbiblical and it's spiritually dangerous. If your church has auditions for the worship team, don't leave, as the blogger suggested, but instead applaud your church and thank the Lord for wise and discerning leadership.

As we move from the justification and precedent for auditions to their application, we start by noticing that the Levites obviously used some method to periodically evaluate skill in order to provide appropriate and ongoing training. We do the same with auditions. The first audition determines current skills and abilities, and as ongoing training is pursued, subsequent auditions determine opportunities for greater responsibilities.

So how do you go about holding auditions? What do you do and why do you do it? How do you decide if someone "makes it," and what do you say to someone who doesn't?

As I share our model for worship team auditions, I'll remind you that I don't have all the answers, nor would I ever suggest that our way is the best way. But it works for us and accomplishes the goal of determining who should be set apart for serving in worship. More than the methods, I hope you'll see and understand the purposes and motivation behind them.

## What are you looking for in an audition?

Our first goal is to determine if the people auditioning have a gift to serve in worship, and then to evaluate their level of skill. If they're singers, for example, can they sing a melody with appropriate timing? We've had a number of singers audition who can only manage to sing in a monotone. Likewise, we've had percussionists audition who apparently consider rhythm to be optional. In both cases, and many others like them, these people simply don't have a musical gift. But for those who do have a musical gift, we then want to evaluate the level of gifting and acquired skill.

Using the parable of the talents in Matthew 25 as our template, we rate the skill level from a five (you should be on stage) to a one (you should not be on stage) and everything in between.

## What do they need to do to get started?

The only way we can accurately evaluate skill is to facilitate a process that allows those auditioning to present themselves at their very best, no excuses. To start with, we provide two songs, one upbeat and one slow, on the Web for them to download. These two songs are unique for each instrument and voice (soprano, alto and tenor) and highlight the technique, range and skill needed to participate successfully. The MP3s are recorded with full instrumentation for only the first minute or so of each song; the intro, first verse and chorus. That's more than enough for us to adequately evaluate. In total, there are approximately two minutes worth of playing/singing time for each audition. Included with the MP3s are charts that show the chords, the melody, the harmonies, the rhythms, and the road map: a good, accurate lead sheet. Reading music is not a requirement, but it's certainly an advantage.

The MP3s contain the full arrangement of the song. However, panning to the left highlights the particular instrument or voice while lowering the level of the track for learning purposes. Panning to the right raises the level of the track and simultaneously reduces the level of the particular instrument or voice, allowing the person auditioning to practice with the track without hearing the pre-recorded part. We also give the auditionees our contact information so they can reach us if they have any questions or concerns pertaining to anything to do with auditions. We encourage everyone to present a reasonable facsimile of what's on the recorded arrangement; we're not evaluating improvisational skills but rather looking for an accurate performance that contributes to and blends in with the whole arrangement. At this point, those auditioning now have all of the tools and resources available to learn and present the two songs to the best of their ability.

Next is scheduling the audition. We hold auditions once every month on a Saturday at 11:00 a.m. We encourage those who desire to audition to first learn the songs and then sign up online for the next audition date. Again, the goal is to eliminate any excuses from having us hear their best performance, so we don't schedule them and we don't give them a time limit. It's the auditionees' choice to sign up for an audition when they feel they're ready.

We also ask every person auditioning to fill out a one-page questionnaire online that gives us some personal information including playing background, church background and testimony.

Although the online process may appear a little impersonal, the vast majority of those that audition have had a lot of personal interaction with me, other worship leaders, team members and staff—all of us encouraging and instructing them in the process well before they begin to access the online resources. The online process comes alongside the personal interaction; it's not intended to replace it.

## How is the actual audition run?

We send everyone who has signed up a reminder a week before the audition, asking them to meet at 10:45 a.m. on Saturday in anticipation of starting on time at eleven o'clock. We welcome them, encourage them, joke with them a little to calm them down and start with brave volunteers. We will generally have anywhere from six to a dozen people at any given audition. We bring them one at a time to the room where they will sing or play. All of the equipment they will need is in that room. Due to their sign-ups, we know ahead of time if someone needs an amp, drum set, keyboard or percussion instruments. In addition to me, the campus worship leaders are present, as well as the interns (so they can observe and learn the process first hand). We have the sound system and the multi-track recordings all set to go for each of the auditionees. Depending on who's playing or singing, we mute that particular instrument or voice on the recording, which allows us to hear the auditionee clearly. As the auditionees each come in, we ask them to introduce themselves, and often we'll ask them a random question to help loosen them up. Then they're given the choice of which song they would like to start with, and off we go.

When they're finished, they're escorted back to the waiting room where they're free to leave or to stay as moral support for the remaining auditionees. Between each audition, the rest of the group and I discuss strengths, weaknesses, level of skill and potential placements. We continue in this way until all the auditions are over. After one final download with the team, we are finished with the auditions. The entire process takes an hour to an hour and a half.

## What determines if a person "made it" or not?

In auditions, we're looking and listening for several elements. Believe it or not, we learn much from just the greeting and brief conversation. How do they respond? Are they serious, lighthearted, funny? What's their countenance? Are they joyful, peaceful, emotional, fearful? Are they self-promoting, name dropping, even flirting? Are they making excuses for their performance before they even start? All of these things give us a bit of a window into who they are and why they're there. For example, if people immediately make an excuse for the upcoming performance, I can guarantee you that they won't make it—it means that they don't take ownership for their own mistakes, whether in music or, usually, in life. Everything's always something or someone else's fault, never theirs. If they were on the team, there would never be an opportunity for correction because, again, nothing is their fault. And since there's no room for correction, their gift is invariably untrained and unskilled. If they're a namedropper or self-promoter, it's generally because their skills don't hold up on their own, so that audition rarely works out either.

People who are friendly and have a peaceful countenance tend to do well. They have a humble spirit and a quiet confidence that generally reflects a great work ethic, and their auditions are usually solid. (But then there's the guy who wore only a black leather sleeveless vest and matching tight leather pants with fur covered boots and who literally winked at the girls as he came forward to audition. Yeah, that one didn't work out so well. . . .) Use that greeting time wisely, there's a wealth of valuable insight to be gleaned.

Once the playing or singing begins, it's not long at all before we have a fairly accurate view of one's gifts and skills. Oftentimes all it takes is literally a few seconds to have a complete and accurate evaluation. For a singer, I'm listening to tone, breath support, pitch, accuracy of melodies and harmonies, long notes, phrase endings, use and frequency of vibrato, style (opera, rock, gospel, etc.), and mic control, to name a few. For an instrumentalist, I'm listening to tone as well, rhythmic accuracy, ability to complement the arrangement and play within the style, pitch, technique and busyness—and that elusive *feel*.

In addition to listening for all of these factors, I'm also listening for the possibility of certain aspects being adaptable, if necessary. Here's what I mean: a couple of years ago one of my newer guys at a satellite campus listened to a girl sing and told her that he couldn't use her because her vibrato was too much for the current sound of worship. I met with her and asked her to sing in a straight tone—she happily obliged and the problem was solved. I still use her to this day on the team. Issues like vibrato, mic technique and busyness can often be adapted and adjusted quite easily. The bigger challenges, though, are rhythmic inaccuracy, note inaccuracy and pitch issues. Some things simply just can't be taught, adapted or fixed.

In some instances, however, someone may have a particular strength and skill that is more specialized and niche but still incredibly valuable. I once had a team member who played acoustic guitar and who had his master's degree in classical guitar performance. What this guy could play was unbelievable! But rhythm acoustic? It wasn't working. He just didn't have a feel for it. On the other hand, I had guys who could play amazing rhythm acoustic, yet they had little or no technique or feel for playing finger style. So on stage and in the studio, I used the one guy for all of the finger-style tracks and ballad-type songs. He even created a few classical guitar licks that worked out beautifully in the studio. And for the acoustic rhythm songs on stage and in the studio, I used different players.

So as you audition people, keep in mind that they don't have to be able to do it all or be one size fits all, nor are you obligated to use them at every service or on every song. For instance, a skilled and gifted violinist or cellist should not be excluded just because you don't have a position for him or her. Instead, welcome this person to the team; you may have an arrangement come up that would come to life with a violin or a cello (or any other instrument), and now you have someone available for when the occasion arises. Just having some of these unique instruments available to you can give you some really creative ideas for writing and arranging, especially during the holidays.

Once the qualifying skills are discerned, it's time to evaluate the level or degree of *talent* as described in Matthew 25. In our case, a five, four, and three-talent level will make it. A five-talent: main campus, satellite campus, get on stage, get in the studio. A four talent: worship choir, larger satellite campuses. A three talent: worship choir, smaller satellite campuses. We try to match everybody and his or her gifts and skills with the appropriate opportunity. Look at how the master in Matthew 25 determined how many talents each servant was given:

> *"Again, it will be like a man going on a journey, who called his servants and untrusted his property to them. To one he gave five talents of money, to another two talents, and to another one talent, each according to his ability." (Matthew 25:14–15)*

"Each according to his ability." That's exactly what we're hoping to do with auditions when assessing levels of talents— assign ministry opportunities to each according to his or her ability.

## When do you tell them whether they made it or not?

I do not communicate any results with anyone at the time of the actual audition. Each audition and auditionee needs to be handled uniquely, and I especially prefer to handle any "rejections" one on one to ensure and facilitate the best possible outcome. Before the auditions even begin, we tell the group that nothing will be decided the day of auditions; instead, they will hear from us with our decision within a week. This allows the auditionees to manage their expectations. Following the auditions, I consolidate everyone's comments, evaluations and suggestions, and then begin to finalize my own evaluations. After taking everyone's input into account, I make the final evaluations and placements, discerning the most appropriate way to communicate the results.

Most communication is done via email, particularly to the ones who did well. We simply thank them for their interest in becoming a part of the worship team, congratulate them on a job well done and give them directions for what's next. We may instruct them to begin attending certain rehearsals, to expect a call from a particular campus worship leader or to respond to any number of instructions. As I mentioned earlier, one-on-one phone calls or personal conversations are generally reserved for those who didn't make the cut, with the hope that a sincere tone of voice will more accurately and sensitively convey the message and mitigate the disappointment more so than a sterile email.

To stretch the time it takes to communicate the results with the auditionees beyond a week would be unfair, frustrating and unnecessarily nerve wracking to them. Be sure to respond in a timely fashion, much like each of us would hope to be treated in a similar situation.

## What about their heart?

As strongly as I feel that people should not participate on a worship team solely because of their hearts regardless of skill, I feel the opposite just as strongly, if not more so: no one should serve on a worship team regardless of skill if his or her heart is not right with the Lord. Paul, in defending false accusations against his ministry and his motives declared:

> *For we speak as messengers approved by God to be entrusted with the Good News. Our purpose is to please God, not people. He alone examines the motives of our hearts. (1 Thessalonians 2:4 NLT)*

There it is: the motives of our hearts. Why do we want to be on stage? Is it applause, affection, attention, approval from man, income, prestige? Maybe even to find a mate?

> *So whether you eat or drink or whatever you do, do it all for the glory of God. (1 Corinthians 10:31)*

The motives of our hearts determine whether we will serve the Lord or serve ourselves, whether we will strive to meet the needs of the body of Christ or the needs of our own flesh and whether we will strive to please God or please people. If it's not for the glory of God, then it's for the glory of man, and that will never end well.

There have been a few people over the years who either fooled me at the beginning of their service on the team or began to wander from the truth during their time of service. Either way, God is not mocked. In every single instance, God exposed their hearts and their deeds. Some went on to repentance and restoration, others continued on in their selfish ways. The sad truth is that most worship leaders who have been serving for any length of time have had their own Judas or two on the team; I've certainly had mine.

**The motives of our hearts determine whether we will serve the Lord or serve ourselves.**

As much as I encourage the team to practice and be prepared, I encourage them even more to pray, to be in God's Word every day, to hold each other accountable and to encourage each other. I'm also a part of the team, and I need to be right in there with them, to reach out when there's a need or a hurt, to pray for them and with them, to take their calls and respond to their emails and texts so that they feel cared for and loved. As important as it is to develop

176

our skills, it's so much more critical for the sake of worship and its effectiveness to build up and guard our hearts in the ways of the Lord.

*May they sing of the ways of the Lord, for the glory of the Lord is great. (Psalm 138:5)*

So keep an eye on their skills, but keep both eyes on their hearts.

## Can nonbelievers audition for your worship team?

No. I would love to meet them, talk to them, invite them to our rehearsal, introduce them to the team and have them come to church to check out the worship. But no, they cannot audition for the team.

"Why?"

I don't use nonbelievers to lead worship. That includes the worship team and the worship choir. The common argument of course is, "But it's a great opportunity to witness, and if even one musician gets saved, then why is it wrong?" Well, let's employ that logic in another related way. You might say, "I know a girl who's a Christian and she married a nonbeliever and he ended up getting saved." Perfect. So are we now to disregard the Word of God and no longer teach the call to be equally yoked in our premarital classes because this one guy got saved? Have we even considered that if the girl had taken a stand for God and His Word, the guy

*Keep an eye on their skills, but keep both eyes on their hearts.*

might have come around anyway—and maybe even sooner? Likewise with the unsaved musician. Befriend him, have him hang around with the team and get to know them, have him come to church, experience the worship and even sit in on a rehearsal, just don't put him on the stage to lead worship. Explain what worship is and whom we worship. Explain how conflicting it would be for

177

him to sing or play a song that says "I love you, Lord" when he doesn't know Jesus. Love on him, witness to him in word and action, and continue to reach out to him. Your relationship with him has a better chance of facilitating a sincere conversion than having him play on your worship team.

I speak from experience. I played for several churches before I was saved. For nine years! And no one ever shared the Gospel with me; I got saved because of the witnessing and example of several college students working at a church for the summer. They befriended me. It was personal and life changing and it had nothing to do with me playing on any worship team.

Maybe it's just coincidence, but I find it interesting that every time someone argues for having a nonbeliever on the worship team, that nonbeliever just happens to be a very talented musician capable of filling a position that's been desperately lacking for quite a while. Just coincidence, I'm sure.

Take to heart these words of Isaiah:

> *The Lord says:*
> *"These people come near to me with their mouth*
> *and honor me with their lips,*
> *but their hearts are far from me.*
> *Their worship of me*
> *is made up only of rules taught by men."*
> *(Isaiah 29:13)*

The Lord is condemning the people of Israel for professing worship and obedience with their mouths while simply going through the motions. No heart, no sincerity. Lip service. And the Lord's rebuke was severe. My exhortation? Don't use a nonbeliever to lead God's people in worship. It's a fraud whose benefits pale in comparison to the consequences. Rather, through prayer and relationship, affect this nonbeliever's life for the Lord. In time, and as a result of your prayers, relationship, example and witnessing, this nonbeliever may soon come to know the Lord personally and someday become a valuable member of your team.

As you can see by the length of this chapter, there is a lot to consider when it comes to auditions. I personally believe auditions are critical to the growth and depth of the worship team, providing a crucial point of entry for so many that would otherwise be left out. Use good, fair and correct judgment and discernment to build up the team for His glory and His glory alone.

"Wait, you left something out!"

## How do you tell a person he or she didn't make it?

I'll discuss the answer to that question in the next chapter.

# CHAPTER 21

# *You're No Good!*

## How to share the truth in love.

You may be thinking, "That title is a little harsh." It is. I used it because those are the exact words many hear with their hearts when they're told they didn't make the worship team. It's a crushing reality for some.

*You've watched and listened to the worship team from afar for years, even dreaming of what it would be like to be on stage worshipping the Lord with all your might—how rewarding, how glorious it would all be! After much prayer, and having been told by well-meaning friends and family that you should try out, you finally muster up the courage and go for it. The audition seems to go well. Although you were struggling a little with nerves, you're pretty confident that didn't taint your performance. All of the "judges" seemed really nice—that's a good sign. You wait, and then the news comes and your worst fears are realized: you didn't make it. "But they told me I did a great job and that I had a really nice voice." You're dumbfounded at first, then confused, then embarrassed. "What will I say to my friends and family who have been praying for me and assuring me I'd make it?" Then you're angry. You don't know what to do next, and you begin to think of leaving the church.*

It should never get to this place; there's just no reason for it. This is a result of poor communication, a lousy explanation and mixed signals in an attempt to temper the "bad news." What's usually missing is truth in love with options. Truth in love is when you're more concerned about the ultimate outcome than just trying to pacify the moment. "You know, you have some skills that need to be developed more, and maybe with some practice and lessons; who knows; because you know, we can do all things through Christ who strengthens us; so, you know, it didn't work out for now; but, you know; you never know about the future," and blah, blah, blah. Translation: "You're not very good and I don't think there's the slightest chance you'll ever be good enough, but I don't want to hurt your feelings (as if they're not already), so instead of giving you other realistic options, I'll just go ahead and give you false hope so I can crush your spirit again in the near future."

This false hope is an attempt, albeit a dishonest one, to mitigate an awkward and uncomfortable situation. One of two things will happen however: one, this person will spend time and money investing in something that you know is not a good investment, only to again be crushed with even greater personal and spiritual fallout, or two, he or she will quickly realize you're insincere and patronizing. Neither one bodes well for your credibility.

Truth in love must be balanced with options; truth in love alone results in rejection. It's like being told you're a sinner and the wages of sin is death and leaving out the part that says the free gift of God is eternal life through Christ Jesus our Lord (Romans 6:23). We need options. Come on, we can't even buy a car without options, yet we can shut down poor souls who want to be a part of our worship team without offering them a single alternative!

*Truth in love* shares with them that serving in worship ministry is not their gift nor where they fit in the body of Christ. And *options* is giving them an alternative: "Let's look at where else in the church you could serve. Do you enjoy working with kids, babies or youth? Are you a people person, maybe an usher or a greeter? There are lots of options for you to serve in this ministry. I'd like to help you find the right one." I go on to give them detailed options: "Since worship's not the best fit, I'd like you to pray about where you'd like to serve, what area of ministry might be a better fit. Then in a week come see me after service and let me know what you've decided and I'll help you get connected with that ministry."

*You offered them redirection instead of rejection. That's our job. More importantly, that's our ministry.*

Most of the time they do follow up and we talk about their new option or options, and I give them the contact info of the person who oversees that particular area of ministry. I then ask them to make contact with me again in a week or two to tell me how it went, letting them know that if that doesn't work out, we'll look at the next option on their list. Don't stop walking with them until they are serving or they disappear (in that case there's not much you can do if they don't want any help). But you offered to help and you gave them alternatives. You offered them redirection instead of rejection. That's our job. More importantly, that's our ministry:

> *Keep watch over yourselves and all the flock of which the Holy Spirit has made you overseers. Be shepherds of the church of God, which he bought with his own blood. (Acts 20:28)*

There's a stewardship responsibility here. As shepherds, we're called to lead, guide and direct. We assess their gifts and skills, give them counsel and guidance, and then serve them and help them through this tough, defining time.

> *Bear one another's burdens, and so fulfill the law of Christ. (Galatians 6:2 ESV)*

Walking people through this process and helping them find their perfect places of service in the ministry is immensely rewarding. I thoroughly enjoy it! And they, in turn, are totally at peace, thriving in an area of ministry they hadn't considered before simply because of a bad case of tunnel vision, poor advice or even a bit of idolatry.

I have walked with many through this rejection/redirection process, and now when they run into me somewhere, there's nothing awkward in the least about it—rather it's a great time of catching up that usually closes with them thanking me for having been honest with them and taking the time to help them find their perfect fit in the body of Christ.

That's what auditions are all about.

# CHAPTER 22

# *Plug 'n' Play*

## Getting a new worship team member involved.

Being invited to join the worship team is a time of great excitement and anticipation, but it can simultaneously be a time of anxiety and intimidation as well. The conflicting emotions are certainly understandable. How do we get new team members to feel like they're a part of the team as soon as possible? How do we set them up for the greatest chance of success?

With any team, certain common denominators have to be in place for a team to function effectively and efficiently, otherwise the team quickly breaks down and confusion reigns—much like a team that plays Olympic volleyball compared to a team that plays dodgeball. Our teams need expectations and guidelines to succeed, and these expectations and guidelines need to be communicated to new team members before they get anywhere near the stage. I would also add that these expectations and guidelines need to be consistent with *veterans* and *rookies*

*Our teams need expectations and guidelines to succeed.*

alike, with the veterans setting the example rather than earning some kind of forgiveness points for every year served.

So how do we get rookies plugged in?

## Introduce Them

Not too difficult. Make sure the new members are introduced to the rest of the team via an email announcement, a musician's fellowship or before rehearsal. Regardless of how, give them a sense of belonging and acceptance right from the start.

## Assign Their Positions

Make sure their roles are understood. If it's an electric guitar player, is it lead, rhythm or both? If it's a female vocalist, is her role soprano or alto? And so on. It's always safe to be overly clear. At this time, don't forget to assess equipment needs for the particular positions; do they need to bring their own drums, keyboards, amps or other gear, or does the church provide that? Do they need to have their own in-ears, or will they use open-air monitors? Consider all that each particular position requires to function properly, then determine and communicate who is responsible for each element of that position.

## Provide Access to Planning Center, Songs and Schedule

Nothing says *welcome to the team* like not having a user name and password for weeks on end while trying to learn songs and figure out schedules. This should be the very first action taken after *you made it* is pronounced. New team members will have the greatest opportunity for success by having the ability to prepare and practice until they're comfortable and confident, and by having a concise schedule of rehearsal and service times.

## Explain the Code of Conduct

It's important to clarify and explain the expectations and what's acceptable behavior on and off the stage right from the very beginning. For example, if the dress code is never explained to a new member and he or she happens to wear jeans for the Sunday service when jeans aren't allowed, whose fault is that? Or if there are no guidelines for personal conduct and a team member posts pictures all over Facebook of himself hoisting cold ones at a party, how do you address that? And if the worship leader requires music to be memorized for the weekend, but doesn't bother to communicate this to the new member who shows up on Sunday with a stand full of charts, what happens now? Every one of these stories and so many more like them are embarrassing and frustrating, and they almost guarantee conflict. These awkward conflicts can all be avoided by ensuring the new team members know exactly what's expected of them.

*Clarify and explain the expectations and what's acceptable behavior right from the very beginning.*

When it comes to conduct, however, my biggest emphasis is a new team member's life off stage:

> *For the grace of God that brings salvation has appeared to all men. It teaches us to say "No" to ungodliness and worldly passions, and to live self-controlled, upright and godly lives in this present age, while we wait for the blessed hope—the glorious appearing of our great God and Savior, Jesus Christ, who gave himself for us to redeem us from all wickedness and to purify for himself a people that are his very own, eager to do what is good. (Titus 2:11–14)*

187

Team members are to be above reproach and without accusation in their relationships, in their social activities, in their personal lives and in their workplaces. But they also need to know that they're not alone, that there's always help available. To that end, it is worship leadership's responsibility to be fully engaged and available for accountability, counsel and correction, ready to assist these new team members in their new season of service.

Hypocritical conduct—being holy on stage, unholy off stage—simply cannot be tolerated. Maintain a biblical standard for your team and don't compromise. Subsequently, your team members will have a great reputation in the church and an effective witness in the community. They are to above all honor and bless the Lord with sincere and uncompromised worship.

Share these expectations with every new member. And then share them again and again and again with not only the new members but with the rest of the team as well.

## Have an Exit Strategy

On any sports team, if a player doesn't fulfill his obligations, meet expectations or follow the agreed-upon guidelines, he will likely be cut, and every player knows this. It's a reality. And it's the same reality for a new worship team member, and one that should also be clearly communicated at the start of his or her service. Some leaders wisely institute a probationary period, usually a month to three months, allowing time to accurately discern a new member's overall fit and ability to serve within the agreed-upon guidelines. Likewise, a new member can use this probationary time to determine compatibility with the direction, vision and style of the worship leader and team, and thus decide whether or not to continue on with the team. Dismissing a new member during a probationary time is much less disruptive than dismissing someone who was under the assumption that the position was irrevocable right from the start. Make sure all new team members are aware of the purpose of this probationary time so they can work diligently and be found faithful at its conclusion.

In closing, the goal is to help each new worship team member acclimate and integrate into the team as seamlessly as possible, easing nerves and anxiety in the process. Above all, we want to help new members achieve through their service in worship all that God has prepared and equipped them for. My hope and prayer is for every new team member to feel and know that he or she is an integral part of the worship team family.

# CHAPTER 23

# *Don't Forget to Change Your Oil*

## Maintaining our teams.

When my wife and I were first married, we owned three cars. Now when you hear that, you might think we were a bit indulgent, but the truth is that all three cars had over 100,000 miles on them—so rather than being indulgent, we were combatting attrition. We each needed a car for work and life, and usually, at any given time, only two of them were working. I had a decent knack for repairing cars, owned a Chilton repair book for each car and even had an auto repair class from the local junior college under my belt, so on any given day off I was repairing and servicing one of the three cars.

I had befriended several mechanics in those days, and they always drilled into me the need for maintenance: "Change your oil every 3,000 miles and maintain your car. Take good care of it and it will take good care of you for years." They were absolutely right. Even now, I maintain our cars, changing the oil and oil filter regularly, making sure levels are where they're supposed to be, checking the air in the tires and rotating them often, inspecting belts and brakes, etc. It takes time and effort, but the result is a smoothly running car with relatively few trips to the repair shop. The alternative, however, is a lot more time in the shop paying for expensive repairs and, in some cases, junking the car prematurely due to a blown engine.

A worship ministry team, or any ministry team for that matter, functions in an identical fashion: it requires maintenance or, better yet, preventative maintenance to run smoothly. Without consistent inspections and service, the team and its equipment will break down when you least expect it.

On the one hand, this maintenance is mechanical: keeping musical gear fully functional, maintained and upgraded. It's better to upgrade gear before it breaks or have back-up whenever possible. It's also important to keep track of gear with proper storage and an up-to-date inventory system. It's all too easy to neglect and forget this area since no ever knows or sees a problem coming until it actually happens, and by then it's too late and painfully obvious to everyone in attendance. It's critical to have someone responsible for this area of the worship ministry who is knowledgeable and passionate about his or her role and the gear involved. Without this person and without enough attention to this ministry, too much time and resources will be spent scrambling to repair or replace broken-down equipment—time and resources that could have been much better spent on maintaining the team.

On the other hand, this maintenance is emotional and spiritual. It's one thing if a soundboard breaks or a microphone goes bad, but it's quite another when a team member "breaks," when his or her focus and purpose goes from the Lord to any number of other distractions. It's much easier to replace a microphone than a person. And a gear glitch will be quickly forgotten, whereas a "broken" and lost person will be a painful memory for a long time.

A number of steps will help maintain your team, and following these steps starts with the leader and trickles (or pours) down to your team.

## Stay in the Word

This is first and foremost. Whether it's a chapter or two a day, a reading-through-the Bible-in-a-year program or some other Bible-reading discipline, being in the Word is an absolute and nonnegotiable necessity. And quite frankly, a devotional is not a substitute. A devotional does the thinking for you, but reading the Bible yourself is an opportunity for the Living Word to speak to you directly. Again, a devotional is fine as additional reading and study but not as a substitute for reading the Bible. Staying in the Word is a daily refocusing and preparation for the immediate challenges ahead, and I can't even begin to tell you how many times the very areas of Scripture I have read in the morning have had a direct application throughout that very day. I can't stress how vital this is. If this is missing, then the rest of the points I make are futile. Without the consistent reading of the Word, there will be no framework for worship. None.

*Being in the Word is an absolute and nonnegotiable necessity.*

So, if you're reading this book hoping to gain some gem or nugget for your worship leadership, or any leadership, and you're not in the Word consistently, then put this book down right now and pick up the Bible. Start in Matthew 1:1 and read the first chapter. Then tomorrow read the next chapter starting at Matthew 2:1, and so on.

> *All Scripture is God-breathed and is useful for teaching, rebuking, correcting and training in righteousness, so that the servant of God may be thoroughly equipped for every good work.*
> *(2 Timothy 3:16-17)*
>
> *Thy word is a lamp unto my feet and a light unto my path. (Psalm 119:105 KJV)*

After a week of daily Scripture reading, then pick up this book again.

## Manage Your Thoughts

> *We destroy arguments and every lofty opinion raised against the knowledge of God, and take every thought captive to obey Christ.*
> *(2 Corinthians 10:5 ESV)*

We see in the first part of this Scripture that the selfish justifications of man and the pride of his heart are all disproved, silenced and made foolish by God's Word, true knowledge—and against that backdrop we reconcile our thoughts to His ways. I am particularly drawn to the phrase "and take every thought captive" for the imagery it provokes.

In our justice system, when people break the law, they are subsequently incarcerated, taken captive as a consequence of their actions and for the sake of rehabilitation. The goal and hope is that they will be released back into society newly inclined to respect the law and contribute constructively to the community. At least that's the theory.

But to take our thoughts captive? Exactly! When our thoughts begin to tempt us to go down a road that's opposed to God's Word and will, then we lock them up. The issue's not that we have wrong thoughts (just as Jesus was tempted, yet didn't give in and didn't sin) but what we do with those thoughts. When we don't lock them up and put them away, the problems begin. When we give these thoughts freedom, we, in fact, give them free rein in our lives and ministries. Then, when their influence overwhelms the Word of God, we begin to struggle, and rather than round up and incapacitate these rogue thoughts, we opt to give them even greater freedoms, all the while vainly attempting to continue on in our lives as if nothing is out of order. Then in a short time and when we least expect it, we have a complete breakdown. Moral failure.

The loss of a job, a ministry, a family and respect. Don't let it happen. Take your thoughts captive and throw away the key.

## Listen Better

> *My dear brothers and sisters, take note of this:*
> *Everyone should be quick to listen, slow to speak*
> *and slow to become angry. (James 1:19)*

I've often found myself in a conversation, particularly when the other party is presenting some thoughts, observations and opinions that are not necessarily in agreement with mine, where, instead of listening, I'm formulating a defense. At the first opportunity (like when the other person pauses to breathe), I present my defense, eager to show the deficiencies in his or her argument. I might have won the battle, but I've lost the war.

Marriage has certainly taught me much on this front. It's pretty obvious that if I'm formulating a defense, I'm not listening, and if I'm not listening, then I'm not learning anything, and if I'm not learning anything, then the same friction and problems will continue unabated. In fact, not listening will create more problems of another nature, that of pride (always needing to be right) and indifference (not caring what the concerns of the other person are). Not a great foundation for a healthy relationship, whether in marriage or in ministry.

When I used to hear a team member ask, "Hey, can I talk to you for a moment?" I automatically assumed there was a problem. My mind would immediately scan my mental RAM for any recent conflicts, behavior or attitude changes or other factors that might shed light on the potential conflict. And once again, a mental preemptive defense based on the limited (and speculative) information available would be constructed. What an absolute waste of time and mental effort. I now actually look forward to those invitations to talk. They are windows into my team members' hearts, opportunities to see and hear things that are happening and being perceived in their lives and a chance to get to know them better, and vice versa. Ninety-nine or more percent of the time I walk away from those conversations in a better and stronger relational place but *only* if I'm quick to listen and slow to speak. I now listen, and listen intently, silently praying, "Lord, help me to hear what this person is saying and sharing, and draw us closer together as we strengthen our relationship and reconcile where needed." Prior to this understanding, I'd easily get angry from only hearing their words and not listening to their hearts. Instead, by listening and not interrupting them, I can fully grasp what they're trying to share, and the end result is always greater understanding and camaraderie.

## Don't Be Easily Offended

> *A man's wisdom gives him patience; it is to his glory to overlook an offense. (Proverbs 19:11)*

Taking a comment or an opinion the wrong way and allowing it to cause offense only serves to nourish roots of bitterness. Even if it wasn't taken the wrong way and what was said was, in fact, offensive; once again, correct if necessary, but avoid at all costs taking offense. The best way to avoid offense is to forgive and forget, and the best way to accomplish that is having this understanding and perspective:

> *Bear with each other and forgive one another if any of you has a grievance against someone. Forgive as the Lord forgave you. (Colossians 3:13)*

> *Be kind and compassionate to one another, forgiving each other, just as in Christ God forgave you. (Ephesians 4:32)*

But be aware, the opposite is true as well:

*For if you forgive other people when they sin against you, your heavenly Father will also forgive you. But if you do not forgive others their sins, your Father will not forgive your sins.*
*(Matthew 6:14–15)*

So forgiving an offense is essential but so is forgetting:

*Whoever conceals an offense promotes love, but whoever gossips about it separates friends.*
*(Proverbs 17:9 HCSB)*

To convey forgiveness yet continue to make an offense an issue, even promoting it to others, only serves to break confidences, betray trust and destroy relationships and reputations—a sure formula for a breakdown.

## Find Someone You Can Confide In

Find someone whom you trust, whom you can say, "I'm struggling with this" or "I'm thinking of doing this; what's your take?" I've had the privilege of having a couple of really close friends, more like brothers, whom I can go to, talk to and get honest feedback from. And that honest feedback hasn't always been easy to swallow. It's tough and it can hurt, but it's so, so important:

*Faithful are the wounds of a friend; but the kisses of an enemy are deceitful. (Proverbs 27:6 KJV)*

The honest advice and observations of a faithful friend can sting, but the goal is for you to ultimately succeed in life and ministry, whereas the goal of a "kiss" from an enemy is to keep you on the path you're on, knowing it could lead to your failure. That's exactly what the enemy (the evil one) is hoping for. Go with the wounds from a trusted friend—it will always pay off in the long run.

## Always Stand Up for What's Right and Protect Your Team

Stake your job on it. Recently a few team members were asked what stood out to them about my leadership, and they agreed that it was how I stood up for them, defended them and protected them. Whether it's protecting some of the women from "wolves" in the flock, insisting that other ministries go through you instead of contacting members of the team directly or shielding them from unreasonable requests or directives from leadership, your team members need to know you support them and have their backs.

In this day and age of video and attention to the projected image, I was once asked to replace someone on the team who, although an incredible musician who contributed mightily to the sound and integrity of the worship and lived a righteous life, had, shall we say, a "face for radio." I wouldn't do it, and I risked my job by my decision. In over thirty years of music ministry, I have put my job on the line for my team more than a few times.

I have also confronted and exposed "wolves" (both from outside and from within) who have attempted to divide the team. I will spare nothing to protect my team and stand up for it. Don't ever throw your team under the bus. Take responsibility for your team members and their actions, and then "clean their clocks" behind closed doors, if warranted. But always have their backs. Look at how 1 Corinthians 13:7 reads in the Living Bible:

> *If you love someone, you will be loyal to him no matter what the cost. You will always believe in him, always expect the best of him, and always stand your ground in defending him.*
> *(1 Corinthians 13:7 TLB)*

First Corinthian 13, of course, is the "love" chapter, often read at weddings. But it's about love, not romance. It's about loving others completely, loving them enough to pull them off the team when that's what's best for them. It's defending them when they're unfairly accused or treated, and protecting them when they're threatened or attacked. Be their friend and advocate at all times.

## Encourage

> *But encourage one another daily, as long as it is called "Today," so that none of you may be hardened by sin's deceitfulness. (Hebrews 3:13)*

Every weekend as I drive home from services, I consider who I want to text, call or email to let them know what a great job they did and how grateful I am that they're a part of the team. It means the world to them. It seems to make their day and, quite honestly, it makes my day as well, hearing or reading their responses to my encouragement. But if I get busy and consumed with a load of responsibilities and neglect to encourage the team for any length of time, it's very easy for "sin's deceitfulness" to creep in. "He must be angry with how worship's been going," "Does anything make this guy happy," or "Would he even notice or care if I quit?" This used to baffle me in my early years, but as I realized how much I appreciated an *attaboy* here and there from my pastor, coworker or even my wife, why would I expect my coworkers and team to be okay with less than that from me? Add to that the fact that the Bible says to encourage one another *daily*, emphasizing the need for consistent, not just occasional, encouragement. Encouragement will keep your team members motivated and excited to serve. We can be quick to point out their mistakes and miscues, but we must be just as quick to

*We can be quick to point out their mistakes and miscues, but we must be just as quick to point out their excellence and value.*

199

point out their excellence and value both musically and relationally.

## Pray

> *For this reason, since the day we heard about you, we have not stopped praying for you and asking God to fill you with the knowledge of his will through all spiritual wisdom and understanding. And we pray this in order that you may live a life worthy of the Lord and may please him in every way: bearing fruit in every good work, growing in the knowledge of God, being strengthened with all power according to his glorious might so that you may have great endurance and patience, and joyfully giving thanks to the Father, who has qualified you to share in the inheritance of the saints in the kingdom of light. (Colossians 1:9-12)*

Paul and Timothy, having heard of the Colossians' faithfulness (the reason behind "for this reason") are now linked to and committed to praying for them. Likewise, we are linked to our teams, and as well need to keep them in constant prayer. Paul prays for the Colossians

- to know His will,
- for wisdom and understanding,
- to live a life that pleases the Lord,
- to bear fruit,
- to know God better,
- to be strengthened,
- to have endurance and patience,
- to have joy,
- and to give thanks to God for His salvation.

Pray this very prayer for your team and your ministry. This is the spiritual maintenance you and your team need; and like Paul and Timothy, don't stop praying this prayer. And finally,

## Give

Give generously, whether it's finances, time, encouragement, support, prayer or love. Don't be stingy, but again, give generously and with joy:

> *Each of you should give what you have decided in your heart to give, not reluctantly or under compulsion, for God loves a cheerful giver.*
> *(2 Corinthians 9:7)*

Tithing should be a priority in worship, and our teams should realize that as well. Tithing is an act of worship, and if we neglect that area of our lives, our worship is incomplete and lacking. Tithing is a matter of faith, trust and gratitude for our Provider and Sustainer. If we fail to worship in this way, we choose to either neglect our responsibility, or worse, we somehow think we're better managers of our finances than the Lord is. Not only is that arrogant, it's also foolish. We're missing out on so much:

*Give generously, not only in your finances but also in your encouragement of others, in your prayers for others and in time spent with others.*

> *Remember this: Whoever sows sparingly will also reap sparingly, and whoever sows generously will also reap generously. (2 Corinthians 9:6)*

Everything we do in this life is a step of faith, and trusting the Lord with our finances is another step of faith as well—but we have His promises to cling to and abide by. Invest cheaply, get cheap returns. Invest generously, get generous returns. Unlike the stock market and your 401k, this is a promise. (I discuss giving as an act of worship in greater detail in "Who You Gonna Serve?")

And give generously, not only in your finances but also in your encouragement of others, in your prayers for others and in time spent with others. Give yourself away and reap the returns!

In closing this chapter, I want to finish by emphasizing consistency. Changing the oil in a car is only effective if it is done regularly, consistently. Think of music lessons. A half hour of practice every day is much more productive than three hours of practice a couple of times a week. In this case, three and a half hours of practice is more valuable than six hours a week, again, because of consistency. Consistency will always trump binging. It's only through consistency that one can develop maintainable habits.

The same is true for our Christian walk, our leadership and our ministry. If we take these suggestions and apply them consistently, we'll see a radical change, not only in our lives and ministries but also in the people we serve with and lead. Our teams desperately need consistent leadership, and we all need consistent maintenance. Let's do all we can to make sure we have both.

CHAPTER 24

# *Count the Cost*

## Managing finances and developing a budget.

There certainly is a personal cost to ministry (or at least there should be). The sacrifice of one's pursuit of comfort and carefree living and the surrender of one's time, resources and heart are necessary and costly, yet well worth the eternal reward. But there is also a literal cost, from buildings, utilities and staffing to furnishings and so on. Worship ministry is no different. Staffing, audio and video equipment, instruments, technology—the list goes on. I want to bring attention to this area simply because it's critical to the framework of worship, yet is often overlooked, neglected or even ignored. At times it's a case of prioritization, but more than often it's a case of just simple ignorance.

The assertion that it costs money to run, maintain and grow a ministry is a reality. One can argue and debate about the extent or extravagance necessary to run a certain ministry, but the fact that there is a cost is, once again, a reality. The challenge, then, is to assess and determine what that cost is:

> *For which one of you, when he wants to build a*
> *tower, does not first sit down and calculate the cost*
> *to see if he has enough to complete it?*
> *(Luke 14:28 NASB)*

I have some friends up north who are preparing to build their new home. As they were planning, they had to consider a multitude of options and make many decisions: one or two stories, how many bedrooms and bathrooms, one- or two-car (or maybe three?) garage, the layout, where on the lot to build, type of doors and windows, what kind of roofing, how large a deck, what type of driveway, and on and on. But none of this planning will come to fruition if there isn't a blueprint for the city and builder and if there isn't enough money to complete the house. The correlation? There has to be a vision for the ministry and leadership and a budget to fund the vision. One complementing the other and both needing to be flexible.

The vision and the budget complement each other when you think through what you would like or hope to accomplish in the upcoming year and what it would cost. For example, a while back I really felt that environmental projection would take our worship to another level by adding a visual component to augment and emphasize the aural experience. I, with the help of my A/V guys, did my due diligence and came up with competitive prices. We also came up with a two-phase implementation. One phase would project on the back of the stage, and the second phase would expand that projection to the side wings as well, covering the entire front of the church. I presented both options and pricing to the leadership, giving them the opportunity to start with a bang, or, if they'd prefer, to phase it in. Between the "phasing it in" approach, along with the cheaper expense, we decided that the first option would be the way to go. Notice that rather than being an "all or nothing" approach, this presentation had options. That was how the vision complemented the budget; there was flexibility in the scope and cost of the vision so that any budget constraints could be appropriately addressed and managed. So now we had our green light, we budgeted accordingly and within a year's time we installed and incorporated environmental projection—and the church loves it!

Here's the process: (1) What's the vision? (In this case, environmental projection.) (2) What's the benefit? (In this case, what will we gain from incorporating environmental projection that we had not had previously?) (3) What are the options in scope and cost? (4) What is the timing of the vision—how soon can and should it be implemented, and why? (5) Can we afford it?

This is no different from my friend's house: (1) What are the plans? (2) Do we need everything on the plans? (3) What are the options (add-ons) and how much will they cost? (4) How soon should we build? (5) Can we afford it?

If my friends don't have enough money to build the house that was planned, they have several options: reduce the size of the house, use less costly materials and amenities, try to negotiate a lower price, wait and build later, or scrap the idea of building a house altogether and just buy an RV!

Above all, think ahead and plan ahead. Then, educate.

*How you handle finances in ministry will reflect your leadership and directly impact your effectiveness.*

I hear worship leaders complain that there's never enough money to cover the basics, let alone do what they want to do. There's always some level of angst as well as a sense of isolation, of being left alone to do a job with no help or support. Here are a couple of things to consider: Did you let leadership know your needs ahead of time? In other words, if you want to record a CD, did you present the vision, the benefits, the costs and the options to leadership? Or did you tell them you want to go into the studio next week and you need $10,000? Then when you're told no, do you feel unsupported and find yourself frustrated when you think about all the other ministries that money is being spent on? Well, you shouldn't, because it's you who dropped the ball, not leadership. To be honest, in this instance, leadership in all likelihood sees you as impulsive, undisciplined, unprepared and a loose cannon. Instead of throwing a fit, consider this alternate course of action:

***Put together a vision.*** A blueprint—in this particular example, a vision for a CD.

***Consider the benefits.*** A CD will facilitate worship outside the four walls of the church. It will draw the team closer together. It will spur some "new-song" writing and bless the body.

***Calculate costs and options.*** It will cost $5,000 if we do a five-song CD and $8,000 if we do ten songs. We can also keep the costs down if we use cardboard cases instead of plastic jewel boxes and do simple monochrome printing instead of full color. (These numbers and options are for example only). We will be able to recoup some or most of the costs through sales.

***Estimate a reasonable time frame.*** We could be ready to start recording in six months (or sooner or longer), and have a finished product within another six months.

This example can translate to a drum set or drum shield, a new digital sound board, a new set of in-ear monitors, a new staff hire, upgraded software, better vocal microphones, a Nord keyboard or basically any vision you have for the ministry.

But if you tell leadership you have to have it now or the world as we know it will end, you'll have a guaranteed denial. Instead, think ahead of what your needs (and even wants) might be in the year (or years) ahead and put a list together with benefits, costs, options and time frames. Now present your proposal to leadership and watch what happens. After they pick themselves and their jaws up off the floor, your chances of finding their support for both the vision and the funding of that vision will be much greater, and their respect for your planning, management and leadership will also increase greatly. Always, always keep leadership in the loop. Keep them informed and educated. It's not only a courtesy; it's a sign of mature leadership.

**If I may, a note to leadership:**

I mentioned earlier the need for vision and budget to complement each other and the need for both to be flexible. I have challenged the worship leader to have a vision with options of scope and cost for these very reasons. I would respectfully ask that leadership strive to be flexible as well. Let me explain: Several years ago I presented the church I worked for a vision and budget that were both ultimately approved. Throughout the year I had been able to purchase some equipment at a substantially lower price than was budgeted, had some budgeted equipment donated and was able to hold off on some approved acquisitions. I came in well below budget. Instead of getting a pat on the back from leadership, I received a sharp rebuke and the following mandate: "Spend it or lose it." I protested saying I didn't need to spend it— that would be foolish and wasteful. Nope. "If you don't spend it, then that means you don't need it and you'll lose it in next year's budget."

How embarrassing and, in fact, stupid! Yet I know many ministries that operate this way. Please don't be one of them. Don't punish your worship leader, or any other overseer, for being a conscientious and wise steward, while rewarding another for unnecessarily wasting finite resources. Instead, be flexible. That is, work with your ministerial team members; commend them for good planning and even more for good stewardship. Some years they may be below budget, and some they may be over. But again, be flexible, adjusting one department's budget where good stewardship has prevailed while adjusting another department's budget where unforeseen challenges and unexpected opportunities have suddenly arisen. That's flexibility, and that's the kind of leadership that will inspire like-minded leadership and continued wise stewardship from the ministerial team and staff.

\* \* \* \* \* \* \* \*

In closing, have a plan, count the cost, communicate clearly, be flexible, collaboratively develop a budget with leadership and then implement it. Be wise in this area and be proactive. How you handle finances in ministry will reflect your leadership and directly impact your effectiveness. And be found faithful, not seeing finances and budgets as a distraction but rather as an instrument for wise stewardship and exciting ministry opportunities, all while responsibly handling the "widow's mite."

# CHAPTER 25

# *Worthy of Wages*

## To pay or not to pay.

This subject sure seems to evoke strong emotions and opinions. On one side you have those who fully support paying worship team members and on the other side a fairly adamant stance that worship team members should never be paid under any circumstances.

Having read numerous articles, books and blogs on the subject, I'm a little disappointed at the position and reasoning the second camp employs. For example, "If we pay the worship team, then all volunteers should be paid as well," or "You can't serve both God and mammon." This thinking is unfortunate and misinformed.

Many years ago I grappled with this very issue personally, and after much prayer, searching of the Scriptures and seeking much counsel, I now, in fact, pay my worship team. Let me explain how I came to that conclusion.

We went through this transition from a volunteer worship team to a paid team several years ago. I had always used volunteers here at Calvary, asking them to serve at one service or two, if necessary. I felt that was a reasonable service. But the church grew and the number of services grew, from two on Sunday, to three on Sunday, then to four on a weekend (one on Saturday evening and three on Sunday). For years I rotated a different team in for each service, and that worked adequately—until we hit four services. Managing, preparing, rehearsing and sound checking four different teams every weekend became more and more unproductive and unsustainable. We also hit another roadblock: as the church and the number of services grew, the expectations grew as well. I've read some comments on various blogs protesting that if worship was acceptable at a certain size, why is it no longer acceptable as the church grows? Well, let me ask you this: as your kid grows older, do you expect him to get smarter? In the same way, why wouldn't the worship team be expected to get better? As the church grows, so does the pool of available musicians and access to greater resources and more seasoned leadership, all to which the following applies:

> *Everyone to whom much was given, of him much will be required, and from him to whom they entrusted much, they will demand the more.*
> *(Luke 12:48b ESV)*

It only makes sense: the more I'm given the more the Lord expects of me. And why not? So how do I get more out of what I have? My only reasonable choice was to have a consistent team on a given weekend; one team that would attend a one-hour rehearsal on Thursday night and then play all four weekend services. Rather than rotating teams every service, which made a dedicated rehearsal impractical, we now rotate teams every weekend. This schedule allows us to take on more challenging songs, arrangements and styles that bless as well as stretch the congregation. And unlike when teams were rotated in for each service, having the same team allows for fellowship between and during services, bringing the team closer together. A win, win! One problem solved. Next problem.

The demands of a rehearsal and four weekend services require a minimum of eleven hours. And travel time. And preparation time. And practice time. It's not unusual for someone to have upwards of twenty hours invested into a weekend service. I find it unreasonable to ask (let alone expect) someone to volunteer that many hours a week on a consistent basis, especially when it means sacrificing work opportunities. We live in a time when fewer and fewer people can afford to be without work or to reduce their hours. Many live from paycheck to paycheck, and although their heart and desire may be to volunteer, their family obligations simply don't allow it. In cases like these, many people simply can't afford to volunteer that many hours. So we either help them make up for the lost income or choose not to use them.

For instance, when my volunteer team rotated each service, sometimes—especially in the summer when there were lots of absences—I would need to use a player or singer for three or even all four services. Although I found it reasonable for them to volunteer at one or two services, I did not, as I stated earlier, feel the same concerning three or four services. The solution: they would volunteer for two services and get paid a stipend per service beyond that.

Fast forward to the transition where we went from rotating teams each service to rotating teams each weekend. I now use that same system for the entire team: two volunteer services and two paid services (and now a paid midweek rehearsal). Notice the distinction—the worship team does not get paid for the entire weekend. Why is that important? Because they're still volunteering for the first two services. Some may think that's just a matter of semantics, but I don't. I want the church to know my team volunteers, but I also don't mind if they know my team receives fair compensation for their work:

> *Now to the one who works, his wages are not counted as a gift but as his due. (Romans 4:4 ESV)*

Finding that balance between reasonable service and work can be tricky, but it doesn't need to be one or the other; it can be a combination of the two. Two to five hours a week is reasonable volunteer service, five to ten hours a week can go either way, and I feel that over ten hours a week crosses over into "work" where compensation is due. Not only is it due, but it also blesses, supports and encourages those who give of their time and talent.

It's important for me to stress that this is my unique situation and solution. Some may feel that it's completely legitimate to pay worship team members for their service regardless of a volunteer component. I don't have an argument with that. I think that's generous and a blessing to the musicians. Jesus illustrates that point in the parable of the vineyard workers in Matthew 20:1–15. I'm not dictating a necessary balance between volunteering and being paid, nor any specific amount or rate of pay, but rather I'm advocating for reasonable compensation for worship team members as the particular situation and circumstances warrant.

*Paying the worship team members for their lifelong investment is not only a blessing and an honorable gesture but also a wise investment by the church and its leadership.*

Especially when excessive time demands and high levels of skill and proficiency are necessary for participation.

How do you respond to the blogger who demands all volunteer roles should be similarly paid if worship team members are paid? All acts of service are equal, right? No, actually they're not. The parable of the talents in Matthew 25 makes that quite clear. Just as there are a multitude of volunteer roles crucial to supporting a ministry, there are also a multitude of gifts and skills necessary to fulfill those different roles. And in the case of a worship team member, those gifts and skills often require a tremendous investment of resources and sacrifices of time in order to participate in that particular position. In my years of experience, the demands and expectations on the worship team have routinely eclipsed those of most other volunteer positions. The notion that if worship team members get paid as a result of their considerable sacrifice of time and finances over a lifetime, then all other volunteer roles should be paid alike simply makes no sense at all. None.

And while we're on the subject of "makes no sense at all," let me also address a common theme that was mentioned at the beginning of this chapter among those who think worship team members and even worship leaders shouldn't be paid: "The Bible says in Matthew 24 that you cannot serve both God and money." Are you kidding! Getting paid is serving money? Paul expresses obvious frustration with similar ignorant thinking in his day:

> *Who serves as a soldier at his own expense? Who plants a vineyard and does not eat of its grapes? Who tends a flock and does not drink of the milk? Do I say this merely from a human point of view? Doesn't the Law say the same thing? For it is written in the Law of Moses: "Do not muzzle an ox while it is treading out the grain." Is it about oxen that God is concerned? Surely he says this for us, doesn't he? (1 Corinthians 9:7–10)*

Yes, he does. For us. It's true; you cannot serve both God and money simultaneously. Trying to do so elevates money and the pursuit of it to the same status as God, and that never has and never will work. You can, however, serve God and be compensated fairly for services rendered simultaneously with no scriptural conflict whatsoever. The same applies to serving God in worship and being paid for that service. Zero conflict.

My staff is full time, and they're paid a competitive full time salary, and my worship team is essentially part time, and they are paid accordingly. I made the decision some time ago to treat all of my worship team members with equal generosity, so worship team singers and instrumentalists alike are paid the same.

With all that being said, there is nothing either inappropriate or unscriptural about the worship team being supported financially along with the staff. The worship, and subsequently the worship team, are an essential and integral part of the church and church services. Paying the worship team members for their lifelong investment is not only a blessing and an honorable gesture but also a wise investment by the church and its leadership.

# CHAPTER 26

# *New and Improved*

## Incorporating technology into worship.

In Old Testament worship, the monophonic voice (all notes sung in unison) was the primary tool used for worship, often accompanied by stringed instruments, including the harp, lute and lyre. Also accompanying the voices were percussion instruments like the tambourine and cymbals.

In the New Testament, as the early Christian church began, the monophonic voice was again the primary tool used for worship, with the early believers choosing to forgo instrumental accompaniment since the instruments of the day were now associated with pagan revelry and debauchery. Over time, vocal harmony that consisted of octaves, fifths and fourths was implemented, and eventually harmonies that consisted of thirds and sixths were also utilized, although with great resistance since those particular harmonies were also associated with pagan music and its unholy activities. Soon instruments began to make their way into worship, starting with the organ, then the early piano and orchestral instruments. Then eventually the dreaded guitar and all of its incarnations; acoustic, electric and bass, along with drums, electronic keyboards and other various contemporary instruments;

began to infiltrate the worship experience, and thus the modern worship team was born.

Every one of these innovations solicited strong reactions; many in favor of and many opposed to. Many people attempted to use Scripture to validate their preferences and condemn innovation, but those hollow arguments never held up over time. Even today, there are still those who vehemently oppose any use of instruments in worship. They stand on their soapboxes proclaiming the lack of any mention of instruments in the New Testament as their premise.

*Technology is revolutionizing the sound, the look, the proliferation, the creation and the community of worship like never before.*

Well okay, if that's your conviction and standard, then I'd better not see you driving a car. Enough said on that subject.

Technology is a new innovation that has made its way into worship relatively recently. And, in my opinion, in an unprecedented short span of time, technology is revolutionizing the sound, the look, the proliferation, the creation and the community of worship like never before.

Many of the blogs, articles and books I've read touch on technology in worship, with many authors viewing technology as an aside—acknowledging a role, albeit a limited one. I tend to view technology's role in a much greater capacity: as technology's tools are more understood and applied, I'm convinced they will become commonplace and a mainstay in worship more so than any previous innovation. Technology offers endless opportunities—limited only by one's imagination and creativity.

How is technology revolutionizing worship?

## The Sound

Whether one incorporates a traditional or a contemporary style of worship, technology can replace missing parts or augment existing ones. When I lead worship at a smaller church where it's not always possible to have a full team, I can use loops or stems (or both) to play the bass, guitar, background vocals or any combination of parts. A program like Ableton Live does an amazing job, using *loops* (programed sounds, instruments and rhythmic support) and *stems* (individual tracks from a multi-track recording that can be transferred into Ableton or used in a stand-alone hardware player). This program or similar programs allow for greater creativity in arranging and greater access to songs and arrangements that would normally be unreasonable to perform.

Imagine having a competent worship team to start with; by using loops or stems you can add a nice complimentary string section or pad, or a subtle percussion track—the list goes on and on. This program helps you keep it all together by providing a click track to the players, allowing everyone to play together while letting the loops and stems lock in to the very same click. Technology has also provided a means to enable all the members of the worship team to have their own individual in-ear monitors, giving each person control over his or her sound, mix and volume level. This eliminates the need for open-air stage monitors that create excess stage noise and cause endless battles over monitor mixes.

Speaking of sound, even sound systems are benefitting from the advancing technology, allowing sound techs to move throughout the sanctuary making minute adjustments to the EQ and other parameters of the sound system by the use of an iPad, app and Wi-Fi.

## The Look

We live in a society that is more and more visually driven and stimulated. Adding a visual component to worship allows those who are still searching in their faith to have a greater sense of engagement and those who are already surrendered in their faith a more comprehensive experience.

A few years ago I led worship in front of the southern steps in Jerusalem and I remember the visual—the steps themselves, where Jesus was believed to have taught when He was in Jerusalem. And behind the southern steps was the massive temple mount wall with all of its beauty and age testifying to millennia of history. The visual took worship to another level. It just did. And that's my heart for environmental projection: to create images, scenes and video that complement and enhance the aural aspect of worship, giving the worship experience a greater depth of engagement and immersion.

In addition to visuals, lyrics can be shown in a creative rather than static presentation, allowing the worshippers to sing along with their heads raised rather than looking down at written words and disengaging from the worship experience. And all of this visual technology can be synced with loop/stem programing, allowing all aspects of the worship experience to be coordinated seamlessly and effortlessly.

As a side note: just as a worship team can play poorly, environmental projection can be executed poorly. Just as skill and talent are imperative to one's involvement on the worship team, the same is true for those who create and program visuals.

The look of worship is quickly becoming as important as the sound. I encourage you to consider how you might augment the visual impact of your worship experience; done well, it will be readily accepted by your church.

## The Proliferation

- *Proliferation*: a sudden increase in the amount or number of something[19]

The sheer number of new worship songs being written and shared has exploded exponentially. Technology in the form of MP3s (songs), MPEGs (videos) and charts (PDFs) shared via the cloud, downloading sites (YouTube, iTunes), social media and organizational programs like Planning Center has opened up a whole new unlimited resource like never before. Gone are the days of ordering piles of songbooks and cheesy accompanying cassettes, spending lots of money, and finding maybe 2 percent of the songs remotely usable—if you're lucky! Now you can search and review countless worship songs and numerous arrangements to find the ones that will best suit your team and church.

Adding to the proliferation of worship is the adoption of notation software, an arranger's best friend. Scores and charts can now be sent anywhere in the world or made accessible to your local team instantly. With a simple click, you can transpose a song into whatever key you desire, perfect for that one vocal soloist who insists on everything a half step lower. Notation software is truly a game changer. Once the music is entered, it's fully editable, fully transposable and easily read. You can also send these digital charts to an iPad and use them as manuscript, turning pages with a simple swipe of your finger. (Just in case you're wondering, I prefer Sibelius for my notation software.)

You definitely don't want to miss out on this. Take advantage of all the resources available to you through technology and enjoy all the new songs and charts you've never heard or seen before.

## The Creation

Writing and creating songs can always be enhanced by some kind of inspiration. Whether that inspiration is an experience, a personal trial or a revelation of the heart, it lends a hand in forming a new song. Putting that inspiration into a listenable and recordable form has often been a challenging and expensive endeavor. But, once again, technology has paved the way for a more effective and inexpensive experience.

For the cost of a laptop computer and a simple recording program (some are even free), the aspiring, as well as the seasoned, songwriter is now free to try new ideas, record them all, listen back, redo, rewrite or rearrange, all in the comfort of his or her home or dorm or wherever. For a little more investment, you can professionally record, produce and mix a single song or an entire project for a fraction of what it cost just a few years ago. This same technology also allows you to record a string section or a drummer and bass player, or any other instruments that you can think of, all by yourself.

It's absolutely stunning what technology can offer to assist you in your creative efforts! Please take advantage of it, and then share it with the world.

## The Community

The worship community is a unique and diverse group of believers who function most effectively when they understand their roles and responsibilities and are connected to the community. Good communication will accomplish all of this, and technology will, in turn, facilitate effective communication with new and innovative ways. Making endless phone calls is no longer necessary in order to schedule teams, distribute song lists and charts, or disseminate important information pertaining to service changes, special events, team meetings, fellowship gatherings, etc. Instead, Planning Center, a group email or a text will now accomplish the same with greater efficiency and accuracy in a fraction of the time. Technology can free you up to make phone calls that accomplish ministry rather than just administration. Few things can frustrate and divide a team like poor and ineffective communication. It leaves your team members in the dark and allows them to think and assume the worst, that they're no longer valued or respected, when the reality is just lousy, late and inaccurate communication. There's really no excuse for it anymore. Make sure to take advantage of the available technologies so communication is rarely a frustration or distraction again.

*Few things can frustrate and divide a team like poor and ineffective communication.*

With all of these technologies available, why would there be resistance? What are the obstacles?

***I'm too old.*** Let's be honest, when people say they're too old, what they're really saying is, "I don't want to bother with it." They're content and not interested in changing the way they do things. But that kind of thinking is not at all limited to age. I've recently heard several people complaining about the new IOS on their iPhones, wanting to keep what they're familiar with— and they're all young (one of them was my twelve-year-old nephew!). I know many an elderly person who is technologically savvy, so if people don't want to change because they think they're too old, that's their choice—but they're missing out on many amazing advances that could immediately enhance their lives and ministries. I know change and technology can be challenging at times, but the reward is so worth it, and I'm convinced that the mental effort and brain exercise used in staying updated and versed on all of the various technologies are keeping me alert and young, not to mention relevant. That alone should be worth it!

***I don't know how to use this technology.*** I completely get that. And so do the businesses that sell it. Many retailers offer in-store classes to explain how to use computers and programs. There are also books and DVDs for practically any program you might use, plus countless online video tutorials that visually walk you through every step of the way. For those that are more seasoned and want to be challenged to a greater capacity, regional workshops are available for a reasonable fee. And don't forget, many others are using the same software you're learning, so you can ask them, you can ask online forums and you can even grab some tips at various conferences. The bottom line is this: if you want to learn, endless resources are available to aid you in that pursuit.

***It seems like technology in worship is overused.*** As with everything, use technology with discretion and balance. For example, if it's just me on a keyboard leading worship, I may use some loops with a subtle pad and a little rhythmic percussion in the background but not a full-on rock band, background vocals and a Trans-Siberian-style orchestra! Nor would I use text and email exclusively so as to never have to talk to my team again. Remember, balance is important in all areas of our lives and ministries, and technology is no different.

A final thought: the apostle Paul's overarching desire was to see people come to faith in Christ. And although the message and saving grace of Christ is unchanging, the method and means to present that message can and do change:

> *I have become all things to all people so that by all possible means I might save some.*
> *(1 Corinthians 9:22b)*

\* \* \* \* \* \* \* \*

Technology has certainly become one of those means, and with its ability to enhance and facilitate worship, there's now an even greater opportunity to impact lives for Christ. But understand, at every step along the way of innovation, there have always been naysayers, doubters and critics, and technology will undoubtedly continue to face the same scrutiny. However, I have no doubt that technology will persist and be implemented with ever increasing effectiveness to further the Gospel like few other innovations have done before it. Don't be intimidated by it and don't minimize its potential impact and value—instead embrace it and employ it. You'll soon realize it's such an incredibly valuable tool that you'll wonder how you ever got along without!

# CHAPTER 27

# *If God Gave You That Song, Why Is It So Bad?*

## Understanding and handling song submissions.

There's that moment when service ends and various individuals approach the stage to talk to me, some to encourage me and some to ask questions concerning song selection, how to join the team, if the blonde singer to my right is single and so on. But the one encounter I used to dread more than any was the people who proclaimed God had given them a song and they wanted me to consider using it in our worship. This was truly one of the most awkward scenarios that I consistently faced.

These encounters would generally manifest themselves in one of the following ways: They would

(1) ask nicely if I would use their song in worship,

(2) insist, even demand, that I use their song in worship,

(3) tell me that they're donating their song and all its proceeds to the ministry, or

(4) say their song was essentially finished, but they needed me
to add chords, help with the melody and lyrics and, in a few
cases, add a bridge and chorus (I'm not making this up).

In each case, of course, the need to hear and evaluate the song
was the initial step in the process. When I first began my
experience in worship leading, I would simply ask, "How would
you like me to review your song?" naively expecting to be handed
a recording or chart. In many cases, though, I was met with a
resounding a cappella vocal rendition of the song right there on the
spot!

In the beginning of my ministry, wanting to honor these
people's sincerity, I would take the time to work with them and
their songs, rework melodies and lyrics, rearrange chords, add
accompaniments, even add a bridge on occasion. It was a lot of
effort and, unfortunately, the results were still always subpar. I
soon discovered the following:

(1) It was taking way too much time.
(2) They were no longer their songs; they were now mine. But
I didn't like them enough to take any credit for them.
(3) I could have written a song that I liked more in less time.
(4) They brought me more songs.

The next step in this evolution was to be less directly involved
and to put the responsibility of making the directed changes on
these possessors of God-given songs (to be referred to by the
acronym *POGGS* from here on out). I would clearly explain what
changes would potentially help the overall quality of the song;
such as reworking the lyrics to make them more effective, trying
different chords and chord structures, adding a bridge, and maybe
even a chorus. The results of this new process were:

(1) It was still taking too much time.
(2) The songs would come back with the suggested changes, but the changes didn't help much.
(3) I could have written a song in the same amount of time.
(4) The POGGS continued to bring me more songs.

By this time the church had grown to a substantial size and the God-given song encounters were increasing exponentially. I needed to reduce my time commitment even more, so I added some reasonable preconditions to submitting a God-given song: The songs would have to be presented in some recorded form. Quality was not an issue whatsoever, a boom box, a handheld recorder, anything, so I could hear the intent of the song. This would eliminate the "live" spontaneous renditions and allow me to listen to all of the submissions at my convenience. I gave out my work number and instructions to contact me after two weeks, allowing me sufficient time to listen to the submissions, and at which time I would share my thoughts and evaluations. This way I was no longer the one responsible for following up.

This looked great on paper and was certainly more efficient, but it created a new set of issues:

(1) Now the POGGS have my phone number and they're calling me. Not after two weeks but every day.
(2) Now I'm dealing with a certain level of guilt. Since I require some form of recording, some are going above and beyond the basic requirements and spending time and money recording their songs in a professional studio. It's not helping the songs much, but there's certainly a lot less hiss.
(3) And while the POGGS were recording, they went ahead and recorded more songs.

No matter what I did, no matter the system I had in place, I was still always confronted with the question that I always wondered silently to myself: "If God gave them those songs, then why are they so bad?" These people were sincere; they meant it with all of their heart. God *did* give them those songs; there was no doubt in my mind and heart about it. But the fact remained, the songs were not good. They were poorly written and poorly arranged, and no amount of intercession on my or anyone else's part was going to change that fact. Considering that maybe it was just me and I was being too critical, I would play the songs for coworkers, team members, family members, even strangers, and every time the consensus was the same: they're not good songs.

I sought counsel from other leaders and found that their solution was to simply have a policy where they don't accept original "God-given" song submissions. I don't have a problem with that solution, but I still felt something was missing—that there was an explanation out there somewhere that could bring clarity to this confusion.

I found myself praying for understanding and wisdom so that I could share something with these people that would encourage rather than defeat and discourage them. Then God led me to 1 Corinthians 14:

> *For anyone who speaks in a tongue does not speak to men but to God. Indeed, no one understands him; he utters mysteries with his spirit. But everyone who prophesies speaks to men for their strengthening, encouragement and comfort. He who speaks in a tongue edifies himself, but he who prophesies edifies the church. (1 Corinthians 14:2–4)*

Finally, it all began to make sense! Prophesy and tongues are both gifts from God; however, they each have different functions. Prophesy edifies the church—everyone can understand it and be blessed—whereas tongues edify the person—it is a personal blessing that only that person and God can understand. Now when people approach me with their God-given songs, it becomes my opportunity and responsibility to determine whether their songs are for the edification of the body (prophesy songs) or for personal edification (tongue songs). If it is a song that I feel everyone will respond to, understand and be blessed by, then I will introduce it to the body. But more often than not, if I feel the song will not be understood or appreciated by, and therefore not bless, the body, I then conclude that it is a song for personal edification and blessing and should be utilized as such.

How do I communicate this? I simply respond by saying, "This song is for you, not for me or anyone else. This song will not be understood or appreciated by anyone but God, because He gave it to you and you alone to share with Him. It is for *your* private worship time with Him, so cherish your gift and worship God with your song often." If necessary, I encourage POGGS to try to not make their songs into something they were never intended to be. Although some will insist on presenting their personal songs to the body, I gently remind them that doing so will only cause *There is now great joy knowing that they did in fact receive a wonderful personal gift from Almighty God—just for them!* confusion, and even frustration, when that's not the use God intended for His song and gift.

Since this personal revelation, I have shared this reality with hundreds of POGGS over the years. And rather than a sense of rejection when their songs aren't played or recorded for the church body, there is now a sense of great joy and discovery knowing that they did in fact receive a wonderful personal gift from Almighty God—just for them!

# CHAPTER 28

# *Turn It Down!*

## Befriending and defending the soundman.

There is no person, other than the Lord, who has more direct influence on the outcome of worship than the soundman. Yet I know of no other position that is more undervalued and overlooked than that very role. A soundman's qualifications are rarely vetted, so someone who worked for Radio Shack can become a shoo-in to a lifelong, irrevocable appointment to the sound booth.

• A *soundman* can also be referred to as a soundperson, audio tech, sound tech, audio engineer and techie, to name a few, and his or her responsibilities often go beyond sound to include lighting, video and studio recording. I'll refer to this all-encompassing position as *soundman* and the sound team as *soundmen* for the sake of familiarity.

More often than not, the relationship between the sound team and the worship team is strained at best and filled with distrust, territorial disputes and opposing visions.

When I came on board at Calvary, I was the first staff position in the worship ministry. As the church grew, my first hire was an administrative assistant. My second hire, a soundman. I initially received strong push back to the position. "Why do we need to pay someone to do a job that's already being filled by volunteers?" But after the hire and the subsequent improvements in every aspect of the sound, there was unanimous agreement that there was no going back to the way things used to be (and sound).

*The soundmen have always been a part of the worship team. It was never the worship team and the sound guys. Never.*

This soundman, Mike Grosso, subsequently served with me in ministry for over twenty years. Together we led worship at Calvary, throughout the country and even in various parts of the world. I was a blessed man to have someone as gifted, skilled and trusted by my side for all of those years who was not only a soundman but also a co-leader, a confidant and a friend. It's a rarity, I know, but I still encourage you to search for that person who has a like-minded vision for what worship should not only be like but should sound like.

That's why I used the phrase, "together we led worship." The soundmen have always been a part of the worship team. It was never the worship team and the sound guys. Never. We worship together, we fellowship together, we have meetings together and we work together. There's no other way to build the unity and trust than to be on the same team. And over the years I have developed and implemented a methodology that has helped to nurture, strengthen and sustain this critical relationship. Here are some steps to consider taking in order to build a relationship with your sound team:

## Intercept Messages

One of the things I protect the soundmen from is everyone on stage. Nothing can be more confusing and maddening for soundmen than when everyone is vying for some personal preference on stage, whether it's their monitor mix, their desire for a different mic or mic placement, a nicer mic stand or any other number of requests (or demands). I am the *gatekeeper* for the soundmen. All requests go through me and I validate the need before I ask the soundman. My sound guys know not to respond to stage requests, only to me. This allows those on stage to maintain a great relationship with the soundmen. If they're going to be annoyed with someone, let them be annoyed with me, not the soundman.

## Solicit Feedback—The Good Kind . . .

I always ask my soundman after rehearsal and service how things went, how things sounded. He can inform me if a particular singer is struggling with mic usage, if the tone of a particular instrumentalist isn't working well, if there's a blending issue with the vocalists and so on. I also ask for his perspective and observations on the "flow" of a worship set. Are the songs blending together or, from his perspective, are the transitions too abrupt? Is there too much of something and not enough of something else? And many more questions. In other words, I ask for his opinion. This gives me valuable insight and perspective and makes him feel valued and respected.

## Be Their Agent

Soundmen are in a unique position. The vast majority of the church and its leadership don't even realize there's a soundman unless something goes dreadfully wrong. A good soundman is invisible, and he knows that. So it's vital that we represent them well, and consistently so, communicating to leadership the extreme skill needed to be unnoticed rather than allowing some in leadership to assume it's a job that anybody able to push buttons and sliders can do. Don't let that happen. The church desperately needs good soundmen, whether they realize it or not.

## Keep Them Happy

This is not about pacification but equipping. The soundman's job is not an easy one, nor is it a cheap one. The equipment required to meet the needs and standards in today's musical climate is expensive and requires constant updating and frequent replacement. Few church budgets will allow us to get everything we want, but most will accommodate some of what we want and most of what we need. Work together with your soundman to determine wants vs. needs, then work with him on a reasonable and workable budget to achieve agreed-upon goals. Be creative with those goals in mind. Trying to do too much at once may likely be cost prohibitive and put the entire project on hold, whereas approaching the goal from a multi-phased initiative that spreads the cost over a few months or longer now makes the goal much more feasible and easier to "sell." This will give your soundman the support he needs, while requiring a little patience in return.

## Have Their Back

"The band is drowning out the singers"; "There's so much bass I feel like my chest is going to explode"; and, of course, "It's so loud I can't hear myself sing."

These are just tiny snippets of the many opinions I've received concerning sound, and these are mild compared to many of the insensitive and rude comments I've been sent. Your soundman shouldn't be left alone to deal with this kind of poison—walk with him through these constant and often thoughtless comments and criticisms, offering him assurance and encouragement along the way. One person's *too loud* is another person's *not loud enough,* and with opposing opinions like this, oftentimes your soundman just can't get a break.

It's up to you to develop your philosophy of sound and mix, with input from your soundman, and to establish the right balance of overall level, with input from your pastor. Then you defend the level, you defend the mix and you defend your soundman. By doing so, you allow the soundman to deflect any criticism back to you, giving you the opportunity to explain the reason and vision behind the sound and mix, and keeping the soundman out of harm's way.

A few years ago I had my soundman bump the volume level for a particular celebratory weekend of worship. The response from the body was overwhelming. They loved it! However, I did get three emails from people that were not so enamored by it. In fact, they were mean spirited, nasty and condemning of the sound, the soundman and me. I told all three that I would love the opportunity to meet with them after service and talk to them in person. Two of them took me up on the invitation, and as I met individually with them following service, they immediately apologized for their emails. We proceeded to have very pleasant conversations where I shared my heart and defended my soundman, and by the time it was over I had two new friends and advocates.

It's important your soundman doesn't have to deal with this kind of personal attack or other criticisms from the body. Give him a way out, handle it for him and defend him—always have his back.

## Don't Be a Master of the Obvious

If during rehearsal there's a hideous outbreak of feedback, there's no need to abruptly stop the rehearsal and shout out, "Hey, there's feedback!" No kidding. Instead, try this: "Hey, is there anything we can do on stage to help you out? Is our stage level out of control?" When there's a problem, and there will be, let your soundman work it out; he's painfully aware of it. And again, simply ask if there's anything you or the team can do to help alleviate the problem. During these breakdowns I'll switch gears and tell the band to take a break and then proceed to work on vocal parts or create some other diversion, thus taking the pressure off the soundman. When he's got the problem solved, he'll tell me and we can then resume where we left off. Nobody lost their salvation, we got in some good rehearsal and the problem was solved.

\* \* \* \* \* \* \* \* \*

The soundman/worship leader relationship is one that needs to be collaborative and mutually edifying. You just cannot have a battle of the wills since everyone loses in that situation. Consistently download with each other your likes and dislikes, your preferences and their feasibility, and whether goals are met or not, and why. There will always be some differences of opinion and philosophy concerning sound, and there's nothing wrong with that. In fact, the process of deliberating those differences and their subsequent resolutions can be extremely rewarding and unifying, as long as they're worked out privately and not on stage.

Pursue this relationship with determination, grace and patience, and you'll soon find, as I did, that you'll not only have a great partnership leading worship together, but you'll also have a great friendship and a lifelong friend, which we could all use more of!

# CHAPTER 29

# Am I Too Old?
# (But I Feel Young!)

## Addressing age discrimination in both contemporary and traditional churches.

Am I too old for this? It's a question many of us ask every time a birthday rolls around. There's such an irony in all of this. When you're young, you try to catch up on experience, and when you're "mature" you long for the days of your youth. The divide has certainly grown wider with the promotion of the youthful look and accompanying visuals (stage lighting, haze, multiple flat screens with motion graphics, environmental projection, props, etc.) by larger churches with greater resources and broadcast capabilities, and further entrenched by publications and conferences focused on promoting the same to present themselves as *cutting edge* and *relevant*. This emphasis and presentation is parroted throughout the worship culture, often confusing, if not alienating, the mature participants and leaders. The emphasis is well intended, purposing to create an experience that is attractive and appealing to the next generation, but the effort can be far from inclusive, literally disqualifying participants based exclusively on their age or look. I

235

know personally of a few local ministries that have either unspoken (or, in a couple of cases, well publicized) age restrictions to serving in worship ministry. But this division can have its drawbacks and shortcomings.

*The old and the young are not to be divided but rather to assist each other with their strength and wisdom.*

A few years ago, my wife and I dropped off our daughter at a college in Southern California. Wanting to find a local church that would be well suited to her, we did some research and found a church that seemed really solid with a particularly strong ministry to college-aged students. In fact, upon visiting this church, we found that it was *all* young people. It was the "happening" church in the area, catering to and attracting young people. So I made a phone call and arranged a meeting with the pastor while we were out there. We had a great meeting and my wife and I felt comfortable with what we heard and discerned. As we closed our time together, I asked the pastor if there were anything we could be praying for, for the ministry and for him. His answer really caught me off guard. He replied, "Pray for more 'mature' believers to start attending. We need more older people." I responded that his answer surprised me. His current situation was what most other ministries and pastors dream of. He then clarified: "We need older believers to disciple these kids. There's no one to mentor them, and we need older believers to support the church since most of the kids are broke. We have a large church and lots of young people, but they're spiritually immature and we're barely scraping by." I was struck by the irony. If many of the pastors and ministries I've known got what they'd been praying for, they'd be in a mess, spiritually and monetarily bankrupt. Be careful what you ask for.

As is often the case, we would do well to strive to find a balance—a balance that has the next generation being welcomed into the church by the mature believers who mentor, share their wisdom and let their lives be an example to the youth, while the

236

youth bring a strength, a vitality and an ability to dream big and accomplish great things.

> *The glory of young men is their strength, gray hair*
> *the splendor of the old. (Proverbs 20:29)*

A great picture of this is the military. The older men are the commanders and leaders who devise the battle plans with their years of experience and wisdom, whereas the young men are the ones who go into battle with their strength, able to defend and defeat. If that scenario were reversed for any reason, the end result would be a disaster.

The old and the young are not to be divided but rather to assist each other with their strength and wisdom.

> *Praise the Lord from the earth,*
> *you great sea creatures and all ocean depths,*
> *lightning and hail, snow and clouds,*
> *stormy winds that do his bidding,*
> *you mountains and all hills,*
> *fruit trees and all cedars,*
> *wild animals and all cattle,*
> *small creatures and flying birds,*
> *kings of the earth and all nations,*
> *you princes and all rulers on earth,*
> ***young men and women,***
> ***old men and children.***
> *Let them praise the name of the Lord,*
> *for his name alone is exalted;*
> *his splendor is above the earth and the heavens.*
> *(Psalm 148:7–12, emphasis mine)*

We see in verse twelve that along with all of creation, the young men, women, old men and children are to praise the name of the Lord *together*; the strong, the beautiful, the wise and the innocent, all as one. Not divided, not separate services, not with age limits:

> *There should be no division in the body, but that its*
> *parts should have equal concern for each other.*
> *(1 Corinthians 12:25)*

We see a beautiful picture of this in the Old Testament:

> *These are the men David put in charge of the music*
> *in the house of the Lord after the ark came to rest*
> *there. They ministered with music before the*
> *tabernacle, the Tent of Meeting, until Solomon built*
> *the temple of the Lord in Jerusalem. They*
> *performed their duties according to the regulations*
> *laid down for them. Here are the men who served,*
> ***together with their sons***.
> *(1 Chronicles 6:31–33a, emphasis mine)*

I have two sons, and one of the greatest privileges and joys I've had in ministry is leading worship together with them. But this partnership is not just with biological children but with other "kids" from the next generation as well. These kids see me as a sort of dad in their lives, training them, mentoring them, correcting them and giving them the same opportunities I was given when I was younger. And just as raising kids from a distance is difficult at best, training young worship leaders from afar is challenging as well. However, training them on stage, both generations together with no division, is the most effective and productive form of mentoring I can think of. It worked in the temple, and it certainly works in our sanctuaries.

Yet division still has a stranglehold on many ministries, a plague that pits generation against generation. What's the problem and how can it be fixed?

## The Problem

Both generations certainly bear some responsibility. The younger generation separates itself by age restriction and youthful pride. They are often bold, arrogant and risk-takers. They tend to have a know-it-all approach to worship ministry and they're reluctant to colabor with the older generation, perceiving the more mature members to be outdated, unyielding and stuck in their ways.

The older generation separates itself not by age restrictions per se but rather by ostracism; they perceive the younger generation's different tastes and preferences as an affront to all they hold dear. They are often arrogant as well, though risk averse and puffed up with their experience and wisdom. This generation often finds the next generation to be a threat rather than a partner, thus becoming more protective than accepting.

The result: the young can be prideful and disrespectful while the mature can be haughty and defensive—a perfect formula for some bad blood:

> *This is what the Lord says: "Let not the wise man boast of his wisdom or the strong man [youth] boast of his strength or the rich man boast of his riches, but let him who boasts boast about this: that he understands and knows me, that I am the Lord, who exercises kindness, justice and righteousness on earth, for in these I delight," declares the Lord. (Jeremiah 9:23–24)*

It's not about the superiority of either a young man's strength or an older man's wisdom but whether one understands the overriding greatness of God, who overcomes all barriers and divisions. Knowing God in this way renders the boasting of one's wisdom or strength as utter foolishness. Yet we persist in our foolishness, continuing in our shortsighted and self-serving ways.

At this point it would seem natural to have a two-part discussion, each part addressing these often-opposing groups. Part one: how to get the youth to adjust to and receive from the mature; and, part two: how to get the mature to adjust to, impart to and not be threatened by the youth. You may be surprised, though, that I don't have a part one. I don't believe the issue is with the youth as much as it is with the older generation. Sure, the next generation could be more respectful and have a greater desire to learn from the older generation, but I put the blame of a lot of the next generation's apathy, disinterest and disrespect squarely on the shoulders of the older generation. Let me begin my explanation with this Scripture:

> *Train up a child in the way he should go: and when*
> *he is old, he will not depart from it.*
> *(Proverbs 22:6 KJV)*

Who's responsible for training this next generation? Their parents? Many have had ineffective or absent parents. What about the older generation? For the most part they've disengaged from the next generation. To make up for this lack of training, it's absolutely imperative that the older generation reengage and reinvest into this next generation. It's their responsibility—it's *my* responsibility:

> *You then, my son, be strong in the grace that is in*
> *Christ Jesus. And the things you have heard me say*
> *in the presence of many witnesses entrust to reliable*
> *men who will also be qualified to teach others.*
> *(2 Timothy 2:1–2)*

That's the essential role of the older generation: to teach and model the wisdom of Christ to the next generation so that they, becoming reliable and qualified, may then disciple and mentor the generation after them. Otherwise, the model the next generation is left with to pass on (and, in fact, is being trained by) is one of division, separation, distrust and even contempt.

I grew up, as did most in my generation, having my preferences derided by the older generation. Especially the music. This music was condemned as "boring, worthless, satanic and void of any skilled artistry." It would never have a chance of lasting for any length of time. (It appears the Rolling Stones, Aerosmith, the Beatles, Elton John, and many, many others would have the last word in that assessment.) There was not just division in taste and preferences but more like a chasm. We hated that kind of opinionated dogma growing up, yet now I'm watching many of my peers approach the next generation and their preferences with a similar disgust.

## The Fix

I'd like for those of us of the mature generation to consider six action verbs as we attempt to navigate the gap between the two groups. And if you're part of the next generation, these actions are certainly applicable to you as well. Implement the ones that can be applied in reverse and enjoy the fruit of broken-down walls and barriers. Those action verbs? Accept, appreciate, adapt, adopt, assist and advocate.

### *Accept*

This is not only a charge to accept the younger generation but, for some, to accept your circumstances first. I recently saw a gathering of a few previously well-known older worship leaders who bemoaned the state of worship today, reminding each other and their audience how genuine and artful worship used to be in their day. I was really disappointed.

And just as recently I received an invitation to a worship conference that via its postcard teaser assumed we were all tired of all the lights and production, and that we all needed to get away from the distractions, grab a guitar and get back to the basics—the way worship was meant to be. I was stunned!

*Stop looking back and wishing for "the good ol' days." They're gone. They've been replaced by good new days with good new people and good new songs and good new technology.*

When did a guitar, a singer and a campfire become the way worship was meant to be? There was nothing remotely biblical or accurate in either of these two assumptions but rather a blatant personal preference that fueled a bad case of missing "the good ol' days."

*Do not say, "Why were the old days better than these?" For it is not wise to ask such questions. (Ecclesiastes 7:10)*

Or as the New Living Translation says it:

*Don't long for "the good old days." This is not wise.*

It's not wise at all; in fact, it's ignorance. It's choosing to ignore the reality of those times, to have selective memory and to distort the "good" times into something to be revered when in fact they were no better than the current times, maybe even worse. Let me allow Scripture to be a little harsher on this:

*Jesus replied, "No one who puts his hand to the plow and looks back is fit for service in the kingdom of God." (Luke 9:62)*

Don't shoot the messenger, but take the message to heart: if we live in the past, idolizing our preferences, then we've disqualified ourselves for serving in ministry today because we will resent the people, the churches and the songs that embrace what is new and contrary to our tastes. We will thus divide rather than unite. We would be better off not to serve and even not to attend rather than carry a chip on our shoulders for all to see and hear, publicizing the grumpy countenance of a bitter soul. Don't be that person. If you are, or if you have leanings toward it, then make adjustments: accept your circumstances so you can accept the younger generation. Be wise. Stop looking back and stop wishing for "the good ol' days." They're gone. They've been replaced by good new days with good new people and good new songs and good new technology. Get a good new appreciation and a good new attitude and make yourself fit for service.

## *Appreciate*

I remember taking music appreciation in college and hearing for the first time early monophonic church music known as Gregorian chant. I initially dreaded the listening labs, having to listen to hours upon hours of this dreadful music in order to identify the particular piece and composer at the drop of a needle (I know, I'm dating myself). All necessary suffering to pass the class. But along the way, a very unexpected thing happened: I fell in love with the music and its style. It grew on me, and still to this day when I hear it in some obscure setting, it just captures me. I can't explain it. However, it taught me a lesson: that appreciation can be learned and developed. It often takes time and effort, but it can be done. Learn to appreciate their music, but first, learn to appreciate them. In order to understand and appreciate this next generation, you need to make the effort to spend some time with them. Schedule a lunch or facilitate some fellowship and then pick their brains. Ask them what their interests are and why, and anything else that comes to mind. Then just listen. Soon they'll start asking you questions as well, and before long, a mutual admiration club has begun.

Take the same effort and time with their music. Listen to it, over and over and over again. You have to train your brain and ears to hear differently, and just like learning a new language takes time and patience in order to understand and implement new inflections and accents, their new music will likewise take time and repetition in order to understand and eventually appreciate. But appreciate you will, and in a short while you'll be surprised as you begin to enjoy and be moved by some of their music. Maybe it will even become your music as well.

### *Adapt*

Just as chameleons can change colors to match their surroundings, it's important for us fit in appropriately without unnecessarily sticking out. Although I won't be changing my clothing or hairstyle to fit in with the fashions of the next generation, I ask for their opinions, their suggestions and their help. I ask them to get me their favorite worship songs, and I make sure to integrate several of them. I ask them their opinions of my arrangement ideas and what they would do differently. Would they use loops, a guitar solo, maybe a breakdown or other options I hadn't considered? By soliciting their input, listening (this is a key factor), considering *all* ideas and then implementing at least some, I have already begun to adapt by acknowledging my surroundings and allowing them to affect and change my natural inclinations.

Earlier this year I took a worship team to Brazil to lead worship at a couple of churches and a worship conference. It was an amazing time with only one frustration, the language barrier. I have since purchased a Portuguese language program and for several months now have been listening to and learning the language so that for my next trip I'll be able to better understand the local people and navigate certain encounters with greater understanding. Likewise with the next generation, though I'm not talking about their particular vernacular but rather their language of technology. This is how they communicate, and it is their tool for music and music ministry. I cannot stress enough the necessity of understanding and integrating this language, and whether it's an i-something, (anything Apple), ProTools, Ableton Live, Sibelius, virtual instruments, keyboards or whatever, it's important to adapt and navigate this language. The next generation will be happy to help you, and by all means let them; they're pretty fluent in this language.

A gentleman on my team is in his sixties, an amazing musician and a great guy. I challenged him a few years ago to learn this language, but he strongly protested, claiming he was too old for these "toys," and besides, he'd gotten along fine without them for all these years, so why change now? With a little persuasion from me and some of the next generation, he went out and got himself an iMac. Then later an iPhone and soon after that, a MacBook Pro. He learned how to use them all with a lot of help from the "youngsters," and, on top of it all, he's now a better musician for it. He's my poster child for adapting, and he also makes my point: if he can learn and adapt, then anybody can. Age is no excuse, nor is intentional ignorance. Learn their ways, speak their language and integrate their tools into your life and ministry. This is key to understanding the next generation, worshipping with them and growing as a musician.

### *Adopt*

When a child is adopted, that child becomes a part of the family with equal rights. It's what we do when we fully accept the next generation; they become part of the team, the family. They become fully grafted in. I have purposed to adopt the next generation in all that I do. I surround myself with them in the office, on the stage, in the Ocean's Edge School of Worship and in my travels. They are fully adopted into our worship ministry, and what an incredible asset to the ministry they are!

> *Consequently, you are no longer foreigners and aliens, but fellow citizens with God's people and members of God's household. (Ephesians 2:19)*

The younger generation can often be made to feel like second-class citizens, aliens in their own land, for which there is no excuse. Put an arm around this group, sincerely reach out to them and make them feel welcomed, loved and a part of the worship and church family, just as Christ has adopted all believers into His family.

## Assist

> *Don't let anyone look down on you because you are young, but set an example for the believers in speech, in life, in love, in faith and in purity.*
> *(1 Timothy 4:12)*

Help this younger generation to grow and excel in these qualities. Teach them and train them, all while loving them.

• *In speech*, train them in the truth of the Word so the things they speak are trustworthy and true.

• *In life*, help them to navigate everyday realities . . . handling finances, buying a home, starting a family, and even helping them fix things.

• *In love*, be available to offer advice on how to love others and how to have godly relationships, in dating and in marriage, in friendships, in ministry and at work.

• *In faith*, you can be a living example of what it takes to trust God and remain steadfast when faced with different challenges and trials.

•   *In purity*, help the younger generation to be pure in thought and motive, to help identify and remove those behaviors that could tarnish and disqualify their service, assisting them to become unhindered in their ability to serve and worship God.

Assist them also in their skills. Help develop their talent by training them to read and chart music, understand chords and basic theory, improve their technique of their particular gifting, maybe even teaching them a different instrument, and so much more.

*Never, ever give up doing everything possible to bring the two generations together.*

Help them in life, love and service, and don't ever be threatened by them. Even if they happen to be your replacements someday, don't worry. You have nothing to fear about being replaced: for to those that give of themselves for the sake of the next generation, God will always have a place in ministry for hearts like that!

## *Advocate*

•   *Advocate*: to speak or write in favor of; support or urge by argument; recommend publicly[20]

This is when unity is finally realized; when you publicly support and recommend the next generation. And how is that accomplished? When they're integrated into the worship experience, nothing shows public support more than when they are on stage with you and the older generation. And "urge by argument"? Fight for them. Defend them against ignorant and close-minded peers. Challenge those in your generation who perpetuate division by setting an example for them to follow. Never, ever give up doing everything possible to bring the two generations together, off stage, on stage and in worship. Recommend it, support it and defend it.

\* \* \* \* \* \* \* \*

In closing, please be assured that you're never too old to serve in worship; age itself is not a restriction. And as you serve, determine to see the value and giftings in each generation, choosing to be a peacemaker by bringing both young and old together to worship God with one voice.

**You're never too old to serve in worship.**

> *For he himself is our peace, who has made the two one and has destroyed the barrier, the dividing wall of hostility, (Ephesians 2:14)*

Bringing both generations together can work and does work. I've seen it firsthand. I pray that you, whether young or mature, are challenged to value the strengths of the other generation and to overcome any prejudices in order to worship in unity and to bring glory to God.

# CHAPTER 30

# *Twinkies Are Back!*

## The danger of entitlement.

Here's a stunning picture of entitlement gone bad: a union goes on strike until certain demands are met. Hostess, rather than meet the demands, declares bankruptcy, and within a period of time sells its assets to a new management company. The new company, in turn, reopens the plants and once again begins producing Twinkies, only this time without the union and without union workers.

I'm not here to make a statement one way or another regarding unions, but I am here to make a statement regarding entitlement: we can feel we're owed something and deserving of something for no other reason than favor, position or tenure, and, like the union did at Hostess, we can stake our livelihoods and futures on it. And we can lose. Lose it all.

• *Entitlement* is defined as belief that one is deserving of or entitled to certain privileges. [21]

We see a picture of this in the Bible in the book of Joshua, chapter 17. After seven years of battle, Israel is now in control of the Promised Land, which is to be divided among the tribes, and it is now up to the individual tribes to drive out the remaining enemies in their allotted lands. But the tribes of Ephraim and Manasseh, descendants of Joseph, felt they deserved more than they had been given:

> *The people of Joseph said to Joshua, "Why have you given us only one allotment and one portion for an inheritance? We are a numerous people and the Lord has blessed us abundantly."*
>
> *"If you are so numerous, "Joshua answered, "and if the hill country of Ephraim is too small for you, go up into the forest and clear land for yourselves there in the land of the Perizzites and Rephaites."*
>
> *The people of Joseph replied, "The hill country is not enough for us, and all the Canaanites who live in the plain have iron chariots, both those in Beth Shan and its settlements and those in the Valley of Jezreel."*
>
> *But Joshua said to the house of Joseph—to Ephraim and Manasseh—"you are numerous and very powerful. You will have not only one allotment but the forested hill country as well. Clear it, and its farthest limits will be yours; though the Cannanites have iron chariots and though they are strong, you can drive them out." (Joshua 17:14-18)*

If you were to look at a map of the division of land among the tribes, you'd see that Ephraim and Manasseh comprise almost half of the entire Promised Land. The challenge was that some of the land needed to be cleared of forest and enemies, and these two tribes felt they deserved land that was already prepared for them. They didn't want to clear land and battle enemies. They felt they were entitled to a stress-free relocation.

I wish.

There are many leaders in the church today that resemble these two tribes: although there's plenty of opportunity, they want someone else to do the work.

> *The teachers of the law and the Pharisees sit in Moses' seat. So you must obey them and do everything they tell you. But do not do what they do, for they do not practice what they preach. They tie up heavy loads and put them on men's shoulders, but they themselves are not willing to lift a finger to move them. (Matthew 23:2–4)*

As leaders, we may have earned or been given certain privileges, but we're not entitled to be lazy. We're called to work, and to work hard. We need to set the example, to be willing to do the small and seemingly insignificant tasks and enjoy the camaraderie that comes along with being in the trenches with the team. The team so respects this.

Some of my team members have been pleasantly surprised to see me help loading up moving trucks for an off-campus event or painting offices on a day off or assembling bookcases for the office. Some have told me during these times, "Don't worry; we've got it," but I do in fact "worry." I want to be a part of the team as I lead the team, not perceived as an entitled leader who's not willing to lift a finger. It's being a part of auditions; it's cleaning the

*As leaders, we may have earned or been given certain privileges, but we're not entitled to be lazy.*

"green room" after services; it's taking the trash out when it's full rather than waiting for facilities to do it and it's even participating on church workdays. It's all of this and so much more.

Now at this point a few might push back by referring to Acts chapter 6, in which some of the administrative duties (food distribution in this case) were delegated so the apostles could focus on the ministry of the Word. Those pushing back might say, "We

251

need to focus on the Word and ministry, and not be distracted by the everyday details and tasks." Here's my question: is that entitlement due to position, or to a sincere need due to priority? The apostles had to make choices: either distribute food or preach the Word. That doesn't mean they stopped doing "menial" tasks or chores, especially in light of Jesus' rebuke of the Pharisees and teachers of the law but rather that they were concerned that their calling and primary responsibility not be neglected.

In the same way, several years ago as Calvary Chapel Fort Lauderdale was doubling in size every year, I simply couldn't continue to adequately fulfill my calling and principal responsibilities unless I had some assistance. So I hired an administrative assistant. She helped me make calls to the team, set up schedules, make copies, set up my calendar and appointments and so much more. Her help enabled me to spend more time working on the worship sets, training musicians, preparing for rehearsal, etc. However, I hadn't shown up on my first day on the job and asked where my company car was, where my reserved parking spot was, who would be handling my dry cleaning, and whom my administrative assistant would be. Nor did I refuse to assist in any task, no matter how menial, as the need arose. Instead, I performed all of the administrative duties and primary responsibilities until I could no longer do both, at which time I, along with my pastor, determined that assistance was necessary. I now had balance, not an excuse to work less.

Some leaders, rather than finding themselves too busy to be able to do all of the work and then making necessary adjustments, start out with a sense of entitlement that makes them feel that they're only required to perform some of the work, especially that which is noble and esteemed (and noticed by others). Other leaders will do whatever it takes. Nothing is beneath them. They are the true leaders.

Entitlement also shows up in tenure. *Tenure* is defined as "status granted to an employee, usually after a probationary period, indicating that the position or employment is permanent."[22]

I first learned about tenure in high school. I had a history teacher who was awful. He only gave reading assignments, which we would occasionally be tested on. There was no teaching and no control, just complete chaos the whole time. It was unbelievable. He just sat at his desk, read the newspaper and was oblivious to all of the commotion around him. He just didn't care. At one of our dinner-table conversations at home, I asked my parents how this guy still had a job. "Tenure," they explained. "Once he's put in a certain amount of time, he's guaranteed a job. Nothing you can do about it unless he breaks the law." That made no sense to me then and it still doesn't today.

That may be the public school system and it may be the union but not ministry, right? Yeah, it happens in ministry too. It happens in every choir, in every worship team and even in the staff.

Tenure is a huge impediment to change since it instills in many a sense of entitlement to their positions and roles until they retire or die. When were we ever guaranteed a position for life? And why would we want the same position for life? (Some call it security. I call it a rut.) And how do we reconcile this position of tenure with Ecclesiastes 3, which is the quintessential model of change? Or, of greater concern, what if God has something amazing for us somewhere else doing something else? How can He possibly get our attention if any suggestion or recommendation for change is met instantly with indignation and resentment because of entitlement and tenure?

*Tenure is a huge impediment to change since it instills in many a sense of entitlement to their positions and roles until they retire or die.*

I recently decided to make a major change in the choir. It had become too large and unmanageable, and the members were inconsistent in participation and preparation. So I instructed my director, Joey, to re-audition everyone prior to our next season (September through June), with the goal of reducing the choir by half (from approximately 120 to 60). The directive, and especially the results, was received with a fair amount of grumbling, primarily along the lines of tenure. Here's a copy of the instructive and corrective email I sent to the choir in response:

> Hey guys,
>
> I wanted to take just a few minutes of your time to help clarify a few things and share my heart once again in this process of "pruning" the choir that you all just went through.
>
> Some of you have shared confusion as to why there was a need to trim the choir in half. To start with, this was not Joey's idea; it was mine. . . . It was also not the pastor's idea as some have suggested, so it is fully my responsibility. There were a number of reasons for this change that dealt with both logistics and commitment: first, it was no longer practical. The choir simply doesn't fit on the risers and there is no more room for more risers. . . . Second, the size of the choir has compromised the quality of sound for quite some time due to the proximity of choir microphones to guitar amps, drums, and ambient sound and vice versa. Third, many of you only show up to rehearsals a week or two before a NOW (Night Of Worship), Easter, Christmas, or choir weekend and attempt to participate at a level commensurate with those who have been attending and rehearsing regularly—that's unacceptable. Fourth, singing is a gift that requires consistency and investment outside of Thursday evenings; that is, singing and practicing at home. So one's attendance might be acceptable, but his or her schedule simply doesn't allow for any other investment. Finally, some of you have had significant changes in your family commitments, your job situation, and finances, to name a few things, that have caused stress and tension that has shown up in a variety of ways, including the aforementioned points. Rather than finding yourself grumbling or complaining, see this as your season to regroup and tend to more pressing needs, allowing for the opportunity to possibly serve again in the future as your personal situation becomes more manageable.

However, it seems that the biggest issue and concern is centered around tenure: that is if somebody has been serving for several years, it is now their right and expectation to continue to serve until they are incapacitated and can no longer serve, that it is somehow their inalienable right to tell us when that time is rather than the other way around. Here's the problem with tenure—it often becomes an impediment for those whom God is calling to different or greater works, and in some cases, to correcting bad behavior.

I'd like to share an example of what happened several years ago: The choir used to be composed of four sections; soprano, alto, tenor and bass. I decided to reduce the choir to three sections; soprano, alto and tenor. I hesitated for over a year not wanting to hurt anyone's feelings, yet I knew I needed to make the change and that I was supposed to do just that. So I did, and initially there was some grumbling, much like now. However, I soon began to receive some amazing emails of former bass singers who now found themselves involved in other areas of ministry in which they were absolutely thriving. One singer decided to serve in the tape-lending library, and in the process he found himself listening to the pastor's teachings for hours every week. It gave him an ongoing interest and love of the Word, and as he began to study more . . . well, he became a pastor.

That's my point. For many of you this new season will be the beginning of something amazing that the Lord desires to do with you and through you—don't miss that opportunity.

To sum it up, this process and the result is one that, honestly, I should have commenced a year ago and one that I stand behind today. How should you respond? Simply this: Psalm 46:10. "Be still, and know that I am God."

To help with greater understanding and also to help with redirection into other opportunities, I will be available on Sunday, October 23rd, following the 12:30 p.m. service in the choir room.

255

Thanks for your understanding and, most of all, for your
service to the Lord,
Clay

Consider the bass singer who became a pastor. He would still be singing bass if he hadn't been pushed out of the nest, and he would have missed out on doing something greater for the Lord. Whatever your role is in ministry, don't let entitlement cause you to miss an incredible opportunity. What might seem unfair and unreasonable may very well be God trying to move you on to greater opportunity. Stop fighting and let Him.

*What might seem unfair and unreasonable may very well be God trying to move you on to greater opportunity.*

Tenure also tends to presume on promotion: solos always go to the singers who have been serving the longest and the opportunity to participate in special events (such as Christmas, Easter and recordings) always go to the ones with the most tenure as well. They most certainly would never go to someone who's new to the team. Would they?

Why not?

I've done that countless times. I've used newer team members over tenured members at times because the new members were more gifted and skilled, other times because they were more mature and sometimes because I just felt like it. And in every instance, it was an opportunity to observe the team's heart and spiritual maturity. When the entire team rallied behind the newcomers, there was unity. When some on the team complained over wrongly perceived inequity, there was correction and redirection. It's simple: we're called to be faithful with what we've been given and with the opportunities that come our way, not to find resentment in what we don't have and the opportunities that don't come our way. What a waste of time and energy. Now, in all fairness, if people are confused, disappointed or even hurt by my decisions, I'm more than happy to meet with them and hear their concerns. In fact, I encourage it. It gives me the opportunity to explain my decisions and clear up any misunderstanding and confusion. It's important for the team to know that I don't lead from a dictatorial position that insinuates, "Don't ever question me; my decisions are always final and indisputable." That's just dumb.

Entitlement through tenure can also presume on job promotions, pay rates, raises and bonuses, office size, which satellite campus one leads or serves at and even whose table someone is assigned to at the annual staff Christmas party.

*Entitlement can quickly eat away at and destabilize the framework of worship.*

I could go on, but, needless to say, entitlement can quickly eat away at and destabilize the framework of worship. It causes us to believe we deserve and have earned certain privileges and guarantees. But the Bible clearly spells out that the only thing we really, truly are entitled to and deserve is death:

> *For all have sinned and fall short of the glory of God. (Romans 3:23)*

> *For the wages of sin is death. (Romans 6:23a NASB)*

Yet God, because of His indescribable love for us, gives us another option:

> *But the free gift of God is eternal life in Christ Jesus our Lord. (Romans 6:23b NASB)*

We're not entitled to anything, yet by God's grace we've been blessed with much, including eternal life with our Lord in heaven! Always hold on to that perspective, living it out and sharing it often.

CHAPTER 31

# *Watch Your Attitude*

## The attitude of praying without ceasing.

Consider all of the various facets involved when serving in worship ministry: seemingly countless roles, conflicting expectations, disconnected leadership, constantly changing schedules and personnel, and a team that places its involvement in worship somewhere behind family, job, bowling league, hunting season, favorite TV series, house renovation, car shopping and dog grooming. We all need to be on our knees praying!

Yet prayer can easily get unintentionally sidelined. Whether because of a jam-packed day (or week or life), increased responsibilities or some unexpected texts and emails that start the day off by dropping grenades on a once manageable schedule, it just happens. We get way too busy. Then we come face to face with the scriptural exhortation:

> *Be joyful always;* **pray continually;** *give thanks in all circumstances, for this is God's will for you in Christ Jesus.*
> *(1 Thessalonians 5:16–18, emphasis mine)*

We can hardly fit prayer in at times, yet we're supposed to pray "continually" or, as other translations say, "without ceasing"? On the surface, that just doesn't seem to make sense, nor does it even seem plausible.

So often we look at prayer as a "wish list" or a "check list," a prerequisite to eating or something we do when every other possible option has been exhausted—a last resort. And this kind of prayer requires a finite slice of our already depleted time. But I submit to you that prayer is not a task that needs to be prioritized and scheduled somewhere in the day but rather an attitude that permeates every moment of the day.

*Prayer is not a task that needs to be prioritized and scheduled somewhere in the day but rather an attitude that permeates every moment of the day.*

Prayer is communicating and communing with God, but that doesn't mean it's exclusively verbal and conscious. I can walk in the door at the end of the day and by the look in my wife's eyes, her posture, her smile, how she greets me, and everything else that constitutes her attitude, I'll know exactly how she's doing. The nonverbal communicates much more accurately then words can and do. I can ask, "How are you?" and she may answer, "Fine," yet everything about her says the opposite. Words can betray, but actions don't lie. And likewise, my walk, my attitude, my nonverbal communication with God, will all mean so much more to Him than all the lengthy Shakespearian-style prayers I could ever offer. That's how one can pray without ceasing. It's not verbal, nor is it confined to a time, rather it's an all-day attitude that communicates clearly and accurately with God.

The other concern with prayer as an exclusively verbal (and conscious) exercise is that it can be easily checked off. Why's that a concern? It can create a false sense of accomplishment, even spiritual pride, when we're able to successfully complete a "time of prayer" every single day for x amount of days in a row. The "streak" can become the goal rather than the sincerity and effectiveness of the prayers themselves.

Let me describe it this way: it's like making your kids hug you every day before they leave for school. They groan "Ooookaaaay," then they slouch as they roll their eyes and half-heartedly dangle their arms around you. But you got your hug. Then they grow up, move away and start their own families. And after they come home for a visit, those departing hugs are very different. Attitude is everything and it'll always trump compliance. And quite honestly, it's no different with prayer: do we go through the motions and check it off, or are our attitudes right and sincere?

*Consider it joy when you face trials, not if. They will come.*

This attitude of prayer communicates to God and communes with God continuously. All day. It doesn't require a set-aside time or a specific prayer list; instead it's an all-day attitude that communicates beyond words. There's no faking it; this attitude can only come from the heart.

And what is it that gives us this attitude? How do we make our hearts right?

## Be Joyful

> *Be joyful always;* pray continually; give thanks in all circumstances, for this is God's will for you in Christ Jesus.
> (1 Thessalonians 5:16–18, emphasis mine)

In addition to praying continuously, we're to be continuously joyful? How do we do that?

> Consider it pure *joy,* my brothers, whenever you face trials of many kinds, because you know that the testing of your faith develops perseverance.

> *Perseverance must finish its work so that you may*
> *be mature and complete, not lacking anything.*
> *(James 1:2–4, emphasis mine)*

Consider it joy *when* you face trials, not *if*. They *will* come. This joy comes from knowing that the Lord's plan for us is good and perfect, and this attitude rejoices in His faithfulness through every trial.

> *I take joy in doing your will, my God, for your*
> *instructions are written on my heart.*
> *(Psalm 40:8 NLT)*

We receive joy, pleasure and contentment from knowing and doing what God has called us to do. It's a joy we experience and an attitude we convey when we willingly lay down *our* own will and desires to instead seek, know and respond to *His* will for our lives.

> *Let us fix our eyes on Jesus, the author and*
> *perfecter of our faith, who for the joy set before him*
> *endured the cross, scorning its shame, and sat down*
> *at the right hand of the throne of God.*
> *(Hebrews 12:2)*

Jesus, faced with the agonizing pain and shame of the cross, knew the joy to come from following His Father's will. Likewise, we know the joy set before us as we daily surrender our will to follow Jesus, enduring various trials with contentment and joy in anticipation of the promise of heaven.

> *Rejoice in the Lord **always**. I will say it again:*
> *Rejoice! (Philippians 4:4, emphasis mine)*

## Be Thankful

> *Be joyful always; pray continually**; give thanks in
> all circumstances,** for this is God's will for you in
> Christ Jesus.*
> *(1 Thessalonians 5:16–18, emphasis mine)*

As with joy, we're also to be thankful in every situation and in
every trial. This thankful attitude acknowledges and is grateful for
the saving grace of Jesus Christ and all that He's done, is doing
and will do in our lives, no matter what we're going through.

> *Do not be anxious about anything, but in every
> situation, by prayer and petition, **with
> thanksgiving**, present your requests to God.*
> *(Philippians 4:6, emphasis mine)*

> *Sing and make music in your heart to the Lord,
> always **giving thanks to God the Father for
> everything**, in the name of our Lord Jesus Christ.*
> *(Ephesians 5:19b–20, emphasis mine)*

## Be Watchful

> *Devote yourselves to prayer, **being watchful** and
> thankful. (Colossians 4:2, emphasis mine)*

Consider the synonyms for watchful: alert, attentive, awake,
observant, vigilant, aware, conscious, sensitive, cognizant,
mindful, careful, cautious, wary, prepared, ready and wide-awake.
By taking each synonym and inserting it in place of "watchful" in
Colossians 4:2, we begin to grasp the breadth and implication of
this attitude.

Paul doesn't say to devote yourselves to prayer, *then* be watchful (or, for that matter, *then* be thankful), but he clearly describes the action of being watchful (and thankful) as being simultaneous with prayer. We are to be watchful while we pray.

### Watch Out for Temptation.

> *Then he returned to his disciples and found them sleeping. "Could you men not keep watch with me for one hour?" he asked Peter. "Watch and pray so that you will not fall into temptation. The spirit is willing, but the flesh is weak." (Matthew 26:40-41)*

### Watch Out; You Have an Enemy.

> *Be alert and of sober mind. Your enemy the devil prowls around like a roaring lion looking for someone to devour. (1 Peter 5:8)*

### Watch Out That You Aren't Disqualified.

> *The Lord said to Gideon, "You have too many men for me to deliver Midian into their hands. In order that Israel may not boast against me that her own strength has saved her, announce now to the people, 'Anyone who trembles with fear may turn back and leave Mount Gilead.'" So twenty-two thousand men left, while ten thousand remained.*
>
> *But the Lord said to Gideon, "There are still too many men. Take them down to the water, and I will sift them for you there. If I say, 'This one shall go with you,' he shall go; but if I say, "This one shall not go with you,' he shall not go."*
>
> *So Gideon took the men down to the water. There the Lord told him, "Separate those who lap*

*the water with their tongues like a dog from those who kneel down to drink." Three hundred men lapped with their hands to their mouths. All the rest got down on their knees to drink.*

*The Lord said to Gideon, "With the three hundred men that lapped I will save you and give the Midianites into your hands. Let all the other men go, each to his own place." (Judges 7:2-7)*

I love this picture. Gideon started with 32,000 soldiers, then 22,000 left because they were fearful, and 9,700 more were disqualified because they failed to stay watchful or to be vigilant. When they drank, they put their faces *in* the water where they could no longer see an approaching threat or enemy, making them vulnerable and unable to defend themselves against an attack. The three hundred, however, kept their heads up and brought the water to their

*This attitude of prayer—it's the lifestyle of worship!*

mouths with their hands, allowing them to stay alert, cautious, ready and watchful, able to see any approaching threat. And likewise, if we keep our heads up and stay alert and watchful, we will as well be set apart, able to defend against any attack and victorious in battles and trials.

\* \* \* \* \* \* \* \*

This attitude of prayer is our ability to pray without ceasing and to live lives that stay in communion with God, whether through trials or in victory. This attitude of prayer is to be a mainstay of our faith and our walk, and a reflection of our relationship with the Living God. This attitude of prayer is born out of a heart that's joyful, thankful and watchful, as we willingly submit to His will for our lives. And this attitude of prayer—it's the lifestyle of worship!

# CHAPTER 32

# *Everybody's Got a Boss*

## In authority and under authority.

We all have a boss. We all have someone or some group to whom we're accountable, who has authority over us. If I took a poll and asked if you'd prefer to be in authority or under authority, I'm guessing most would prefer to be *in* authority, thinking you'd likely be more productive, more efficient and maybe even more effective. But then comes along the centurion in Matthew 8, who turns the concept of authority upside down:

> *When Jesus had entered Capernaum, a centurion came to him, asking for help. "Lord," he said, "my servant lies at home paralyzed and in terrible suffering."*
>
> *Jesus said to him, "I will go and heal him."*
>
> *The centurion replied, "Lord, I do not deserve to have you come under my roof. But just say the word, and my servant will be healed. For I myself am a man under authority, with soldiers under me. I tell this one, 'Go,' and he goes; and that one,*

> *'Come,' and he comes. I say to my servant, 'Do this,' and he does it."*
>
> *When Jesus heard this, he was astonished and said to those following him, "I tell you the truth, I have not found anyone in Israel with such great faith.*
>
> *Then Jesus said to the centurion, "Go! It will be done just as you believed it would." And his servant was healed at that very hour.*
> *(Matthew 8:5–10, 13)*

The centurion, although a man of authority, was also under authority. That authority was Rome. He was employed by Rome and Rome "had his back." The centurion's authority (i.e., his boss) gave him support, backing and direction. You mess with the centurion, you're messing with Rome. And messing with either could have deadly consequences, so simultaneously a centurion was revered and feared. As you can imagine, his soldiers did exactly what he said.

***To be effective in authority, one must first learn to function capably under authority.***

Jesus is "astonished" at this centurion's faith because the centurion gets it. He understands. When the centurion says, "For I myself," he's saying, "in the same way you are," or "just like you," meaning, "I am also under authority." He's acknowledging that Jesus isn't some mad man making this savior thing up as He goes along. He is Jesus, the Son of God, under the authority of God. Jesus has the backing, the will and the full support of God Almighty, His Father. You mess with the Son. . . .

So it's not one or the other—being in authority or being under authority—but rather, it's both: being in authority and under authority at the same time. But to be effective in authority, one must first learn to function capably under authority, to know and understand the person of authority, as well as his or her

268

expectations. In other words, how well do you know your boss? How well did Jesus know His Father, His authority (i.e., His boss)?

> *"If you really know me, you will know my Father as well. From now on, you do know him and have seen him."(John 14:7)*

By knowing Jesus, we know the Father, Jesus' authority. How well will someone know your boss by knowing you? Will someone be able know your boss's vision and heart by talking to you and spending time with you? Now, for some of you, that might sound a little creepy; but seriously, you should know your boss—his or her likes, dislikes, vision and expectations. And not only that, you should represent your boss rightly and respectfully to those whom you know and with whom you have contact.

I've had the privilege of teaching at many worship conferences over the years and I always try to allow for a Q&A time. And the number one question? "How can I get along and work better with my pastor?" Let me respond to that question with another question: how can you serve your boss effectively if you don't know his vision or expectations? Yet another question: how can your boss back you and support you if he doesn't feel you have his best interests at heart? Therein lies the heart of the conflict: do you even know each other? So, how do you overcome this? For starters:

## Communicate

Imagine for a moment this scenario: a police officer sees something suspicious in a dark alley. He's goes to investigate but doesn't call it in, doesn't call for back up and leaves his gun in the car. He gets beat up.

Now here's another scenario: July fourth is on a Sunday, and in addition to patriotic songs, you decide to incorporate pyrotechnics, confetti and streamers dropping from the rafters and dancing girls (a la the Rockettes) in red, white and blue sequins. But you don't pray about it, you don't clear it with your pastor and you leave your brain in the car. You, as well, will get beat up. (I'm serious; it really did happen. And just in case you're wondering; no, it wasn't me. And yes, the music director was fired following that service.)

Can the takeaway be any more obvious? If you don't communicate, if you don't secure back-up (support) and approval, the chance that things will go terribly wrong increase exponentially.

On a more personal note, as you know, ministry isn't a nine-to-five five-day-a-week occupation. With every intention of doing so, I can tell my wife that I'll be home by six for dinner. And more often than not, something or someone happens and my arrival time gets pushed back. When I get home an hour later than she was expecting me, she's disappointed and frustrated. Not because something or someone came up and not because I was late but because I didn't respect her and her time enough to let her know I would be late. That's all she's asking for, a little respect. That's all your boss is asking for, some respect. Whether your boss is a pastor, a worship leader or any other leader or overseer, put some practices in place to facilitate more consistent and effective communication.

As Calvary continued to grow and campuses multiplied, the expectations of the worship ministry grew as well. In order for me and my pastor to stay on the same page, we both felt it necessary to meet on a weekly basis to review and evaluate the past week's services and events, as well as to preview and coordinate upcoming services and events. This meeting is scheduled for only fifteen minutes. That's it. Every week.

I recommend the same for you. The length of the meeting is totally up to you, but meet weekly. These times become an opportunity to receive understanding and impart understanding in order to minimize misunderstanding.

## Ask

A vacation, a day off, anything out of the ordinary during service, a correction or discipline of a staff or team member, a new hire, a dismissal, any significant ministry purchase, a "guest appearance" at another ministry—the list goes on and on. Ask. It shows respect, it informs, and it also allows for additional input and direction that can favorably influence your decisions.

## Submit

> *Obey your leaders and submit to them, for they are keeping watch over your souls, as those who will have to give an account. Let them do this with joy and not with groaning, for that would be of no advantage to you. (Hebrews 13:17 ESV)*

Let's say you're asked to cut a song or play a song that your pastor requests or even dress a little nicer on the weekends. So what? Be sure not to turn a "no big deal" into a "big deal." It's just not worth it. I prefer to follow the old saying and pick my battles wisely. If you defend every request and issue as if it's a life or death scenario, you'll only make your boss's job miserable, and what will you have accomplished then? What advantage will you have gained? None. Except a boss who would rather remove you than support you. If instead you submit consistently and willingly to your boss, you're more likely to have a receptive ear when the time comes to share a concern.

## Don't Slander

> *Whoever slanders their neighbor in secret, I will put to silence; whoever has haughty eyes and a proud heart, I will not tolerate. (Psalm 101:5)*

There's just no place for this kind of behavior. It accomplishes nothing, yet destroys much. Take a look at the list of synonyms for *slander*: defame, libel, malign, smear, belittle, disgrace, shame, humiliate, scorn and, to sum it all up, dishonor. Slander dishonors the very person God called you to honor, tearing him or her down just to build yourself up. It's a serious offense and one that will not only derail your ministry but your life as well. When the Lord says He will "silence" and "not tolerate" those who behave this way, you really want to take this seriously:

> *Therefore, rid yourselves of all malice and all deceit, hypocrisy, envy, and slander of every kind.*
> *(1 Peter 2:1)*

Take an honest assessment of yourself before the Lord, or ask someone you know who will be gut-level honest with you. If you are involved in this behavior in any way, please, please, get some counsel, along with some accountability. Rather than tear down your boss, build him or her up.

## Don't Whine

> *Do everything without complaining or arguing.*
> *(Philippians 2:14)*

Several years ago, there was a guy on the team who was quite talented, but he found fault with practically everything and everybody, and he voiced it regularly. Every time he served was an opportunity to voice another complaint. It was endless. Finally I called him into my office and calmly informed him that I was pulling him off the team because I needed a break from him. I just couldn't take the incessant complaining anymore. How did he take it? He was incredulous that I would let someone as good as he was go, so that became just one more thing for him to complain about.

When the rest of the team members found out that he was gone, they were thrilled and relieved.

Over the years I've had several team members who acted as if complaining and arguing about everything were a gift, and they regularly exercised their gift for all to see and hear. When they would leave the team, whether voluntarily or by compulsion, nobody missed them. The team was once again relieved. But when there were team members who brought joy, encouraged others and were peaceable with everyone, their departures were mourned. There were tearful goodbyes, hugs and promises to stay in touch. And those people are still in touch today. I call them honorary team members. They will always be welcome on our team. What a difference between the two groups! If you're one who complains and argues to excess, then the "groaning" sound that Hebrews 13:17 mentions is coming from your boss whenever he or she sees you coming. Don't be that person, but instead

> *let's keep on pursuing those things that bring peace*
> *and that lead to building up one another.*
> *(Romans 14:19 ISV)*

Don't complain or argue, but be peaceable. Be *that* person.

## Try to Be Relatable (Then Try Harder)

After teaching a session at a conference I was approached by a young worship leader who looked (and smelled) like he had just rolled out of bed. Every third or fourth word he spoke was the word *like*, and during the conversation he admitted that he didn't have a regular time of Bible study or devotion. His question: "My pastor and I just don't seem to relate to each other. Do you have any suggestions?" I loved his question and his heart. But still, I couldn't help but think, "Seriously?"! I was very honest with him and challenged him to look at all of the potential areas of disconnect: his attire, his hygiene, his scriptural ignorance, his lack of complete sentences, and which, if not all, of those areas could be even slightly modified to give his pastor the impression that he was really trying to be more relatable. It's not about him giving up his identity, personality or uniqueness; it's about him taking a shower and using deodorant, for crying out loud! I especially challenged him to study and apply the Word. Although a comb and deodorant would certainly help externally, he needed the Word to transform him internally. Not only would that thrill his pastor, but it would give the two of them a starting point of growing relatability.

*Give a little, if not a lot, for the sake of your relationship, thus relatability, with your pastor.*

Again, I'm not asking or suggesting someone "sell out," but in the spirit of *"consider(ing) others as more important than yourselves (Philippians 2:3 HCSB),"* give a little, if not a lot, for the sake of your relationship, thus relatability, with your pastor. Chances are, he'll return the gesture.

\* \* \* \* \* \* \* \*

> *For rulers hold no terror for those who do right, but for those who do wrong. Do you want to be free from the fear of the one in authority? Then do what is right and you will be commended. (Romans 13:3)*

Honor the Lord, honor your boss and do what's right. In this way you prove yourself under authority. When that happens, you will likewise be honored. And when you behave like that, if you're not in authority yet, you soon will be. And if you're already in authority, you will soon be given even more responsibility. When you honor the Lord and you honor your boss, you'll in turn *be* a great boss!

CHAPTER 33

# *Who You Gonna Serve?*

## How worship and giving go hand in hand.

*No one can serve two masters. Either you will hate the one and love the other, or you will be devoted to the one and despise the other. You cannot serve both God and money. (Matthew 6:24)*

This Scripture makes it clear that we can only serve one master. We can only be devoted to and love just the one. Then it goes on to spell out the competing masters: God and money. If you were to poll your worship ministry with that very question: "Who or what are you devoted to, God or money?" The answer would likely be unanimously in favor of God. Yet take another poll and ask, "Do you tithe?" and I guarantee the answer would no longer be unanimous, with the possible exception that it's unanimous that none of your team is tithing.

This is a problem. A huge problem. One's tithing or giving record can quickly and clearly reveal one's level of faith, trust, commitment, spiritual maturity and obedience, as well as one's pride and selfishness.

On the subject of tithing, some are quick to point out that tithing was part of the law, and we are no longer under the law but rather under grace—so tithing is therefore no longer valid and should not be taught nor practiced. However, the law is still holy and valid as a guideline for moral and godly living. Christ came to fulfill the law, not abolish it. The law no longer condemns because of Christ's sacrifice, but the law is still a compass for morality. To conclude that tithing is no longer necessary is no different than concluding that murder and adultery are no longer forbidden. If the law no longer applies to one part, then it no longer applies to any of the parts. I'm more inclined to think that the motive of some of these advocates is not so much scriptural compliance as it is an excuse to be stingy and cheap.

I will refer to the heart of tithing and giving as simply "giving" going forward.

This chapter is by no means a call to obligate or require that a person give but rather to take a look at the purpose of giving and the spiritual implications related to this act:

> *Each of you should give what you have decided in your heart to give, not reluctantly or under compulsion, for God loves a cheerful giver.*
> *(2 Corinthians 9:7)*

How does one become a "cheerful" giver? First, let's examine the word *cheerful*:

- feeling or showing happiness
- feeling or showing that you are willing to do something without complaining
- causing good feelings or happiness[23]

I also found these various phrases describing what it means to be a *cheerful giver*:

- to give with a cheerful countenance, to give willingly
- to give voluntarily
- to give as an act that takes delight in helping others
- to give for the love of God
- to give with a heart like God's

It's giving with the right heart, a heart that's willing, generous and desiring to help others, not out of abundance but sacrificially. And therein lies the essence of giving: Christ gave sacrificially for our salvation out of love for us, and when we truly have the mind of Christ, our desire, likewise, is to give sacrificially to others out of love and gratitude for Christ and what He's done for us. Christ gave sacrificially for us and we give sacrificially to Him. That's worship.

*If our giving is cheap, our worship is likewise cheap.*

When it comes to giving, God wants us to be generous and sacrificial but not because He needs our money. That must be understood—otherwise we have this perverted image of God, not unlike many televangelists who emotionally declare that their ministries will shut down unless we dig deep and send in our support right now (add tears . . .). That's not God, not even close:

*I have no complaint about your sacrifices*
 *or the burnt offerings you constantly offer.*
*But I do not need the bulls from your barns*
*or the goats from your pens.*
*For all the animals of the forest are mine,*
*and I own the cattle on a thousand hills.*
*I know every bird on the mountains,*
*and all the animals of the field are mine.*
*If I were hungry, I would not tell you,*
*for all the world is mine and everything in it.*
*Do I eat the meat of bulls?*
*Do I drink the blood of goats?*
*Make thankfulness your sacrifice to God,*

*and keep the vows you made to the Most High.*
*(Psalm 50:8–14 NLT)*

The Israelites were bringing animals to sacrifice and did so with an attitude and heart that assumed that God needed them to bring to Him that which He already owned. What they missed was that these continual animal sacrifices were pointing the way to a "once and for all" sacrifice: Jesus. But God was exhorting the Israelites then and still exhorts us today, "Make thankfulness your sacrifice to God, and keep the vows you made to the Most High."

This call to sacrifice is illustrated poignantly in First Chronicles chapter 21. For all the wrong reasons, King David took a census to determine the number of fighting men. David had in his heart to trust more in his military might than in God's protection, much like our propensity to trust in our money rather than in God's provision. The end result was a disaster, and God required a sacrifice from King David to show a changed and repentant heart:

> *Then the angel of the Lord ordered Gad to tell David to go up and build an altar to the Lord on the threshing floor of Araunah the Jebusite. So David went up in obedience to the word that Gad had spoken in the name of the Lord.*
>
> *While Araunah was threshing wheat, he turned and saw the angel; his four sons who were with him hid themselves. Then David approached, and when Araunah looked and saw him, he left the threshing floor and bowed down before David with his face to the ground.*
>
> *David said to him, "Let me have the site of your threshing floor so I can build an altar to the Lord, that the plague on the people may be stopped. Sell it to me at the full price."*
>
> *Araunah said to David, "Take it! Let my lord the king do whatever pleases him. Look, I will give*

*the oxen for the burnt offerings, the threshing
sledges for the wood, and the wheat for the grain
offering. I will give all this."*

*But King David replied to Araunah, "No, I
insist on paying the full price. I will not take for the
Lord what is yours, or sacrifice a burnt offering
that costs me nothing." (1 Chronicles 21:18–24)*

Araunah offered to give everything to David: the property, the
oxen, the wood to burn and the wheat. All of it. But David
wouldn't take it. He wasn't about to offer a sacrifice to the Lord
that cost him nothing. That's not a sacrifice. He insisted on paying
the full price. Not a discounted price, full price.

Are we willing to do the same, to bring to the Lord a sacrifice
that costs us something? Even full price?

*And he sat down opposite the treasury and watched
the people putting money into the offering box.
Many rich people put in large sums. And a poor
widow came and put in two small copper coins,
which make a penny. And he called his disciples to
him and said to them, "Truly, I say to you, this poor
widow has put in more than all those who are
contributing to the offering box. For they all
contributed out of their abundance, but she out of
her poverty has put in everything she had, all she
had to live on." (Mark 12:41-44 ESV)*

Clearly, this picture of giving has no correlation to the amount
but entirely to the sacrifice of giving, to what it costs us.

Years ago I was involved in a capital funds drive at a church,
and I used to marvel at (and be embarrassed by) the attention and
accolades given to those few whose giving was in the top tier. But
I knew a couple of these guys, and what they gave in relationship
to their income and net worth was hardly generous. They simply

gave from their abundance. I also knew a few folks who gave way over-the-top generously when compared to their income and net worth. They gave all they had, but there was no attention given to them. It seems we've got this all backward: man honors the amount, but God honors the sacrifice.

As we've just seen, God honors a sacrificial heart:

> *Through Jesus, therefore, let us continually offer to God a sacrifice of praise—the fruit of lips that openly profess his name. (Hebrews 13:15)*

How is praise a sacrifice? When it's an act that sacrifices our natural desires and tendencies to live and care for ourselves and meet our own needs above all else. When it's a heart and attitude of thankfulness, grateful for salvation and a hope of heaven where *"there will be no more death, or mourning or crying or pain" (Revelation 21:4).* And it's when you *"keep the vows you made to the Most High" (Psalm 50:14 NLT).* And what are those vows? Those are the vows you and I made when we surrendered our lives to the Lord, when we said, "I'm yours Lord, everything I am, everything I have. . . ." Not part of our lives but all of it. Even the part that holds onto money and material possessions out of fear and for lack of faith.

*We've got this all backward: man honors the amount, but God honors the sacrifice.*

That's why giving and worship are inextricably linked. There's just no way around it. We are to give sacrificially from our possessions and our hearts. Yet if our hearts are hesitant and fearful in giving and sacrifice, then our worship will be compromised. Our sacrificial worship is dependent upon a sacrificial heart. I submit that if our giving is cheap, our worship is likewise cheap.

Giving is one of the most vital structures in the framework of worship, yet it is one of the most misunderstood, least taught, and rarely practiced acts of worship in the worship community and church at large.

Why are we so hesitant? What keeps us from giving? Disobedience, neglect and fear.

Disobedience is simply knowing what to do and choosing not to do it. In the case of giving, it's selfishness. It's thinking of one's self rather than thinking of others.

> *But if anyone has the world's goods and sees his brother in need, yet closes his heart against him, how does God's love abide in him?*
> *(1 John 3:17 ESV)*

Neglect is being distracted, not making something a priority and failing to take care of something which we had every intention of doing. We mean well, but we don't follow through. This takes attention and, again, prioritization:

> *Do not neglect to do good and to share what you have, for such sacrifices are pleasing to God.*
> *(Hebrews 13:16 ESV)*

Fear seems to be the biggest stumbling block for the believer. It deceives and paralyzes, causing decisions to be made in the flesh rather than in the Spirit. What are we fearful of?

Down deep, many of us truly don't believe God can take care of all our needs. If we give, there won't be enough left for us, especially for our bills. But Paul addresses that fear:

> *And my God will meet all your needs according to the riches of his glory in Christ Jesus.*
> *(Philippians 4:19)*

And how does God meet all of our needs?

> *He who did not spare his own Son, but gave him up*
> *for us all—how will he not also, along with him,*
> *graciously give us all things? (Romans 8:32)*

It's all right there: God sacrificed His own Son for us . . . of course He'll provide for our needs. He'll give us everything we need. Maybe not everything we want but certainly everything we need. To think less, to believe less, to trust Him less, is making God out to be a liar, incapable of providing for all of our needs as He said He would. If we have surrendered our lives to Him, yet we still cling to our money and possessions, our worship is lacking and incomplete. Withhold nothing from Him in your worship; give and worship generously and sacrificially from the heart with great joy and thanksgiving:

*If we've surrendered our lives to Him, yet we still cling to our money and possessions, our worship is lacking and incomplete.*

> *For God so loved the world that he gave his one*
> *and only son, that whoever believes in him shall not*
> *perish but have eternal life. (John 3:16)*

God *gave* His only son for us. Let's give our whole life to Him, not withholding anything, making *cheerful* and generous giving an integral part of our worship.

# CHAPTER 34

# *Is It Okay to Lift My Hands?*

## Overcoming the confusion and misconception of physical expression in worship.

As I've had the opportunity and privilege over the years to visit and lead worship at many churches of different denominations, age groups, sizes and nationalities, I've marveled at how different these various worship experiences can be, from very sedate, formal and passive all the way to overly energetic, passionate and demonstrative—and everything in between. Our worship preferences and even our worship theology can often be reactionary. A previous bad experience at a church with a particular expression of worship now has the two inseparably linked, thus inappropriately associating scripturally sound worship with wrong doctrine and bad teaching and behavior. In other words, the particular expression and style of worship in a particular service may have been acceptable, but other aspects of the service were so distracting and unacceptable that the overall experience left a bad taste in our mouths—including, by association, the worship.

We can also develop our worship philosophy based on oral tradition, observations, preferences, biases and even prejudices passed down (or along) as truth, often morphing into a self-realized doctrine. Then there are those good ol' fashioned "false teachers" that teach and promote worship practices nowhere to be found in the Bible. Whatever the case or cause, a lot of confusion exits over what's acceptable in our expression of worship.

*Oftentimes, the physical representation of worship can be as compelling and moving as the music itself.*

How we express ourselves physically in worship can be an indicator of our personality, our heart, our doctrine, our relationship with the Lord, our whole being. Oftentimes, the physical representation of worship can be as compelling and moving as the music itself. A sincere heart overflowing in worship perfectly yoked to an accompanying and appropriate physical expression is nothing short of awe inspiring; it's even a shadow of things to come. But what's appropriate? And when is it too much or not enough? There are plenty of opinions about these very questions and the various physical expressions in worship, but rather than deal with opinions, let's address some of the specific physical responses that the Bible mentions and prescribes in worship.

## Lifting Hands

Of all the physical expressions, this one probably generates the most confusion and division. For many years I struggled with it as well. As a new believer, I once experienced worship at a very "expressive" church. Quite frankly, it was totally out of control (as was the teaching), and in addition to running around, standing on pews, shouting, yelling, screaming and so on, those in the congregation were also raising hands. So I associated hand-raising with bad doctrine and unscriptural and purely emotional worship, an inappropriate association that nevertheless gave me pause.

I didn't want to be one of "those people," but as I continued to grow and study the Word, I began to see and grasp the scriptural precedent for lifting hands in worship. But I was still prejudiced. And I was self-conscious of what others might think.

Then one Sunday morning when I was by myself at a church, during a particularly moving song where everyone was engaged and worshipping, I clearly heard the Spirit encourage me: "Lift your hands." My initial reaction was to pretend I was hearing voices and ignore it. His voice came again and now I was nervous and a little freaked out, yet I wanted to lift my hands—I really did—I just didn't know how. What was the right technique? Should my fingers be together or spread apart, palms facing out or in, elbows locked or bent? Now I was really starting to freak out. But His voice was persistent, so finally I went for it, but it was a cautionary attempt, more like a *maître d'*-holding-a-drink-tray kind of lift. One last time, "Lift your hands." Finally, without any care for what someone else might think and putting aside my prejudices, I lifted my hands straight up with total surrender. It was glorious! I honestly felt free to worship like never before. And my form? It took care of itself. I just lifted my hands and worshipped and the form was right because my heart was right.

Yet I was still a little hard-pressed to fully explain the dynamics of lifting hands. Certainly an element of surrender and "letting go" was happening, plus a sense of being "freed up" from the yoke of self-consciousness, but it wasn't until I was married and had kids that it finally made complete sense to me. One day as soon as I came in the front door, I saw my two little kids running toward me with their hands raised, wanting me to pick them up and hold them, to make them feel safe and secure and to tell them how much I loved them. And I picked them up and held them for a long time.

*Lift up your hands in the sanctuary and praise the Lord. (Psalm 134:2)*

Sometimes as we prepare to sing a song that has a verse or chorus with an exhortation to lift our hands, I will begin by reading this Scripture. I'll follow it with a brief rendition of my story and then encourage the congregation to respond as the psalmist exhorts, and as my kids did, with raised hands. The invitation is offered with scriptural understanding and practical explanation. It's certainly the people's choice not to raise hands but more importantly, it's now their freedom and invitation to do so—and the response has always been beautiful. There are just no words to describe a sanctuary filled with people with open and sincere hearts all lifting their hands to the Lord, wanting to be comforted and loved. On many on those occasions, they're just like I was. They finally "get it" and it's a new chapter in their walk and in their worship.

> *In every place of worship, I want men to pray with holy hands lifted up to God, free from anger and controversy. (1 Timothy 2:8 NLT)*

Paul understands the significance of this physical expression and the accompanying heart. That's why he uses the phrase, "I want." He doesn't say, "Hey, if you don't mind," or, "If this isn't too awkward for you," but again, "I want." It's an imperative and that's why I teach it, explain it, encourage it and apply it. Only through the Word can our fears and prejudices be overcome.

More than anything, I want as many as possible to experience this childlike heart of worship, reaching out with raised hands to our Father to be held, comforted, reassured and loved.

## Kneeling

This posture denotes surrender and submission, one that defers any and all semblance of authority to the One before whom we kneel.

> *Come, let us bow down in worship, let us kneel*
> *before the Lord our Maker; for he is our God and*
> *we are the people of his pasture, the flock under his*
> *care. (Psalm 95:6-7)*

A proud heart cannot find in itself the ability, desire or reasoning to release control and ownership, but the amazing economy of God is this: a heart that kneels before the Lord is not one of surrender in the sense of being vanquished or defeated but rather quite the opposite.

> *Humble yourselves before the Lord, and he will lift*
> *you up. (James 4:10)*

I have, on a number of occasions subsequent to this Scripture being shared, asked the church (if physically able) to kneel right where they were as the worship continued. Each time the atmosphere in the sanctuary immediately changed. This physical expression put the entire church as one into a humble state before the Lord, with a right heart and countenance to be lifted up in the midst of our circumstances and trials by the Lord our Redeemer. It is always tremendously moving, and it's merely a sampling of things to come:

> *Therefore God exalted him to the highest place and*
> *gave him the name that is above every name, that at*
> *the name of Jesus every knee should bow, in heaven*
> *and on earth and under the earth.*
> *(Philippians 2:9-10)*

Kneeling is a beautiful private and public physical expression that would do us and the church well to practice more often.

# Movement

I was at a worship conference where my team and I were slated to lead worship after one of the main-session speakers. We sat in the back listening to the speaker, an older pastor, as he began to list a multitude of things that bothered him in worship. There were the usual suspects like guitar solos, loud drums, too many new songs, unsingable melodies, immodest dress and so on. All of a sudden he hit on one that sent a shudder through the team: he hated when the singers move; it draws unnecessary attention to them. He instructs his worship leader to make sure the singers stand still and reverent without any body movement whatsoever at all times and during all songs. We were about to go on stage and lead a time of worship that included a couple of rousing, celebratory gospel songs that cannot be sung standing still. They simply can't. Neither those on stage nor those in the sanctuary would be able to stand still. It'd be like trying to stand still as your favorite football team wins the Super Bowl. It's just not gonna happen.

I calmly explained to the team that we were to lead worship as we had planned, that neither the motive nor the scriptural precedent for our physical expression had suddenly become suspect following a teaching on preferences. It was not disrespectful but rather our conviction—so I simply encouraged the team to do what we'd been called and invited to do and trust that God would supply mercy and understanding to all involved.

We came onto the stage and I nodded in appreciation and respect to the speaker as he left the podium. We took our places, and after a brief welcome we began our time of worship. It was then that I noticed the speaker had taken a seat further back on stage, right behind the singers, of course. He was about to have quite a view!

The worship time with all of the conference attendees was just incredible. The time of celebration and rejoicing felt completely holy and sincere as we truly acknowledged God's goodness and faithfulness with our whole being. Ironically, if my singers had, in fact, stood still, their stoic, stiff-as-a-board responses to a living, loving God would have drawn more attention to them than their natural physical expression of movement did.

Ecclesiastes 3:4 tells us there's *"a time to mourn and a time to dance."*

At a funeral, it's an appropriate time to mourn and clearly an inappropriate time to dance. But in worship? When we're rejoicing, celebrating and acknowledging the greatest love and hope *ever*, who promises eternal life in heaven where there will be *"no more death or mourning or crying or pain" (Revelation 21:4)* for all who call upon His name? How can you *not* move? How can you *not* dance? How can you stand still!

> *You have turned for me my mourning into dancing.*
> *(Psalm 30:11 ESV)*

> *Let them praise his name with dancing.*
> *(Psalm 149:3 ESV)*

By now, you may have this vision of our sanctuary filled with crazy people dancing up and down the aisles during worship. But no, not even close. While movement is completely valid and scriptural and, in fact, practiced in our sanctuary, there once again needs to be an appropriate balance.

> *But all things must be done properly and in an*
> *orderly manner. (1 Corinthians 14:40 NASB)*

For me personally, as well as for my pastor, "dancing in the aisles" in a sanctuary setting is an expression that (1) is potentially harmful—somebody's going to get hit, knocked down or worse; (2) draws unnecessary attention to oneself and away from God, causing one's motive for this particular expression of movement to be suspect; and (3) is presumptuous, out of context and out of order in our setting.

However, over the years, and in partnership with the ushers, we now allow those who are courteous to ask and whose motives seem pure to dance to their hearts' content in the very back of the sanctuary. There they won't get hurt or hurt anyone, nor will they be a distraction. It's been a wonderful solution that benefits everyone and manages that fine line between being a distraction and being able to worship freely.

So whether rejoicing before the Lord while holding a mic or instrument or right where one stands in the sanctuary, whether dancing for joy before the Lord privately or publicly or even on stage in the sanctuary as a skillful, coordinated expression of worship, movement is an essential and natural physical expression of worship.

## Standing

We stand when the judge enters the courtroom, we stand when the bride begins her journey down the aisle, soldiers stand when an officer appears and we even stand when the Hallelujah Chorus is performed. Yet it's not unusual for me to get some push back when I have the church stand for the worship time. If a handful of church-goers got their way, there would be a lot less standing and a lot more sitting. To them it's an unnecessary formality that has no real purpose. I don't see it that way. Why do we stand?

### *Awe*

> *The priests took their positions, as did the Levites with the Lord's musical instruments, which King David had made for praising the Lord and which were used when he gave thanks, saying, "His love endures forever." Opposite the Levites, the priests blew their trumpets, and all the Israelites were standing. (2 Chronicles 7:6)*

290

This took place during the dedication of the temple by King Solomon, and the people stood in amazement and awe of what had just happened. The sacrifice had earlier been consumed by fire from heaven, and now the people were experiencing a glorious time of worship in the presence of not a mere human king but the King of Kings! If one stands in response to the call to *all rise* as a judge enters the courtroom, how much more respect and honor should we have in standing before the *"judge of the living and the dead"* (Acts 10:42)!

### Awareness

> *This is what the Lord says: "Stand at the crossroads and look; ask for the ancient paths, ask where the good way is, and walk in it, and you will find rest for your souls." (Jeremiah 6:16)*

Standing is a position of being attentive to the rightness of our ways, to seeking godly instruction and counsel as we purpose to walk in the way that leads to life. This posture is opposed to one of laxness, slouching and taking the easy way. Kinda like sitting. . . .

### Allegiance

> *Sometimes you were publicly exposed to insult and persecution; at other times you stood side by side with those who were so treated. (Hebrews 10:33)*

> *But the Lord stood at my side and gave me strength, so that through me the message might be fully proclaimed and all the Gentiles might hear it. And I was delivered from the lion's mouth. (2 Timothy 4:17)*

291

There's no greater ministry you can offer someone than to stand at his or her side. This posture shows love, loyalty, support, faithfulness and friendship, which is exactly the same posture the Lord takes with us.

Standing as an expression of worship before the Lord shows an awe for who He is and what He's done, and an awareness and attentiveness to His ways. It shows an allegiance and loyalty to Him through all of life's ups and downs and a determination to never desert the faith. In this context, it sure beats sitting.

## Clapping

Clapping is usually exercised in our society as an expression of approval, encouragement and sometimes courtesy (if the performance is less than what we expected or hoped for). But clapping in church has been a major source of contention for many, evidenced by numerous lengthy dissertations available on the Web espousing the evils it brings upon countless unsuspecting churches. Sheesh, one might get the idea that sexual sin, faithlessness and gossip in the church isn't the problem; it's clapping! Evil, demonic clapping!

Sorry, I'm back. I'm not going to defend clapping. I'm simply going to present the scriptural mandate for clapping and leave it at that.

> *Clap your hands, all you nations; shout to God with*
> *cries of joy. (Psalm 47:1)*

Clapping in church and in worship is a physical expression that acknowledges the breadth, length, height and depth of Christ's love, and reflects a heart filled with awe and gratitude. This clapping is, or should be, a response to the Lord, the center of our worship, not the performance of such. This is a critical distinction and a justifiable source of contention.

Yet there's one more twist to all this: clapping can also be affirming and encouraging, a physical response much like that of a verbal "amen!"

So how do we keep all of this straight?

Clapping that acknowledges and honors the Lord and "amens" a particular message or truth pertaining to the Word brought by the worship team, a soloist, the pastor or some other means is reasonable and acceptable. Clapping during worship that honors the "performance" or the "performers" is suspect and best avoided.

Clapping is an uplifting expression of worship when exercised in a right way and with understanding. But we're not the only ones who clap unto the Lord; even creation gets into the act:

> *Let the rivers clap their hands,*
> *Let the mountains sing together for joy.*
> *(Psalm 98:8)*

Amen!

## Shouting

Think about when we shout. Living in South Florida, I've been able to go to several Miami Dolphins football games. The enthusiasm (certainly some of it alcohol inspired) when the home team scores is loud, unbelievably loud, with everybody making noise, shouting and cheering! Or how about the time you got your sorely needed tax refund just in time? Or when you got a job or a promotion at work? Or when you found out you were having a baby? And on and on. We shout for joy! We shout like crazy people, but we don't care because we're so happy!

Then we show up to church and oftentimes it's quieter than a law library. Wow . . . what happened?

> *Come, let us sing for joy to the Lord; let us shout*
> *aloud to the Rock of our salvation. (Psalm 95:1)*

> *My lips will shout for joy when I sing praise to you—I, whom you have redeemed. (Psalm 71:23)*

> *Shout to the Lord, all the earth; break out in praise and sing for joy! (Psalm 98:4 NLT)*

Wow! That's more like it! With the backdrop of a shared Scripture on *shouting*, encourage your church to consider its salvation and future hope, have the worshippers all let out a joyous shout together that rivals any touchdown celebration, and then "break out in praise and sing for joy!" I'm totally serious!

\* \* \* \* \* \* \* \*

The Bible records many more physical expressions of worship—too many to mention here—but, similar to the ones that have already been discussed, they likewise reflect the heart of the sincere worshipper in a demonstrative way. As you read and study the Bible, purpose to discover all the various physical expressions; how, why and in what circumstances were they were exercised and if they, too, can be incorporated into your times of worship.

*We are called to love and worship the Lord with our whole being.*

The question was asked earlier: "When is it too much or not enough?" We've seen the validity and value of these various physical expressions throughout Scripture, but the balance between too much and too little is determined by spiritual discernment and sensitivity to our surroundings and circumstances. We saw somber worship and subdued physical expression the Sunday after 9/11, yet great rejoicing and an energetic physical response on Easter morning acknowledging a risen Savior. Allow sensitivity to guide you when you're torn between what's permissible and what's beneficial. For example, you might consider toning it down a little at a small Baptist church in Ohio but then ramping it up at any church in Brazil!

*My whole being will exclaim, "Who is like you, O
Lord?" (Psalm 35:10a)*

*Love the Lord your God with all your heart and
with all your soul and with all your strength and
with all your mind. (Luke 10:27a)*

We are called to love and worship the Lord with our whole
being—with everything that makes us who we are—including our
strength and our bodies.

Our physical expression in worship is not to be neglected, nor
is it to attract undue attention. Instead it's to mirror a heart that's
sincere in all of its affections, bringing due attention and honor to
our Creator and Savior.

# CHAPTER 35

# *I Messed Up*

## A journey of repentance.

I'm sitting in my office going over some routine tasks when a team or staff member pokes his or her head in my door and asks, "Can I talk to you?" The look in the eyes, the body posture and the countenance all say that a long and sad meeting and an even longer journey is about to begin. What comes next is usually a stumbled-over apology followed by, "I messed up." The next words are mine: "Tell me what happened." And thus the journey begins.

*Addressing moral failure is a sad reality in ministry.*

Addressing moral failure is a sad reality in ministry. This is not skipping rehearsal or lying to get out of jury duty but rather those decisions that have a very real possibility of not only destroying one's life but the lives of others as well. Moral failure is an action or behavior that generally violates a scriptural precedent. Moral failure commonly refers to these three areas:

(1) Sexual sin. Adultery, fornication (sex between two single people) or homosexuality.

(2)  Sins of the heart. Envy, dissention or rebellion.

(3)  Sins of idolatry/addiction. Drugs, alcohol or pornography.

Obviously this is not an exhaustive list, but the vast majority of sins on the team resulting in disqualification from service fall right into this list.

Now, you may say that sin is sin, and I agree: sin is sin. But the very real consequences vary according to what the sin is, as does the potential for "collateral damage." The temptation in dealing with moral failure is to take the easier road by having the guilty party removed and banished as an example for all to see and learn from. While that way is more convenient, it also guarantees the greatest amount of fallout possible with little to no chance of redemption. God would have us take the road less traveled, one that takes time and personal investment with no guarantee of success. But the hope of repentance and restoration and the unspeakable joy a redeemed life brings makes for an irresistible invitation to take this journey—one that I'll always take without hesitation.

I've taken this journey with both male and female friends, associates, team members and even initial strangers. Neither gender has a corner on this unfortunate market. Although I will begin this journey with either gender, further down the road I feel it is appropriate, even necessary, to have same-gender counseling in order to continue on in this journey. We must be above reproach and avoid temptation, and as the discussions and revelations become more intimate and emotional, it is simply unwise for opposite-gender counseling to continue. Later in this chapter, I will share my thoughts as to when this parting of ways should take place. In presenting my experiences in this process, I will proceed with the assumption of same gender, male-to-male, counseling for the sake of clarity in this essential journey of repentance.

As we begin our journey and continue in conversation and discovery, I purpose to show in my demeanor neither sympathy nor condemnation. Instead I show a sincere concern for the person's well-being, knowing very well the fragility of the situation at this very moment and in the days ahead. We talk it all through; I get all of the facts and history that are pertinent and necessary; I assure him that there's nothing he's done that God hasn't already died for and, after a time of prayer, we plan the next step in our journey.

This journey is all about turning from sin to God. It's about repentance.

- *Repentance*: Sorrow for anything done or said; the pain or grief which a person experiences in consequence of the injury or inconvenience produced by his own conduct[24]

Repentance is a sobering realization that one has made a hurtful, selfish, foolish and purposeful choice, contrary to God's Word and God's desire for us, and is now reaping the consequences of those actions. Without repentance, there is no opportunity for change, healing or restoration. Thus, this journey is all about arriving at a place of repentance and dealing with the devastating aftereffects of sin.

At subsequent meetings with this person, we begin to confront his sin and consider his choices and who he's hurt. It's important that I consistently express hope throughout our journey, a journey that understandably appears hopeless to him:

> *And we know that in all things God works for the good of those who love him who have been called according to his purpose. (Romans 8:28)*

We're starting a deliberate, step-by-step process that requires the utmost sincerity and honesty, without which true repentance will not and cannot be realized. Anything less, anything contrived, will short-circuit the process and cut the journey short.

These are the steps we work through and that I look for, in this order:

## The Need to Own It

He needs to take responsibility for his actions and decisions. There can be no shared responsibility or blame to go around. He has to own his sin and own it all unconditionally.

> *If we claim to be without sin, we deceive ourselves and the truth is not in us. (1 John 1:8)*

This is the "icebreaker," if you will; once he's taken full responsibility and now fully owns his sin, it's likely going to be a fruitful and healthy journey.

## The Need to Understand It

He needs to know what happened, what caused him to drive off the road and how his decisions and behavior were destructive and hurtful. He needs to know that what he did was wrong and why it's sin. This complete understanding of the chronology of his actions and decisions and the thinking (flawed or not) that led him down this path will not only serve to point out the defects in his spiritual armor but to help him become better equipped and prepared to defend against the future temptations that *will* come.

> *So, if you think you are standing firm, be careful that you don't fall! No temptation has seized you except what is common to man. And God is faithful; he will not let you be tempted beyond what you can bear. But when you are tempted, he will also provide a way out so that you can stand up under it. (1 Corinthians 10:12-13)*

It's important for him to understand what the temptation was that "seized" him, why he didn't take the way out provided and how he might stand up under similar temptation next time. And he needs to understand how to be aware of and overcome his arrogance, thinking he has everything under control, and thus relying on his own strength while neglecting God's faithfulness to deliver him from sin.

## The Need to Show Remorse

I absolutely need to see and discern a sincere sense of "I really messed up bad and I just can't believe I did this," rather than a less than contrite, "Yeah, I messed up, but it's not that big a deal and God's already forgiven me, so can we just move on?"

> *The sacrifice pleasing to God is a broken spirit. O God, you do not despise a broken and sorrowful heart. (Psalm 51:17 GW)*

This is where repentance is realized: where he truly, sincerely and with a broken heart comes face to face with the gravity of his sin and the painful consequences of his actions, not only of how his own life has been affected but of how others, often dear to him, have been hurt and devastated.

> *I now rejoice, not that you were made sorrowful, but that you were made sorrowful to the point of repentance. (2 Corinthians 7:9 NASB)*

Paul was not *rejoicing* for their sorrow with some sort of sick pleasure but rejoicing for what their sorrow produced: repentance. It's at this point in the journey that I have witnessed many a person sitting across from me begin to "break," weeping over their sin, finally and fully feeling the entire weight of the consequences and devastation to themselves and to others and the pain and disbelief of having so completely let God and others down. Inside I rejoice, I really do, because I know this is when healing can truly begin and when God is pleased because He now has them back. Without this sincere *sorrow*, there's an absence of the need to be redeemed and restored, perpetuating a continued broken relationship with God. It's one or the other: a broken heart and a right relationship with God or a proud heart and a broken relationship with God. Allow this time of brokenness to take its course. Don't limit it, abbreviate it or interrupt it in any way. It's essential for this person to let his heart break completely in order to be restored completely.

## The Need to Confess

To confess or acknowledge our sin condition is to put God in His proper place. He's God. This is the relationship He's established: we're sinners, God sent His Son to die for our sins and if we believe and confess our sins, He's faithful to forgive us. This relationship and confession proclaims our need for a Savior and our dependence on Him rather than on ourselves and our own strength. To do any less than put our complete dependence on God essentially puts our dependence on ourselves, and in doing so we are now proclaiming, whether overtly or subtly, that we don't need God.

*It's one or the other: a broken heart and a right relationship with God or a proud heart and a broken relationship with God.*

> *If we confess our sins, he is faithful and just and will forgive us our sins and purify us from all unrighteousness. (1 John 1:9)*

Scripture conversely demonstrates that anything short of honest and complete disclosure is now an act of deception and subterfuge, to what end one can only guess (possibly to minimize the embarrassment or consequences of the sin). But Scripture makes it clear that this behavior is once again an attempt to stay in control and manipulate the outcome, showing that a complete surrender of one's self over to the control of a faithful Savior is foolishly delayed:

> *He who conceals his sins does not prosper, but whoever confesses and renounces them finds mercy. (Proverbs 28:13)*

Confession clearly shows the ultimate condition of the heart, and at this point in our journey I encourage this person to "get it all out." I have found that with some encouragement and assurance of God's faithfulness, a deeper and broader issue with a greater history often surfaces that is also in desperate need of being addressed and confessed. Confession becomes that opportunity to "dig deep" and to get to and get out all that is hijacking his relationship with Jesus.

*Some may look on and soberly realize that the only difference between them and the person confessing his or her sin is that one got caught.*

At some point in this process there should also be an opportunity for confession to the team, since healing also needs to take place between this person and the team. This is a valuable lesson for the team members. They see the consequences of sin first hand, they see God's mercy played out, they gain respect for their leader's compassion and godly behavior and they also have a bit of *fear* instilled that will generate some self-evaluation of their own walk with the Lord. Some may look on and soberly realize that the only difference between them and the person confessing his or her sin is that one got caught. It's a very spiritual process that should draw the team members closer to each other and, more importantly, to God. It often opens the door for others to want to come forward and get right with God themselves. Make sure the invitation to do so is extended. Don't hide or shield the team members from this process in any way, rather bring them along for their own edification.

Finally, there needs to be confession to those who have been hurt and offended by this person's sin and behavior. Oftentimes the hurt persons can look on and see the offender receiving all the care, counsel and support while they themselves are left alone in their pain, confusion and anger. Those who have been hurt will need the same care, whether from you or from another spiritually mature leader, in order for them to receive healing and for all who have been affected to embrace restoration.

If you have been counseling a person of the opposite gender from the beginning of this journey, during this time of confession you will find it advantageous and wise to bring in a competent biblical counselor of the same gender as the person being counseled. This can facilitate more intimate and honest confession as well as bridge the transition to an ongoing relationship that is more professional and engaging and spiritually wise. Continuing on in same-gender counseling will now open the door to a fruitful and lasting relationship that is healthy, above reproach and God-honoring.

## The Need to Make Permanent Changes

In this journey it makes no sense to put a Band-Aid® on a gaping wound. There needs to be change, wholesale and sincere change. For him to walk out with the words, "I'm gonna change," doesn't cut it. There must be an overwhelming desire to change, a plan put in place to help facilitate that change and accountability to support and encourage that ongoing change.

> *Produce fruit in keeping with repentance.*
> *(Matthew 3:8)*

There will be evidence of sincere repentance. There will be a changed heart, a changed countenance and a gratitude for God's grace and forgiveness that will manifest itself in his behavior and attitude as this person purposes with God's strength to never return to nor repeat his foolish and destructive behavior again.

This part of the journey is not as intensive, no longer needing weekly meetings, but the follow up is imperative for encouragement and accountability. This stage is more akin to moving someone from the emergency room to the hospital, and eventually to rehab and then to being discharged. There still needs to be periodic check-ups along the way, and there will likely be one or two redirects to keep him firmly established on his new path. By now it's been anywhere from six months to a year or more on this journey, and though the intensity and frequency subsides, the friendship and trust that has been established continues, allowing for informal visits, calls and conversations that recall and rejoice over God's faithfulness and love for us that never gives up.

The penultimate goal of repentance is restoration, first and foremost to a right relationship with God, then with one's spouse, then with family and friends, and then finally, a restoration to service:

> *Therefore this is what the Lord says: "If you repent,*
> *I will restore you that you may serve me;"*
> *(Jeremiah 15:19)*

When the time is right to begin restoration to ministry and all parties involved and affected are prayerfully in agreement, bring about that restoration with great patience and deliberation. I usually have this person serve once to see how it all goes, and if things are good I'll schedule him again in another month. I'll do this for three or four months and then slowly begin to increase his participation. With continued follow up and care, it will usually take a year for this person to feel fully integrated again—at no fault of the team or leadership—it simply takes a season of time for healing and restoration to run its full course. I'm happy to say that

I've been a part of several of these complete restorations. God's Word really works, and these restored people are stronger in their faith than they ever were because of this process, the love and care of others and, above all, God's love and mercy.

If anyone on your team or staff or in your circle of influence needs you to go on this journey with them, don't hesitate. Jump right in. This person desperately needs you, your guidance, your support and your love. It's a great way to reach out tangibly with the love and compassion of Christ and, quite honestly, it also serves as a sobering personal reminder of the consequences of sin. During and after each journey, I'm reminded of what I've been blessed with and how easily and quickly I could lose it all by just one foolish choice. Stay vigilant and guard your heart.

> *Because of the Lord's great love we are not consumed, for his compassions never fail. They are new every morning; great is your faithfulness. (Lamentations 3:22–23)*

Moral failure can, in fact, consume us and disable us with its devastating potential to render everything and everyone we've known and loved to but a footnote in our lives. But we have this incredible promise to hold onto: God's unending love, His great faithfulness and His enduring compassion can redeem the unredeemable and restore that which was lost. What an amazing journey!

# CHAPTER 36

# *Road Trip*

## Time to take a break.

*For in six days the Lord made the heavens and the earth, the sea, and all that is in them, but he rested on the seventh day. Therefore the Lord blessed the Sabbath day and made it holy. (Exodus 20:11)*

Let's establish right from the start: rest is holy. To not rest, therefore, is unholy. I'm therefore very unholy. And I'm sure I'm not alone, not even close.

I enjoy watching and playing various sports, so I tend to follow the latest sports news, and one of the recent issues in the headlines has been the treatment of sports injuries. A generation ago, an injured athlete was expected to "tough it out," to play through injuries for the good of the team. That was certainly noble in that era, but today it's being seen in a very different light. Athletes these days are getting better advice, treatment and rehabilitation before coming back to the field of play. Where the tough-it-out mentality might have helped the team short term, it hurt the team long term as injuries were compounded, often becoming degenerative and causing careers to end prematurely. With today's advances and greater understanding, athletes now take the necessary time for their bodies to fully recover before returning, and subsequently their career spans and productivity have both increased significantly.

We would do well to follow their example.

Many in ministry, in the misguided attempt to be noble and sacrificial and to "take one for the team," end up burning out, or worse. They reinjure themselves time and time again, responding and reacting more and more in their own strength and less in the Lord's strength, ultimately ending their ministry prematurely as they depart wounded, or worse, disqualified.

## Rest for the Tired

- *Tired*: needing rest

The Sabbath is intended as a day of rest, but that doesn't assume spending all day in a hammock (although, there's nothing that says you can't). A Sabbath is a day to rest from the weekly work activities and responsibilities that employ our physical, mental, emotional and spiritual capabilities. Again, this is not some catatonic state of being but rather a refocusing. It's taking a break from work and focusing on the Lord. But what about those whose "job" requires them to work on the Sabbath? Especially those in ministry?

Extensive theological discussions and debates abound on this subject, but here's what I've gathered, summarized and experienced: Whether or not the Sabbath is still a requirement for today is an argument for those who have the time. I don't. Regardless, the purpose, the value, the example and the fruit of a Sabbath are undeniable. Insisting on a specific day and only that day for the Sabbath to be observed is refutable:

> *Then he said to them, "The Sabbath was made for man, not man for the Sabbath. So the Son of Man is*

Jesus was speaking to the Pharisees, so once again He was addressing blatant hypocrisy. We should not find ourselves focused on the legalistic application of the Sabbath but rather on the how the intent of the Sabbath can accomplish the will of the Lord in our lives. As Mark 2:27 makes clear, the Sabbath was made for our benefit, not just as another hoop for us to jump through in an empty, works-driven faith.

What day you take your Sabbath is simply not an issue, but what's important is that you honor the intent and take a day off from your weekly obligations to spend with the Lord, your family and your friends, doing those things that bring relaxation and rest to the body, soul and spirit. Since I serve on weekends, my Sabbath is on Monday. Or sometimes Tuesday. Maybe for you it's Saturday. But you get my point.

That's a weekly Sabbath. It's similar to an athlete who takes some time off every week to rest and avoid overworking the muscles. But occasionally, even an athlete needs to take a week or two off to rehab some of those accumulated nagging injuries. Those injuries aren't necessarily keeping him from performing on the field but left unattended for too long, those minor injuries can soon become tears, separations or worse. They can sideline him for weeks or months, or even longer, possibly ending his career.

That's why vacations, extended times to get away, are critical. Taking a vacation doesn't have to be an issue of budget; it can be a "staycation." It's a time for us to be recharged by God, to appreciate, savor and enjoy family and friends, and to reconfirm or even reevaluate our calling. Those who have an allotment of vacation time and don't take it are foolish. There, I said it. And in saying so, I have also indicted myself for past behavior. Many of the vacations I've taken began with a sense of, "I don't have time for this," and ended with a conviction of, "I've got to do this more often." Simply put, taking time away is a discipline, and it's survival. Don't neglect it, or like an athlete who neglects his body, you'll break down when you least expect it.

## Rest for the Weary

In worship (and any other) leadership, it's one thing to be tired, just plain physically exhausted, but it's an entirely different thing to be spiritually weary:

- *Weary*: no longer interested in or enthusiastic about something[25]

This is a scary place to be. There's little motivation, less and less of the Lord's strength, and more and more pressure to do and perform the very thing that has caused your weariness.

> *"Come to me, all you who are weary and burdened, and I will give you rest. Take my yoke upon you and learn from me, for I am gentle and humble in heart, and you will find rest for your souls."*
> *(Matthew 11:28–29)*

"Come to Me." And leave everything else behind. And stay awhile. And, as I see it, one of three things will happen:

### *You'll Be Refreshed*

It's like sitting in the shade and having an ice-cold glass of lemonade in the middle of a hard day's work in the sun. It's simply refreshing, giving a small yet significant respite from a laborious and productive day. It helps our outlook and attitude as we prepare to continue on in our labors. And so it is with the Lord:

> *I will refresh the weary and satisfy the faint.*
> *(Jeremiah 31:25)*

Once again, as I mentioned earlier, getting away with friends and family for a vacation or some other kind of getaway can be wonderfully refreshing. This can also be a time to get some honest input and wisdom from those who truly care for and love you. If you're married, listen especially intently to your spouse's input, discernment and observations during this time (since this is the one who'll have to deal with you if you burn out). Like that cold glass of lemonade, this is a time to just relax, be still and hear the voice of the Lord. Sit back, bask in it and then head back to work encouraged and refreshed.

### *You'll Be Renewed*

- *Renew*: To renovate; to restore to a former state or a good state, after decay or deprivation; to rebuild; to repair [26]

Sometimes we need more than a break, more than a vacation. Sometimes our roles and responsibilities have so increased, our creativity has been so marginalized, and we've become so entrenched in a rut that the need to take an extended leave, a sabbatical, is paramount to being able to continue on with any effectiveness in our current role.

For some, the traditional role of a sabbatical is often associated with the academic profession, where every seven years a professor takes an extended period to write, study and be refreshed from the rigors of academia. For others, the sabbatical is viewed as a much-needed break and diversion for those who have been tirelessly working away for years without much of a rest.

However, for most, the reality of the need for a sabbatical is more akin to an athlete who's pushed it too hard for too long, who's broken down and is no longer able to effectively continue on in his or her responsibilities.

> *Do you not know?*
> *have you not heard?*

> *The Lord is the everlasting God,*
> *the Creator of the ends of the earth,*
> *He will not grow tired or weary,*
> *and his understanding no one can fathom.*
> *He gives strength to the weary,*
> *and increases the power of the weak,*
> *Even youths grow tired and weary,*
> *and young men stumble and fall;*
> *but those who hope in the Lord*
> *will renew their strength.*
> *They will soar on wings like eagles;*
> *they will run and not grow weary,*
> *they will walk and not be faint.*
> *(Isaiah 40:28–31)*

It's all about whose strength we're working and serving in.

> *I can do everything through him who gives me strength. (Philippians 4:13)*

The converse then is true: I can do nothing in my own strength. Before we even realize it, our schedules, agendas, responsibilities, the urgent, and other's expectations and demands can slowly (or quickly) begin to crowd out any opportunity of being refreshed and strengthened, causing our times with the Lord to become cursory at best, and soon, nonexistent. We tough it out for the team. I mean, it is ministry, right? Despite the subtle and not-so-subtle hints from our spouses, friends and coworkers, we continue down this path, fooling ourselves into thinking it'll let up as soon as we get through this season. The only problem with that is that the next season soon overlaps the current one.

*As we spend less time with the Lord and function more in our own strength, we begin to lose the Lord's perspective.*

Here's the double-edged sword: as our schedules get more insane, as we spend less time with the Lord and function more in our own strength, we begin to lose the Lord's perspective. We now start to believe that our work, ministry and efforts are so crucial that we ourselves have become irreplaceable. Now we have no choice: we *must* keep going or everything will utterly collapse. No. We can *never*, ever serve in ministry thinking we're irreplaceable or invaluable. This mindset creates undue pressure and stress, and it's a flat-out lie. The moment we think He needs us is the very same moment He begins to show us that He, in fact, doesn't need us.

*It's time to realize that the Lord doesn't need us for His ministry but rather He desires us for His ministry—and never for our glory, only for His.*

And as He begins to move His hand from us, we begin to strive more and more in our own strength until we eventually break down and burn out. In time we'll lose our ministry and more than likely we'll also lose our family.

And then we'll blame it all on God.

It's time to stop. It's time to realize that the Lord doesn't need us for His ministry but rather He desires us for His ministry—and never for our glory, only for His. This is so critical for us to understand that I feel the need to restate it: He *wants* us, but don't ever be mistaken; He doesn't *need* us.

It's time to repair, rebuild and make new.

For those who are in this broken condition, it's time to come out of the game, and not for just a week or two, not even for a month or two but for a season. This isn't about being refreshed or taking an extended break but about being renewed and restored. And this renewal, this sabbatical, will take much more time and require significantly more attention.

During this time, the church should come alongside to intervene and help, supporting its pastors, ministers, leaders and worship leaders through this much-needed time of renewing. The church has a lot to gain from a leader who returns renewed and wiser.

> *Look to the Lord and his strength; seek his face*
> *always. (Psalm 105:4)*

One of the sobering, and at the same time liberating, realizations of this process is that you'll find the ministry will get along fine without you. It always could have. But the same isn't true for your family. So get help and pursue renewal, get to know your family again and enjoy a renewed sense of calling and service in ministry as you seek the Lord's face and strength in all things and at all times.

## *Or You'll Resign*

Sometimes we realize that our weariness is not so much being overburdened or operating in our own strength rather than the Lord's but instead from a mismatch in a particular ministry or a discontentment in our calling or even a realization that our season of ministry has come to a close. For some, they just don't fit into the culture and personality of a particular ministry. If the worship leader is younger, has a heart and passion for contemporary music and is serving at a denominational ministry that prefers hymns and orchestral accompaniments, then honestly, it's time to move on. No wonder he or she is weary.

For others, they realize they just don't enjoy leading worship. They have the ability and skills for it, but it just doesn't seem to be a fit, a calling or a passion. They find instead that they have a heart for youth or counseling or, in many cases, to pastor a church or be a stay-at-home mom.

And yet for others, they've led worship for a few decades, and although they're not ready to retire, they feel their season of serving as a worship leader might be over. They're ready for another career, even one apart from ministry. And that's perfectly fine. We could use more strong believers impacting the secular workplace for Christ.

Any of these scenarios will make anyone weary. They're life-changing struggles that we can easily resist because of comfort, familiarity, financial security and a whole slew of other reasons. And none of these particular situations will be resolved with a two-week vacation or a much longer sabbatical—instead they need a lifelong change of vocation. This takes a bold step of faith, and I, for one, personally applaud and support those who recognize their weariness for what it is and do something about it. It's admirable and honorable, and God will surely bless their faithfulness.

* * * * * * * *

Several years ago, a few days before my family and I were to leave on our vacation, I got a call from the church: a local fireman had been tragically killed in the line of duty. Due to the size of the expected turnout, the memorial service would be held in our church sanctuary . . . on the day after my planned departure. Our pastor was asked to officiate and I had been asked to provide the music. Because of the size of the service, the impact on the community and the fact that my pastor had accepted the invitation, I accepted as well. My wife and family were understanding but disappointed. The service was very moving, the family and my pastor were appreciative of my involvement, and since I didn't know anyone, I left right after the service to finish preparations for our delayed road trip.

The next morning we started our trip, and about an hour or two into our drive my wife very calmly turned to me and asked if she could share something with me. "I'm sure the family appreciated your playing for the memorial service, but they would have been just as appreciative if someone else had played. And the pastor would have been fine if someone else had played as well. But you left your family and delayed our trip for two days for people you've never met, who won't even remember that you were there a week from now. But your family will remember, and that hurts."

My wife wasn't angry or combative in the least, although I think I actually would have preferred that. But those words really, really sunk in. I didn't have any inclination to be defensive because it was truth and wisdom from the Lord through my wife, and I took it to heart from that moment on.

There are times for sacrifice and legitimate reasons to delay or cancel a road trip or vacation, but those times should be rare and the exception rather than the norm, which is what it had become for me. And my family paid the price. Don't do that to yourself, don't do that to your family and don't do that to your ministry. Take a road trip, get away and be refreshed. Don't let anything stop you. There will *always* be reasons to postpone or not go, but once you're on the road those "reasons" will suddenly disappear in your rearview mirror, and you'll soon realize that the earth didn't cease to exist because you weren't there to handle everything.

> *He gives strength to the weary and increases the power of the weak. (Isaiah 40:29)*

If we depend on our strength less and less and on His strength more and more, we'll find rest for our weary bones. Now enjoy the trip!

CHAPTER 37

# *Hand It Off*

## Planning for coverage in and out of season.

Maybe it's time for your vacation, a conference, an anniversary or a kid's big recital or game. Maybe you're sick or you got injured or some other emergency has just obliterated your plans. In these situations and others, do you have someone available and equipped to step in for you?

For planned absences, finding coverage can be as simple as calling a fellow worship leader you know in the community or arranging for a guest artist to come from outside the community. In either scenario, you'll want to provide your guest worship leader a contact person to handle personal and musical needs and assist him or her with the on-site logistics. Not only will this give your guests, and ultimately your church, a great experience in your absence, but it will likely make them eager to return to help with future coverage needs.

For the emergency absences, however, it becomes imperative that you have someone on your own team ready to step in at a moment's notice. This person doesn't need to be an experienced worship leader or even an accomplished musician, but he or she must be a competent and respected leader. This role is not so much one of an *overseer* but more of a *deacon* or *deaconess*, that is, "one who serves:"

> *Deacons, likewise, are to be men worthy of respect, sincere, not indulging in much wine, and not pursuing dishonest gain. They must keep hold of the deep truths of the faith with a clear conscience. They must first be tested; and then if there is nothing against them, let them serve as deacons.*
> *(1 Timothy 3:8–10)*

These qualities are a fitting barometer for your team and volunteers, especially those who may be called to a higher level of leadership. The opportunities to assist with worship leadership in an emergency may very well be the testing that eventually "promotes" someone to a greater role, even that of overseer.

Remember that people covering for you in an emergency do not have to lead from an up-front position, one that denotes singing and playing. They can lead from any position and function more as a music director, assigning various roles (such as who will sing lead on which songs) and making various arrangement decisions (such as whether to use a solo vocal or group vocals or whether to repeat a chorus), and so on. They should be prepared to switch gears and song lists, having at their disposal a collection of worship songs that are simple, easy to play and easy to sing for both the team and the church.

*The goal is to have a time of worship that doesn't bring attention to the fact that you're gone.*

When there's an emergency, rather than try to plow through what's already been planned around your particular strengths and giftings, allow, and in fact encourage, your emergency substitute to be ready at all times with a song list that he or she is comfortable with. The goal is to have a time of worship that doesn't bring attention to the fact that you're gone but instead continues to be a seamless temporary transition that has people unaware that you were even absent. This might be a blow to the ego but a promotion to your leadership.

> *Be prepared in season and out of season.*
> *(2 Timothy 4:2b)*

This is an admonition for both you as leader and your deacon as substitute: have a plan in place for your absence; whether a vacation or other planned absence (in season), or sickness or other unexpected absence (out of season). And likewise, your substitute should have at all times at least one, if not two or three, song lists prepared so that he or she is ready to lead worship at any time. In fact, you would be wise to also have a second deacon prepared at all times in the unusual event that your deacon of first choice is unavailable. But, in the unlikely event that you haven't made any contingency plans for an emergency, you can always have your pastor lead the church in a couple of simple a capella songs. Then when you return, be sure to get your résumé dusted off and updated. . . .

Many years ago, I left for a vacation and put one of my team members in charge. I trusted him to keep the transition reasonably unnoticeable, and off I went. Upon my return, I was horrified to learn that my sub had taken familiar worship songs and given them various musical treatments and arrangements that were so extreme and inappropriate that the entire congregation was left with their jaws on the ground. I was completely embarrassed, yet I learned a valuable lesson. From then on, I have always approved the set lists and arrangements before my departure. In the rare event of an unplanned absence, there's now a clear understanding of which worship songs and arrangements should and should not be used. And I now also have a team that is trained and tested so that those fears and concerns are no longer present.

I recommend having similar awareness, approvals and contingencies. I also suggest having team members who are relatively new to leadership lead a few practice worship sets in various settings with you present to evaluate and tweak. That way you'll become comfortable with their leadership and they'll become comfortable with your expectations.

The whole point of having people prepared to lead worship in your absence is to give you peace of mind while you're away. Train them and prepare them, leaving nothing to chance and giving them every opportunity to succeed. In doing so, you'll end up with competent assistant worship leaders and you'll be freed up more often to attend to other needs and opportunities—oh, and you'll still have your job when you return!

CHAPTER 38

# *Did You Remember?*

## Remembering and honoring our partners in ministry.

It was the Wednesday before Thanksgiving, and I had been asked to teach the Word that evening at our midweek service. I was honored, a little nervous and excited all at the same time. As I ran sound check before service, the worship team seemed almost more excited than I was. "How're you feeling?" "You nervous?" "Don't embarrass us!" "You're not gonna go long, are you?" "We're praying for you!"

And pray they did. I usually pray with the team before service, but that night they asked if they could pray for me. I gladly obliged. We then made our way to the stage; the worship went well, and following worship when I took my place behind the pulpit, the church was surprised and then curious: "Let's see what he's got!"

When the teaching was done, the body seemed responsive and appreciative, and after making my way back to the keys we closed in worship and I said goodnight. Afterward I received several hugs and attaboys from the team, who had been back stage watching, listening and cheering me on during the teaching. I was sincerely touched by their support, their encouragement and the camaraderie.

The very next morning, Thanksgiving morning, the first thing I did was make my way to the computer and write a note of appreciation to the team, telling them what they meant to me and how I couldn't do what I do without them, and then I emailed it to them. What surprised me was how surprised they were by my email. In their responses, beside their surprise, they were appreciative and grateful for my kind words and encouragement. So much so that a few of them shared with me that my email had brought them to tears.

*Whether divinely imbedded or consciously placed, what's in our heart is what we value and remember.*

Here's what I quickly came to realize: I do love my team, I do care greatly for them and they do bless me tremendously. They really, really do. I just don't tell them nearly enough, and that has to change.

> *I thank my God every time I remember you. In all my prayers for all of you, I always pray with joy because of your partnership in the gospel from the first day until now, being confident of this, that he who began a good work in you will carry it on to completion until the day of Christ Jesus. It is right for me to feel this way about all of you, since I have you in my heart. (Philippians 1:3–7a)*

It starts with an understanding that this is a partnership—I'm not on stage by myself, nor am I in ministry by myself. I need to constantly acknowledge and remember this reality and those who partner with me. But how do I get to the place where "remembering" is a way of life rather than just another thing to add to my to-do list?

Paul, by writing these words, *"It is right for me to feel this way about all of you, since I have you in my heart,"* has given us great understanding and insight. Whether divinely imbedded or consciously placed, what's in our heart is what we value and remember.

When the Lord imbeds something in our hearts: a mission trip, a call to ministry or a desire to adopt an orphan, for example, we don't forget. We remember and we respond. Likewise, when we know and determine the things in our lives that are of great value and importance: our marriages, our anniversaries, our families, our friends, and our partners in ministry (to name a few), we consciously and purposely put those things in our hearts to remember and to respond to as well.

But when we forget or neglect the great value of something or someone in our lives and hearts, it's often the result of something or someone else capturing our attention, inappropriately vying for a place in our hearts. Left unchecked, these diversions can overrun and eventually occupy our hearts, and, invariably, we let our family and friends down. And that's when things can go terribly wrong.

That's why we need to be so careful to guard our hearts at all times and to be wary of the world and its temptations. We need sensitivity to the Spirit and sober judgment to determine what to let in and what to keep out of our hearts.

How do we best accomplish this?

> *Praise the Lord, O my soul,*
> *And forget not all his benefits—*
> *who forgives all your sins*
> *and heals all your diseases,*
> *who redeems your life from the pit*
> *and crowns you with love and compassion,*
> *who satisfies your desires with good things*
> *so that your youth is renewed like the*
> *eagle's. (Psalm 103:2–5)*

To remember the Lord, all His benefits and His goodness and faithfulness is to have Him in the center of our hearts. And likewise with our partners in ministry, to remember them, all their "benefits" and faithful service, is to, as Paul expressed earlier, have them in our hearts as well.

*Let's not forget those in our own backyards and on our own stages who quietly, humbly, faithfully and sacrificially carry out ministry.*

Throughout Scripture we see beautiful and compelling stories of those who have served the cause of the Lord in some small or great way. Noah, Joseph, Rahab, Gideon, Ruth, Mordecai and Esther, John the Baptist, Mary, the apostles, Stephegn, even the thief on the cross (and so, so many more) are all remembered and honored for their various acts of service, sacrifice, courage and faith. We do well to remember these great men and women of the Bible: their mighty deeds and bravery, their perseverance and faithfulness, their humility and sacrifice. But let's not forget those in our own backyards and on our own stages who quietly, humbly, faithfully and sacrificially carry out ministry with many of those same qualities and virtues every single day.

My heart is for us to be more diligent to remember those who serve the Lord and partner with us in ministry every day, to honor them and to share our joy, love, gratitude and appreciation with them as Paul did with the Philippians.

\* \* \* \* \* \* \*

On that Thanksgiving morning, the Lord laid the worship team on my heart and I wrote them an email that shared my sincere appreciation and gratitude. From then on I determined to never forget them again but to remember them, honor them, pray for them and by some means (note, card, text, email, call, word of encouragement, etc.) to let them know they're in my heart.

*We continually remember before our God and Father your work produced by faith, your labor prompted by love, and your endurance inspired by hope in our Lord Jesus Christ.*
*(1 Thessalonians 1:3)*

Consider who your partners in ministry are: your family, friends, worship community, pastors, missionaries, coworkers—and the list goes on. Keep them in your heart, never lose sight of their value to you and your ministry and never take them for granted. Remember them, honor them, and above all, tell them.

# CHAPTER 39

# *Let's Find Our Seats*

## The role of worship in our services.

For many in the church, worship has been relegated to the cue for the time of fellowship to wind down and for all of us to find our seats. Others see it as a warm-up for the reason we're all there: to hear and be inspired by the teaching. Still others see worship as setting the mood, creating a pleasant diversion from life's irritations. Some pastors see worship as an extension of their favorite iTunes playlist, and thus assume a major role in planning the song lists. And some worship leaders see it as an opportunity to promote their new songs or CDs.

For many pastors and people in church leadership, worship is expendable. If the teaching, along with announcements and other added elements, is clearly going to go long, then the first and often only option is to cut a song. An attitude that I consider most egregious (especially since it's so widespread) is: "Let's be sure to start the service with worship rather than announcements, since we wouldn't want any latecomers to miss any of the announcements."

Many, if not most, worship leaders face this challenge weekly. It's easy to feel marginalized and tolerated at times, yet the solution isn't to give up or to complain incessantly but rather to (1) determine what role worship should actually have in the service; (2) purpose to diligently pursue "worship in spirit and in truth"; and (3) consider how to go about initiating change in the midst of the prevailing culture.

## The Role of Worship

Worship should invite us, encourage us and even compel us to express our love with sincere emotions: from sorrow for our sins to thanksgiving and joy for the Lord's salvation to praise and adoration for His faithfulness, and everything in between., Our worship is based solely on and in response to the truth, the understanding and the full knowledge of Christ Jesus, His Word and His promises. This is the essence of worship:

> *For God is Spirit, so those who worship him must worship in spirit and in truth. (John 4:24 NLT)*

This truth we worship in—God's Word, and the understanding, acceptance of and belief in who God is, who His Son Jesus is, and His crucifixion on a cross and resurrection for our salvation—is the very foundation and anchor of our faith. And to know God is to love:

> *The person who does not love does not know God, because God is love. (1 John 4:8 ISV)*

God is Spirit and God is love; for us to be able to worship, we must first know these truths. And if we know these truths, then our spirits, awakened by God's Spirit, respond in like-kind love, sacrificial and unconditional, yoked to our unique emotions and personalities, which are willingly surrendered to God. And when we love God, we love others; and when we love others, our worship is now a lifestyle, not just fifteen minutes of singing on Sunday morning. We need our minds to comprehend these truths and our spirits to convey our love to God and to others. Thus, these truths and our spirits work and worship in tandem.

If people worship only with intellectual truth, they are often rigid and pharisaical, arrogant in their superior intellect. Those who worship only in the spirit are often uncontrollably emotional, being tossed around by every popular doctrine that comes along, prideful in their spiritual intimacy. Visit various churches in your community and your travels and in many cases you'll experience worship that emphasizes either spirit or truth. It will be unmistakable, incomplete and sad. Instead, truly strive for the role of worship in your ministry to be one that fully embraces the marriage of spirit and truth. Scripture clearly says it's a must.

> *Our attractions and distractions are exposed in the presence of God and are appropriately judged and pardoned as we worship.*

## When We Worship in Spirit and in Truth

### God is honored and praised.

> *But you are a chosen people, a royal priesthood, a holy nation, God's special possession, that you may declare the praises of him who called you out of darkness into his wonderful light. (1 Peter 2:9)*

Our attractions and distractions are exposed in the presence of God and are appropriately judged and pardoned as we worship. Painfully aware of our past and even our present, yet filled with hope for our destination whose path is paved with forgiveness, mercy and grace, we respond rightly when God is the center and purpose of worship.

God and God alone is to be honored and praised—not the worship team, not the soloist, not the worship leader, and not the

329

fashionable look or the current sound or style. Sincere worship points not to itself in any way or capacity but to God. Just God.

### Hearts are changed.

> *Create in me a clean heart, O God, and renew a right spirit within me. (Psalm 51:10 ESV)*

The days are dirty; they just are. We can't roam through a dry and dusty land without attracting and retaining some of the dirt, no matter how lightly we tread. It's a fallen world, and we live in the middle of it. Worship is that time of cleansing, that time to acknowledge our dirt and to rebuke our own efforts at cleansing. His love purifies and our worship places us under His grace.

> *I will give you a new heart and put a new spirit in you; I will remove from you your heart of stone and give you a heart of flesh. (Ezekiel 36:26)*

Sometimes we can get used to the dirt, becoming comfortable with its look, its feel and even its smell. We become anesthetized to it: "What dirt?" we ask. This dirt not only coats our hearts but can even invade them, permeating them to the core. Worship can bring a sobering and shocking awareness to our dulled spiritual senses as we struggle to grasp how far and long we've been away from God's cleansing grace. Where most would see an irreparable condition, God's solution is simple: time for a brand new, soft and pliable heart! Worship is that time where our new hearts are conceived and born, soft hearts now as receptive to God's Word as tilled soil is to the sowed seed.

> *Search me, O God, and know my heart; test me and know my anxious thoughts. See if there is any offensive way in me, and lead me in the way everlasting. (Psalm 139:23–24)*

Worship is that time when we're honest with God, choosing to be vulnerable rather than pretentious (as if God is genuinely fooled). Some superficially engage in worship to impress leadership or the potential mate seated nearby. Others go through the motions of worship to fulfill some kind of spiritual obligation, hoping to approach God as a sort of genie in a bottle, seeking to have their wishes and wants granted. But sincere worship convicts the heart and exposes our real motives. It compels the worshipper to "get real" and stop "playing church." It ultimately changes our focus from ourselves to God, from being self-centered to being God-centered, taking our offensive ways and motives and trading them in for His righteousness.

*Worship is that time where our new hearts are conceived and born, soft hearts now as receptive to God's Word as tilled soil is to the sowed seed.*

### Battles are won.

*After consulting the people, Jehoshaphat appointed men to sing to the Lord and to praise him for the splendor of his holiness as they went out at the head of the army, saying: "Give thanks to the Lord, for his love endures forever." As they began to sing and praise, the Lord set ambushes against the men of Ammon and Moab and Mount Seir who were invading Judah, and they were defeated.*
*(2 Chronicles 20:21–22)*

I can only imagine what was going through the worshippers minds right before the battle. Some may have been wondering if it wouldn't make more sense to have a time of worship back at camp and then send the army into battle—but to go into battle in front of the army to have our time of worship? To the human mind, that's counterintuitive and suicidal. Yet to God, that's exactly what He wants us to do. We have two choices: go into battle void of worship and in our own strength, or put worship out front and then go into battle in His strength. How many battles and trials have we lost in our own strength? Likely too many to count. The battles you face will always seem overwhelming, but before you invest time and resources planning a counterattack, stop. Just stop. Now retreat and put worship out in front. Then, and only then, proceed. Worship will always win battles and rout the enemy. The army was only for show; the real battle always did, still does and always will belong to the Lord!

*The army was only for show; the real battle always did, still does and always will belong to the Lord!*

## How to Bring Change

Trying to bring responsible change to an established culture is an admirable endeavor not for the faint of heart. Bringing change takes a real heart for the people and a development of mutual trust that only time can build. It also requires that your pastor have a similar vision. Even then, expect the process to be like getting a 300-foot barge (not a WaveRunner) to change directions.

Communication to leadership is important; we must calmly and consistently share the value and purpose of worship in the service, determining not to whine or throw a hissy fit as a strategy for change. But even more compelling than communication is demonstration: show them. And show the church. Consider presenting a special evening or midweek service set apart for just worship—an opportunity to help bring greater understanding to the purpose and role of worship in our lives, in the church, and, subsequently, in our weekly services. This service can be led by your own worship team or a guest worship artist, or a combination of the two. Then present another night of worship, and then another, as frequently as you and your leadership feel would be appropriate. Purpose to make these nights part of the fabric of your church, allowing your church body to enter into a deeper and more personal time of worship than they would normally experience on a weekend. And over time, these nights will give birth to a desire within the congregation to experience some of the same in their weekly worship services.

* * * * * * * *

Let your church see, experience and benefit from sincere worship. Let them see Jesus lifted up, lives changed, hearts of stone softened and battles won. Once they've experienced life-changing worship and witnessed its fruit, they'll want more. It's not about forcing worship upon them but rather allowing them to yield their hearts and minds to the power and impact of worship in their lives. And when that happens, then ever so slowly the barge begins to turn.

# CHAPTER 40

# *Closing Song*

Worship changes lives, radically. It does so by keeping our eyes, hearts and minds responsive to Jesus, desiring above all to honor, follow and please Him rather than ourselves. That's radical in our world and in our culture where "me" is worshipped above all.

But Jesus was radical. He turned culture and tradition upside down. He taught us to think of others more highly than ourselves and to love others as ourselves. And to serve. And He practiced what He preached, laying down His life for us so we would no longer be condemned to die in our sin. We don't worship an ideal, a philosophy or a lifeless idol, we worship the Living God! This profound reality gives us hope in a hopeless world—and when we worship, we're immersed in that hope, a hope that is absolutely indescribable and literally unimaginable:

*Sometimes bended knees and raised hands are all we can say.*

> *No eye has seen, no ear has heard, no mind has conceived what God has prepared for those who love him. (1 Corinthians 2:9)*

Words fail miserably when we're confronted with this kind of inconceivable glory; sometimes bended knees and raised hands are all we can say. We sing songs and testify with voices and countenances that our hearts are true, but our behavior and attitudes toward others in our everyday lives confirm whether we perjured ourselves during worship. Worship is not three or four songs sung on a Sunday morning but rather a lifestyle, and when this lifestyle is embraced and adopted, when our worship is sincere and authentic, our lives and destinies are transformed, never to be the same again.

Over the years, I've received numerous letters and emails attesting to this life-changing power of worship. These testimonies have nothing to do with a ministry, a leader, a team or a denomination but rather with worship itself, life-changing worship:

> When we come into the sanctuary and the music starts, we can feel the "stuff" of the week just break away. We are just transported in the spirit to worship, and it is so transforming. We don't leave the way we came in.

> I have been unable to be at church the last few weekends (lung cancer). . . . I seem to be seeing the doctors more than anyone else, but that is ok. I was able to sing only part time last night as my lung capacity is going down. I have been able to enjoy and share in services online more than I would like, but I am thankful the technology is available for me and thousands around the globe to be able to do that!

> One of the sweetest blessings was at the Night of Worship back in October—my (adopted) daughter Melissa, then 6, walked forward and accepted Jesus as her Lord and Savior! She said the music sent God into her heart! Her name is in His book, and that date will always be one to celebrate for our family.

> I came to know the Lord in 2001 through Calvary Fort Lauderdale. I did not understand why or how to worship

when I was saved. Through the years, CCFTL's worship has brought me closer to the Lord, helping me put a voice to my fears, sorrows, joy and praise!

Even in the most difficult times, I would walk into church, hear your music and the service and I would leave feeling revived. I can't even count how many times I have wept through worship because the Spirit brought me closer to Jesus. It is an emotional, tender, powerful and cleansing time with the Lord.

Friday night I watched my grandchildren both, for the first time, raise their hands as they worshipped the Lord. It made my heart sing!

Praise and worship opened up my heart like the Grand Canyon to God so that I could worship like never before.

Worship has inspired me, made me laugh and cry. It has lifted me up when I was really down and increased my faith when I needed it.

On Sept. 6th, the Lord took my husband to his heavenly home. And I can't begin to tell you what a comfort worship has been.

One of the most profound supernatural experiences I've yet had with Him was while I was worshipping Him. Part of my testimony is growing up in a very dysfunctional home with lots of abuse. When I was saved, He filled the bottomless pit in me that had been looking for unconditional love my whole life! I definitely know He loved me! It had been deeply engrained in me to not trust. And I'll never forget the time in worship, arms and heart raised to Him, with lyrics about trusting Him. And the revelation, "Oh, this is what trust is!" It was during worship that He revealed to me that He had slowly, gently and powerfully taught me to trust! And my walk with Him grew exponentially from that point!!"

Worship encouraged me to abandon teenage insecurity and lift my hands to the Lord for the first time.

Not having experienced contemporary worship before, I was sure God was offended by your guitars and drums. But you opened my eyes to true worship and taught me that it is not the instruments, but the heart that pleases God, and whether we worship with an organ or rock band—if we do it in genuine love and respect for God, He is pleased.

And for the first time in my life I actually WORSHIPPED! Not sang—worshipped. The first couple of times I came I was a bit uncomfortable by all the "hand raisers." It wasn't long before I was one of "them."

During worship, I do so feel the Spirit's presence and often feel that perhaps heaven itself pauses for a moment to worship with us!

These notes and emails speak of changed lives, changed generations and changed destinies, all from worship. Take this to heart if you're discouraged and weary; in your church there are countless stories like these that haven't been told yet. And remain steadfast. Be diligent in building a strong and sturdy framework so that the worship you lead and experience will be life changing rather than a passing fad, no deeper than veneer that only changes the look and sound but not the heart. This sincere, life-changing worship is when God is truly honored, His Son Jesus is exalted and the Holy Spirit is freed to move about and within our hearts, transforming stone into flesh.

Serving in worship ministry is a glorious and humbling calling, filled with great blessing, yet constant temptation. It's an honor to direct praise to our Creator and Savior, yet we need to remain vigilant so that no misguided praise comes to rest on us. The framework must be built on nothing but the Word of God. Without that foundation, the framework is compromised and dangerous.

We're to be steadfast and diligent, persevering in our calling and giftings. And we're to be joyful, fully aware of our undeserved deliverance and our inconceivable hope and home to come.

> *Come, let us sing to the Lord! Let us shout joyfully to the Rock of our salvation. Let us come to him with thanksgiving. Let us sing psalms of praise to him. (Psalm 95:1–2 NLT)*

Yes, we are to sing, shout and be thankful! All of us. And through instruction, exhortation and example, we're to lead others to sing and shout and be thankful in worship, doing so in God's strength and by His Holy Spirit.

When you stop and really think about it, leading and serving in worship is absolutely amazing and awesome, as well as a little (if not a lot) scary and intimidating at the same time. But with a sure foundation in place and a solid framework to support it, leading and serving in worship is beyond rewarding: it's a calling, a way of life and a profound honor!

May you be blessed in all your endeavors, and may your life be a living expression of worship for others to follow as you faithfully lead.

Amen!

# *An Addendum*

## I didn't see that coming . . .

Since I completed the initial rough draft of this book, there have been some drastic changes in my life and in the very ministry where much of my experience and growth as a worship leader, pastor and overseer have transpired.

I resigned from my position as worship leader at Calvary Chapel Fort Lauderdale in the fall of 2013. It was a decision I could never have imagined making, let alone implementing. Yet I did. My wife and I, after much, much prayer and agonizing over the decision for months, finally sensed that it was, in fact, time to move on. I had my reasons, but none of that really matters. What matters is that I could not find peace while debating the decision, and upon making the decision I was flooded with peace. But even in the midst of indescribable peace, it was nonetheless an excruciatingly painful process to say goodbye to coworkers, staff, teammates and an unbelievable body of believers.

But say goodbye I did, and thus began a new chapter for my wife and me. I took my newfound time to complete the writing of this book, to catch up on lost time with my family and to do some traveling. I essentially did what I wrote about: I took a sabbatical. And coming from someone who has now reaped the rewards of a much-needed sabbatical, I can highly recommend the same for those of you who have let way too much time go by without being refreshed and renewed.

But, unfortunately, my resignation wasn't the only change. My former pastor of twenty-three years made several decisions over the last few years that were self-centered and foolish. His behavior, which included ongoing sexual sin, ultimately led to his resignation in the spring of 2014. I don't have the words to express the sadness, disappointment and, at times, even anger over this revelation. But in the midst of the shock and disbelief, I'm reminded of Jesus' words:

*"Come, follow me." (Matthew 4:19)*

Jesus says numerous times to follow Him. Not follow His disciples, but follow Him. Not follow the famous televangelists, the best-selling Christian authors or the celebrity pastors, but follow Him. Yet too many times there are those who follow great charisma and convincing passion all the way up to a lofty pedestal, one not meant for man. The higher the pedestal, the more spectacular the fall. And the fall was inevitable. And once again the world has had yet another front-row view of a well-known pastor falling from great heights. And the world rejoices.

And yes, the story of redemption now has another opportunity to publish itself, although that story is likely to receive a lot less publicity—it's boring and not nearly as juicy as a fallen pastor.

My life will go on, Calvary Chapel Fort Lauderdale will continue on, my former pastor will likely regroup and press on, and your life will as well go on. And each one will likely go on in very different directions than were planned or expected. But when it's all said and done, what will you be remembered for? What will be your legacy? What will you accomplish, how will you accomplish it and for whom? Will it be unto self or unto the Lord? I shared this Scripture in an earlier chapter and it bears repeating:

*Whatever you do, do it all for the glory of God.*
*(1 Corinthians 10:31 NIV)*

Follow Jesus, not man. Pursue humility, not fame. Give God the glory, not anyone or anything else. And finish strong, leaving an honorable legacy. The world thinks that's boring. God doesn't. And that's all that matters.

Some of you may ask me, "What's next for you?" I don't know. But I'm excited, a little anxious and very curious all at the same time. With my faith in Jesus even more entrenched, tested and proven, with my wife at my side as she has been for over thirty years and with incredible, loving and supportive kids, I'm not worried.

> *Thy word is a lamp unto my feet and a light unto my path. (Psalm 119:105 KJV)*

I can only see the path directly in front of me, so rather than strive to see way down the road, I'll just take one step at a time and see where the Lord's path leads me.

> *"For I know the plans I have for you," declares the Lord, "plans to prosper you and not to harm you, plans to give you hope and a future."*
> *(Jeremiah 29:11)*

How can I argue with that? And how can I not look forward to that? That's why I'm not worried, nor should you be. Keep following Jesus every step of the way on your path and look forward with great excitement to the plans He has for you in the next chapter of your life!

# Endnotes

1. *American Heritage Dictionary Online*, s.v. "framework," http://www.yourdictionary.com/framework#americanheritage.

2. *Cambridge Dictionary Online*, s.v. "framework," http://dictionary.cambridge.org/us/dictionary/american-english/framework_1?q=framework.

3. *Wordsmyth Dictionary-Thesaurus*, s.v. "framework," http://www.wordsmyth.net/?level=3&ent=framework.

4. Vocabulary.com, s.v. "framework," http://www.vocabulary.com/dictionary/framework.

5. Ibid.

6. *Wordsmyth Dictionary-Thesaurus*, s.v. "framework," http://www.wordsmyth.net/?level=3&ent=framework.

7. About.com Christianity, "What Is God's Sovereignty?" by Jack Zavada, http://christianity.about.com/od/glossary/a/Sovereignty.htm.

8. The Free Dictionary by Farlex, s.v. "ambition," http://www.thefreedictionary.com/ambition.

9. *John Gill's Exposition of the Bible*, s.v. "2 Timothy 1:7," http://www.ewordtoday.com/comments/2timothy/gill/2timothy1.htm.

10. *Webster's New World College Dictionary*, s.v. "correct," http://www.yourdictionary.com/correct.

11. Ibid., s.v. "confront," http://www.yourdictionary.com/confront.

12. *Merriam-Webster*, s.v. "tradition," http://www.merriam-webster.com/dictionary/tradition.

13. Ibid.

14. Ibid., s.v., "humility," http://www.merriam-webster.com/dictionary/humility.

15. *Webster's New World College Dictionary*, s.v. "artist," http://www.yourdictionary.com/artist.

16. The Free Dictionary by Farlex, s.v. "perform," http://www.thefreedictionary.com/perform.

17. *Merriam-Webster*, s.v. "vision," http://www.merriam-webster.com/dictionary/vision.

18. *John Gill's Exposition of the Bible*, s.v. "Matthew 7:1," http://www.ewordtoday.com/comments/matthew/gill/matthew7.htm.

19. *Longman Dictionary of Contemporary English*, s.v. "proliferation," http://www.ldoceonline.com/dictionary/proliferation.

20. Dictionary.com, s.v. "advocate," http://dictionary.reference.com/browse/advocate?s=t.

21. *Merriam-Webster*, s.v. "entitlement," http://www.merriam-webster.com/dictionary/entitlement.

22. Dictionary.com, s.v. "tenure," http://dictionary.reference.com/browse/tenure?s=t.

23. *Merriam-Webster*, s.v. "cheerful," http://www.merriam-webster.com/dictionary/cheerful?show=0&t=1410220083.

24. The King James Bible Page, s.v. "repentance," http://av1611.com/kjbp/kjv-dictionary/repent.html.

25. *Oxford Advanced Learner's Dictionary Online*, s.v. "weary," http://www.oxfordlearnersdictionaries.com/definition/english/weary_1.

26. The King James Bible Page, s.v. "renew," http://av1611.com/kjbp/kjv-dictionary/renew.html.

36403162R00200

Made in the USA
Charleston, SC
02 December 2014